AN INTRODUCTION TO THE
# World-System
# Perspective

# About the Book and Author

Full attention is given to the controversies surrounding the world-system approach to the study of modern social change in this introductory text designed for undergraduate and graduate level students.

The book traces the general antecedents of world-system theory and describes the system's basic characteristics and the relationships within it. Dr. Shannon characterizes changes within the system: social and economic trends, cycles of great-power leadership, and events and policies by which states rise or fall in importance. These processes are illustrated by numerous examples, with a focus on five points in history (1400, 1560, 1763, 1900, and the present).

The author's explanation of the world-system includes an overview of some of the most prominent criticisms of the theory and the responses to these criticisms by proponents. Dr. Shannon concludes with an overall assessment of the world-system approach and relates it to other attempts to understand global change. Concise and clearly written, the book assumes no advanced knowledge of sociological theory or world history on the part of students.

Thomas Richard Shannon, professor of sociology at Radford University, is the author of *Urban Problems in Sociological Perspective* and *American Social Structure.*

# AN INTRODUCTION TO THE
# World-System
# Perspective

**THOMAS RICHARD SHANNON**

**Radford University**

91-807

**WESTVIEW PRESS**

Boulder, San Francisco, & London

Copyright © 1989 by Westview Press, Inc.

Published in 1989 in the United States of America by Westview Press, Inc., 5500 Central Avenue, Boulder, Colorado 80301, and in the United Kingdom by Westview Press, Inc., 13 Brunswick Centre, London WC1N 1AF, England

Library of Congress Cataloging-in-Publication Data
Shannon, Thomas R., 1945–
  An introduction to the world-system perspective.
  Includes bibliographical references and index.
  1. Economic history.  2. Socialism.  3. Social
systems.  I. Title.  II. Title: World-system perspective.
HC51.S474  1989      303.4      89-16715
ISBN 0-8133-0794-5
ISBN 0-8133-0795-3 (pbk)

Printed and bound in the United States of America

The paper used in this publication meets the requirements of the American National Standard for Permanence of Paper for Printed Library Materials Z39.48-1984.

10  9  8  7  6  5  4  3  2

# Contents

# Tables and Illustrations

# Preface

This book grew out of my experience teaching undergraduates world-system theory in my social change course. Although my students seemed interested in the ideas of world-system theory, most of them found what had been published in the area confusing and difficult to read. I also found myself having to spend inordinate amounts of time in class providing the basic historical background necessary to understand the theory. This book represents my attempt to provide students with an accessible introduction to world-system theory that is firmly embedded in history.

I have set about trying to create a particular kind of book. I wanted it to be brief. That gives the instructor the flexibility to use it as part of a course and/or in combination with other reading. I have striven to write in a simple, accessible prose style. That way I could be reasonably certain that students could read the material on their own, without the necessity of in-class clarification of every topic. I have also avoided assuming very much prior background on the part of the reader. I have learned that one cannot assume even the most basic historical or geographical knowledge when addressing an undergraduate audience. Consequently, Chapters 3 and 4 are heavily descriptive and are designed to provide the background necessary for the discussion of system dynamics in Chapter 5. In addition, I have not assumed a background in modern sociological theory. Chapter 1 provides a brief overview of the theories most directly relevant to an understanding of the origins of world-system theory. More sophisticated readers may not feel the need for this kind of assistance and are invited to skip over this material.

World-system theory itself imposed another requirement on this book. While currently the dominant approach in the study of modern social change, it is also a very tentative and a controversial theory. I think everyone who reads about world-system theory should be aware of the debates surrounding it. Hence, I have devoted a substantial portion of the book to criticisms of the theory. I conclude with my own overall evaluation of the world-system approach and mention some of the alternative approaches that have recently appeared.

*Thomas Richard Shannon*

# Acknowledgments

To my colleagues in the Sociology and Anthropology Department at Radford University I am grateful for being granted unusual flexibility in my teaching schedule and other departmental responsibilities, which gave me the time to write this book. The interlibrary loan office of Radford University Library also gave me more than my fair share of time and assistance.

The students in my social change classes played a special role in creating this book. They suffered through a number of drafts of the various chapters and provided me with consistently helpful feedback. My student Steven Light did yeoman service in assisting me with final editorial revision and manuscript preparation. Iya Jefferson, a student in the Geography Department, prepared the maps.

Of course, as is the case in any textbook, the "real" authors of this book are all those scholars whose original work provided the basis for the derivative task of text writing. I apologize if I have misrepresented them. The anonymous reviewers of the manuscript for Westview Press made major suggestions for improvements in it that I think substantially strengthened it.

*T.R.S.*

# The Origins of World-System Theory

C. Wright Mills (1961) once described sociology as the attempt to link history to individual biography. This book examines one recent attempt in sociology to make sense of the social, economic, and political history of modern societies—world-system theory. Like its theoretical predecessors, world-system theory adopts a particular approach to history. Theorists of this school claim that out of the welter of events contained in the historical record, certain general trends and historical patterns can be identified and shown to be causally related. According to this view, history is a relatively orderly general process in which certain events make others possible or likely.

World-system theory is a continuation of the central concerns of such early social theorists as Karl Marx, Max Weber, and Emile Durkheim. They maintained that a fundamentally new kind of society had emerged in Western Europe in the centuries after 1500 (the modern era). They sought to identify the nature of this new society, explain its origins, and explore the consequences of its emergence.

World-system theory is also part of a general theoretical development in sociology that began in the 1970s. During the 1940s, 1950s, and 1960s structural-functionalism was the dominant approach in U.S. sociology. This theoretical perspective provided a general model of the nature and operation of all societies and constituted the conceptual underpinnings for an explanation of the evolution of contemporary societies called modernization theory. In the late 1960s both structural-functionalism and modernization theory were the objects of increasingly harsh criticism. Much of this criticism came from a growing group of sociologists who sought to replace these theories with a revised and updated Marxist sociology. World-system theory emerged in the 1970s as part of this Marxist intellectual revival. The theory's specific role was to provide an alternative to modernization theory's interpretation of social change in the modern era.

This chapter will trace the origins of world-system theory, beginning with a consideration of structural-functionalism and modernization theory. The chapter will then examine how world-system theorists have drawn upon a number of previous models in the Marxist tradition to create an alternative to modernization theory. World-system theory represents an explicit effort to extend, modify, and synthesize these earlier efforts.

## Structural-Functionalism and Modernization Theory

World-system theorists reject the structural-functionalist theory of modernization, which considered societies relatively stable systems of interrelated parts. Each part, such as the kinship system, did something necessary (had a "function" or social consequence) for the other parts and for the system as a whole. Each part was related to and dependent upon the others. Social change was therefore the process by which the social system gradually adapted to a changing environment. Because of the system's interrelatedness, once one element of the system changed, the others had to change (Parsons, 1951, 1966; Moore, 1974: 72–93; Applebaum, 1970: 67–70).

Modernization theorists attempted to apply this basic view of society to an understanding of changes in the modern era. To formulate a general model of the emergence of contemporary societies, theorists focused on explaining the process of industrialization in Europe. One of the best known practitioners of this approach, Wilbert E. Moore, characterized the process of modernization as the

> "total" transformation of a traditional or premodern society into the types of technology and associated social organization that characterize the "advanced," economically prosperous and relatively politically stable nations of the Western world. . . . It is . . . a general transformation of the conditions of life and the way life is socially organized (1974: 94).

At the most general level, these theorists described modernization as a process of "differentiation." In this view, the social structures of "traditional" societies were relatively simple, or "undifferentiated." In an undifferentiated social structure most of the key activities necessary for societal survival were concentrated in a limited number of insti-

TABLE 1.1
Levy's Comparison of Relatively Nonmodernized and Relatively Modernized Societies

| Comparison Dimension | Relatively Modernized Society | Relatively Nonmodernized Society |
|---|---|---|
| Specialization of organizations | Highly specialized | Few specialized |
| Degree of interdependence | High | Low |
| Relationship emphases | Universalism; functional specificity | Particularism; functional diffuseness |
| Patterns of centralization | High | Low |
| Generalized media of exchange and markets | Use of money and markets high | Use of money and markets low |
| Bureaucracy | Widespread | Limited |
| Family considerations | Important, but decreasing number of functions | Important and significant number of major functions |
| Town-village interdependencies | Urban, industrial, with flow of goods, services, and knowledge from urban to rural | Rural, agricultural, with flow of goods and services from rural to urban |

*Sources:* Based on Applebaum (1970: 40–41) and Levy (1966).

tutions, especially the family and kinship systems. The roles within each institution were also limited in number and performed several different functions. Hence, modernization entailed the creation of more numerous, specialized (differentiated) institutions and roles (Parsons, 1966; Smelser, 1973).

Modernization theorists attempted to identify certain key social, cultural, economic, and political changes that they felt were central to the emergence of contemporary societies in the West. Most theorists did so by constructing an "ideal type" (generalized, abstract model) of the process. In the model, premodern societies were characterized by certain general features that were typical of all traditional societies. As a result of industrialization and social change, a new societal type with different features emerged—the "modern" or "industrial" society. Table 1.1 summarizes one view of these societal types.

These theorists also attempted to specify the preconditions for these changes and the events that typified the process of modernization itself (see Table 1.2). Modernization theorists believed that they had identified the common elements of an essentially universal process of change about which it was possible to make meaningful general theoretical

TABLE 1.2
Moore's "Sequential" Model of Modernization

---

  I.  CONDITIONS NECESSARY FOR INDUSTRIALIZATION
    A.  Values
        1.  Desirability of economic growth and individual mobility
        2.  Identification with and legitimacy of state
    B.  Institutions
        1.  Economic
            a.  Property transferable
            b.  Labor geographically and socially mobile
            c.  Markets and money
        2.  Stable political system with a just legal system and the ability to maintain social order
        3.  Institutionalization of "rational" organizations
    C.  Organization
        1.  Bureaucratic administration
        2.  Appropriate fiscal organization of the state
        3.  Adequate provision of infrastructure and public services
    D.  Individual motivation
        1.  Achievement orientation
        2.  Innovative orientation

  II.  CONCOMITANTS AND CONSEQUENCES OF INDUSTRIALIZATION
    A.  Economic organization
        1.  Commercialization of agriculture
        2.  Reduction of agricultural labor force
        3.  Upgrading of the skill levels in the labor force
        4.  Differentiation of the occupational structure
        5.  Commercialization of consumer goods markets
        6.  High labor mobility
        7.  Mechanisms for continual capital investment
        8.  Rising consumption and standard of living
        9.  High degrees of economic specialization and interdependence

*(Continued)*

statements. With some room for minor variations, all societies presumably either had already gone through or were going through modernization (Harrison, 1988: 1–32; Abraham, 1980: 1–29).

### APPLICATION TO THE THIRD WORLD

Modernization theorists interpreted the problems and events in Third World countries in light of this presumed universality. (World-system theorists classify such countries among the so-called peripheral and semi-peripheral societies. We will follow that usage here.) These societies were viewed as typical traditional societies just beginning the process of modernization. Their difficulties in achieving the conditions existing in the already industrialized societies were simply the result of "historical backwardness." According to this view, such Third

TABLE 1.2
Moore's "Sequential" Model of Modernization (*Continued*)

   B.   Demographic and ecological structure
       1.   Initially: declining death rates, high birth rates, and rapidly growing population
       2.   Later: family limitation and declining growth rates
       3.   Initially: young population age structure because of high birth rates
       4.   Rapid urbanization and geographically uneven development
   C.   Social structure
       1.   Weakening of kinship ties
       2.   Temporary family disorganization
       3.   Improving status of women
       4.   Cultural heterogeneity and the need for formal social controls
       5.   Voluntary mate selection
       6.   Increasing apathy and alienation
       7.   Mass communication creating a standardized popular culture
       8.   Sharp division between work and leisure
       9.   Rise in number of voluntary organizations
     10.   Secularization of values but continued religious belief
     11.   Increasingly complex stratification systems
     12.   Mass mobilization and participation in politics
     13.   Centralized, bureaucratic state

 III.   DYNAMICS OF INDUSTRIAL SOCIETIES
   A.   Attempts at partial restoration of traditional patterns
       1.   Conjugal family but continued kin ties
       2.   Some personalization of market relationships
   B.   Continuous social change
       1.   Technological change
       2.   Continual specialization and differentiation
   C.   Attempts at organized and planned social change
   D.   Divergence between industrial societies based on:
       1.   Conditions before modernization
       2.   Preexisting social tensions
       3.   Technology available at the beginning of modernization
       4.   Political regimes

*Source:* Based on Moore (1974: 94–118) and Applebaum (1970: 46–50).

World societies needed to overcome the traditionalism of their social structures, cultural values, and political institutions (that is, the characteristics that marked all societies prior to modernization). Then these societies would be in a position to take advantage of transfers of industrial technology from the West and to begin improving their economies. If local political elites were appropriately educated and socialized, they could speed up the process by first changing the political system to copy Western political structures and then using it to foster economic and social change. The advanced societies of the West ("core" societies in world-system usage) could also help by advising the local political elites on how to reform the political system; providing technical training and expertise; donating some of the capital and industrial equipment to start industrialization; investing in the local economy; providing the assistance to create a more efficient service infrastructure (roads, schools, airports, electrical grids); and so on.

Apart from altruism, it was in the interest of the industrialized societies to provide such assistance in order to counteract the decreased social equilibrium brought about by the process of modernization. If modernization was not encouraged and shaped by Western efforts, the rising discontent that derived from the breakdown of traditional value systems and institutions and from increased expectations among the impoverished masses could lead to support for Communist-inspired revolutions and the creation of totalitarian dictatorships hostile to the West (Chirot, 1977: 2–4; Abraham, 1980: 1–29; Sanderson, 1988: 168).

## CRITICISMS OF STRUCTURAL-FUNCTIONALISM AND MODERNIZATION THEORY

By the late 1960s both the general model of structural-functionalism and the specific claims of modernization theory were encountering a number of criticisms in U.S. sociology. (World-system theorists generally agree with these criticisms and have attempted to avoid making the same mistakes in formulating their own theory.) The general model was faulted for overemphasizing the degree of orderliness, cooperation, and stability in society. Critics pointed to the frequency of very abrupt social changes and open conflict in history. Other critics added that the apparent preference for stability and order in structural-functionalist theory led its practitioners to view conflict and rapid change as inherently dangerous and abnormal. Behind this failure, said the critics, was a failure to recognize the importance of vast differences among various groups and social strata in terms of power and the benefits received from society. These differences in fact guaranteed a high level of group conflict (Dahrendorf, 1959; Buckley, 1967; Coser, 1956).

Structural-functionalists were also criticized for their general analytic approach, which was characterized by theoretical statements that were no more than complex, abstract statements of the obvious and sterile systems of categories. In particular, critics castigated structural-functionalists for their lack of a sense of history and of the uniqueness of particular societies and time periods (Mills, 1961).

Of most relevance to world-system theory, however, were the criticisms of modernization theory. The central complaint was that it attributed the conditions and problems of peripheral societies to factors internal to them (their traditionalism). Critics charged that such a view ignored several centuries of cultural contact, trade, colonization, and political-military intervention by Europe and (later) by the United States. Hence, said the critics, these countries had stopped being true traditional societies well before the twentieth century. Rather, they had been changed into new kinds of societies that fit neither the traditional nor modern categories of modernization theory (Chirot, 1977: 3–6; Wolf, 1982: 386–391; Sanderson, 1988: 140).

Emerging out of this central criticism of modernization theory were a number of other, related ones, particularly that structural-functionalists had assumed that the Western process of industrialization (especially that of Great Britain) was the pattern all other societies had to, would, and should follow. This assertion, critics charged, ignored a number of factors. First, Britain had developed without competition or inter-vention from other, more technologically advanced societies, whereas peripheral societies were attempting to industrialize and compete with wealthy, technologically advanced, and militarily powerful countries. Second, the social, economic, and political conditions that existed in Great Britain in the eighteenth and nineteenth centuries did not exist in the periphery in the twentieth century. Third, peripheral countries differed considerably among themselves; they had unique historical heritages that created special problems for their modernization efforts. Fourth, modernization theorists implicitly assumed that the results of Western industrialization (individualism and materialism, for example) were inherently desirable. In fact, such results were not necessarily compatible with the cultural values of many people in the periphery (Abraham, 1980: 176–204).

Critics of modernization theory also rejected its attribution of a benign role to the core countries as the supposed purveyors of mo-dernity. That view, critics charged, ignored the centuries of abuse and exploitation by the core of the periphery and also failed to explain why core governments had so frequently supported corrupt and ex-ploitative authoritarian regimes in the periphery. Hence, these critics claimed, many of the problems of the periphery were the result not of historical backwardness but of the "imposed backwardness" caused by core exploitation and repression (Burns, 1980; Magdoff, 1969; Sander-son, 1988: 159–185; Frank, 1966).

IMPLICATIONS FOR WORLD-SYSTEM THEORY. These criticisms of structural-functionalism and modernization theory became part of the initial agenda of those who were to develop world-system theory. Specifically, these criticisms suggested that an adequate alternative approach should (1) be grounded in the historical experiences of the societies in the periphery; (2) consider the differences between present-day conditions and those that existed when the core industrialized; (3) explicitly address the role of relationships *among* societies in explaining change within them (such as the role of the already industrialized countries in creating conditions in the periphery); and (4) take into account the role of power, exploitation, and conflict in the relationships both within and among societies. In their search for such an approach, sociologists in the late 1960s and early 1970s began to reexamine a number of previous theoretical efforts, beginning with the work of Marx.

## Classical Marxism

Marx's basic model of society emphasized the role of power in social relationships, the exploitation by one social class of the rest of society, and the constant conflict generated by that exploitation. For Marx, the basic nature of society was shaped by the "mode of production"—the type of technology and organization of labor used in economic production (the "productive forces") and the set of rules governing who controlled and benefited from that production (the "social relations of production"). In turn, the relations of production determined the nature of the social class system in society. In Marxian sociology a "social class" was defined in terms of its relationship to the means of production. Those who controlled the productive process, economic decisionmaking, and the distribution of the goods produced constituted the "ruling class" of society. This class concentrated the benefits of economic production in its hands and did so by "exploiting" the labor power of workers (who, depending on the type of society, were peasants, serfs, slaves, or paid employees). By exploitation Marx meant that the ruling class kept the bulk of the wealth created by the workers' labor because of its control over the means of production (Marger, 1987: 33–34; Ritzer, 1983: 80–91; Freedman, 1961; Szymanski, 1983).

To continue this process of exploitation the ruling class had to have effective control over society. In part, the ruling class's direct supervision of the process of production provided it with day-to-day control over the workers. The ruling class also used its economic resources to shape the basic institutions and culture of society (the "superstructure"). Hence, religion, family relationships, the laws, the policies of government, education, and cultural beliefs and values all reflected the interests of the ruling class. As a consequence, the superstructure functioned to shape the behavior and beliefs of the exploited members of society so as to encourage their acceptance of the economic system and the power and privileges of the ruling class. The most critical institution in the superstructure was the state, which promulgated and enforced laws benefiting the ruling class (Marger, 1987: 35–36; Ritzer, 1983: 80–91; Giddens, 1971: 35–60).

Yet, for all the power of the ruling class, its control of society was not stable or permanent. Productive forces continually evolved. Marx identified several basic stages in this evolution; as the productive forces moved from one stage to another, the relations of production also changed. (There was a best or most appropriate set of relations of production for each general stage in the development of the productive forces.) But change in the relations of production would undermine the position of the ruling class—whose power ultimately rested on a particular set of relations of production. Hence, the ruling class resisted changing these relations. Eventually, that resistance proved futile because a new class, associated with the new productive forces, emerged and began to challenge the power of the ruling class. This new class stood to benefit by a change in the relations of production. Because of its association with the newer, more effective productive forces, this class gradually became larger and more economically important in society, more aware of its true class interests (to change the relations of production), and thus more politically organized. Finally, it became powerful enough to stage a political revolution and seize state power. Once in power, the new class was then in a position to change the relations of production to benefit itself and reshape the superstructure to protect its interests. Thereby, it became the new ruling class (Marger, 1987: 36–38; Giddens, 1971: 35–60; Freedman, 1961).

Thus, Marx viewed society as being in a constant state of tension, with the potential for class conflict always present. At any given time, one class was exploiting the rest of society. It succeeded for a time, yet it eventually was challenged by a new class, which ultimately displaced it.

For Marx, the nineteenth century (when he wrote) represented yet another phase in the evolution of the productive forces (machine technology and factory production) with a distinctive set of relations of production (the system of private property). This "capitalist" mode of production represented the most advanced one yet to appear. Throughout the world it was rapidly supplanting the preceding "feudal" mode of production.

As conceptualized by Marx, capitalism had certain central defining features. First, ownership of the means of production was in the hands of a single class (the "capitalist class" or "bourgeoisie"). No one else had the necessary tools and equipment to engage in production. Second, lacking the means of production to support themselves, laborers (the "working class" or "proletariat") had no choice but to sell their labor power. Under capitalism labor had become a commodity that was bought by the capitalist and sold by the laborer. Third, capitalists determined the allocation of the results of production. They owned the means of production (and could call on the power of the state to enforce their ownership rights), and workers had to work for them to survive. Capitalists consequently needed only to pay workers enough to "reproduce" their labor (enough for them to keep working and raise the next generation of workers). In turn, this guaranteed that the workers had to continue selling their labor power because they could never acquire their own means of production.

Fourth, because workers could be required to work longer than was necessary simply to reproduce their labor, capitalists ended up with the difference between what they paid the workers and the value of what the workers produced ("surplus value"). Fifth, capitalists were under a fundamental imperative to engage in the "accumulation of capital." Surplus value could not simply be used for the private consumption of the capitalist class or to purchase what was necessary to maintain the current level of production. Capitalists were in intense competition with one another to maintain and increase their share of the market by reducing prices, which required reducing production costs. Capitalists attempted to do so, in part, by forcing wages down. Nevertheless, long-term success also depended upon investing part of the surplus value into new, more efficient equipment and facilities ("capital") to increase worker productivity. Growth in the size of the production unit also yielded "economies of scale" in which larger productive units were more efficient than small ones. Hence, a basic dynamic force in capitalism (other than the simple avarice of the capitalist) was to accumulate more and more capital (Freedman, 1961; Mandel, 1975: 591–599).

In Marx's time, European capitalism was incorporating more and more of society into a system of wage labor and industrial work and was reshaping society to fit the interests of a capitalist ruling class whose members were the owners of industry and whose instrument of control was the state. Yet, in this process, a new class of industrial workers also came into being. According to Marx, the basic nature of capitalism required that the capitalist class steadily increase the intensity and severity of its exploitation of the working class in order to maintain the rate of profit (extraction of surplus value). As a consequence of this tendency, as well as the alternation of periods of prosperity with increasingly severe economic depressions, the working class would come to see that the system was not working to its benefit and would eventually succeed in overthrowing the capitalist class. Capitalism would be replaced by a system controlled by the workers. This "socialist" mode of production would then gradually evolve into a "communist" society characterized by total equality and the absence of economic exploitation (Marger, 1987: 37–38; Giddens, 1971: 31–34).

Outside of Europe, Marx saw the system of European colonialism as part of the process by which societies with less advanced modes of production were slowly being transformed into capitalist societies. Eventually, when they became fully developed capitalist societies, they, too, would experience the sort of class conflict already emerging in Europe.[1]

IMPLICATIONS FOR WORLD-SYSTEM THEORY. World-system theory incorporates the major elements and basic terminology of the Marxist theoretical approach. World-system theorists share with Marx the notion that the nature and functioning of capitalism are the fundamental factors in understanding contemporary societies. Like Marx, world-system theorists are deeply concerned with accounting for the rise and spread of capitalism, and they see capitalism as an inherently exploitative system that has been responsible for most of the conflict and misery— and economic expansion—in the modern era.

On the other hand, world-system theorists do not accept many of the detailed claims of Marx's theory. In fact, this rejection is one of the major sources of controversy about world-system theory and has led a number of more conventional Marxist theorists to reject or severely criticize the world-system approach. The theory represents a major modification of the traditional Marxist approach, rather than a simple application of accepted Marxist principles.

## Lenin on Imperialism

The starting point for almost all post–modernization-theory thinking about the relationship of the core countries to the periphery has been Lenin's theory of imperialism.[2] Writing several decades after Marx, V. I. Lenin (the leader of the Russian Revolution) proposed a Marxist interpretation of the wave of European colonization in the periphery during the second half of the nineteenth century. Lenin argued that capitalism had reached a new (and final) stage in its development characterized by the domination of the core economies by large, monopolistic corporations funded and controlled by a few giant financial firms. This "finance capitalism" was, according to Lenin, faced with a serious problem. Maintaining the rate of profit required continued economic growth to provide investment opportunities. Because of the extremes of wealth and poverty in capitalist countries, the vast bulk of the population lacked sufficient purchasing power to absorb the production generated by continued investment. If capitalists invested solely in the domestic market, they faced declining profits because of insufficient market demand. At the same time, profits were further threatened if increased production drove up the price of raw materials.

According to Lenin, the solution to the problem had been to open up new markets, obtain new sources of raw materials, and generate new opportunities for investment in the periphery. In this effort, the finance capitalists were able to use their political control of the core states to enlist them in the effort to colonize the periphery. Once colonized, the peripheral areas were required to allow foreign investment at the expense of local enterprises, accept the goods produced by the colonizing countries, and produce raw materials cheaply. Peripheral countries provided cheap raw materials and cheap labor and imported expensive goods from the core countries. Consequently, the relationship between the core and the periphery was exploitative. Wealth flowed from the colonies to the capitalists of the colonizing countries. This new system of exploitation was the "highest stage" of capitalism: "imperialism."

Imperialism, said Lenin, had several short-term consequences. Wealth flowing in from the colonies allowed the capitalist class not only to maintain a high rate of profit but to "buy off" small businesspeople and the upper levels of the working class with a higher standard of living. Hence, intense exploitation of the colonies made it possible to reduce exploitation at home and still maintain profits. This higher standard of living for domestic workers and small businesspeople reduced social and political unrest at home. Colonial wars and rivalry among the core powers for control over the colonies also contributed to feelings of nationalism in the core working class. This deflected workers away from internal struggles against the capitalist class.

In the longer term, however, imperialism would undo itself and thereby lead to the collapse of the whole capitalist system, according to Lenin. The competition among the core powers for colonies would lead to devastating and financially draining wars between them. The losers of those wars would face economic difficulties because of the loss of their colonies. The winners would face growing anticolonial wars of national liberation by the oppressed peoples of the periphery. These wars would drain the winners economically, and they would eventually have to surrender control over their colonies. The core's loss of its colonies would lead to economic stagnation, declining living standards, social unrest, and, ultimately, a revolution by the working class and the destruction of capitalism. As a consequence, imperialism only temporarily postponed the conditions Marx had predicted would lead to revolution.

IMPLICATIONS FOR WORLD-SYSTEM THEORY. Lenin's notion of imperialism casts an extremely long intellectual shadow over world-system theory. World-system theorists see the relationshp between the capitalist core and the periphery as basic to an understanding of the conditions in both sets of countries. They agree with Lenin that this relationship is exploitative and central to the economic success of the core countries. But world-system theorists do not agree with Lenin that imperialism and peripheral exploitation were characteristic of a particular stage of capitalism in the nineteenth century. World-system theorists view peripheral exploitation as a central feature of capitalism through its centuries-long history and nineteenth-century colonization as just one aspect of a longer term pattern in the modern era.

## The *Annales* School

A number of world-system theorists, most notably Immanuel Wallerstein, explicitly characterize their work as an extension of the concerns of the *Annales* school of French historical thought. (*Annales* is a journal in which scholars of this school have published much of their work.) Although the *Annales* school is not an explicitly Marxist theory, those working in this school share with Marx a concern for the origins and development of capitalism and employ many concepts ultimately derived from Marx. Among these scholars, the work of Fernand Braudel is of the greatest direct relevance to world-system theorizing. His three-volume work, *Civilization and Capitalism, 15th–18th Century* (1981, 1982, 1984), is the fullest statement of his approach and contains a number of ideas that reappear in world-system theory.[3]

For Braudel, society is an *ensemble des ensembles*—that is, a collection of parts assembled into an interrelated system—and societies are subsystems of a larger system. The unity of this larger entity is created by the prevailing type of world-economy, which shapes the nature of the relationships among the parts of the system and the nature of the parts themselves. Braudel describes the contemporary world economy in terms of three dimensions: "horizontal," "vertical," and "chronological."

The horizontal dimension consists of the organization of the world-economy into a geographic "center" surrounded by a periphery. The center is made up of economically strong and militarily powerful states that have the most advanced mode of production (following the Marxian usage of that term). The center (usually dominated by one particularly powerful state) benefits the most from the way in which the world economy is organized and attempts to maintain that organization. As one moves away from the center, societies have progressively less advanced modes of production. These modes are not just holdovers from the past; they are essential parts of the whole world-economy and exist to serve the interests of the center. Thus, the different modes of production in the world-economy are interrelated and interdependent.

The vertical dimension, the organization of the economic system into levels, comprises (1) a bottom level consisting of the everyday activities of individuals engaged in production and subsistence (the "material civilization"); (2) a middle level made up of the system of market relationships; and (3) a top level consisting of the general system of ownership and control in the economy. The basis of the whole system is the bottom level, which shapes the basic nature of economic activity.

The chronological dimension, the organization of the world-economy into identifiable periods with certain typical economic, social, and political characteristics, is made up of "long cycles" of events that lead up to the dominance of a particular state in the center, followed by a period in which that state's power gradually declines. He identifies four states that were associated with particular long cycles: (1) the northern Italian city-states (fourteenth century), (2) Holland (seventeenth century), (3) Great Britain (nineteenth century), and (4) the United States (twentieth century).

Braudel's central concern is to create an economic-historical account of these historical cycles and the accompanying development of a capitalist system of world-economy during the modern era. His thesis is complex and not subject to simple summary. Essentially, Braudel portrays the development of the current world economic system as series of chronological phases. Each of these corresponds to a set of changes in the horizontal and vertical dimensions and to a period of dominance by one state in the center.

IMPLICATIONS FOR WORLD-SYSTEM THEORY. The work of U.S. world-system theorists has numerous parallels with that of Braudel. Both assume that it is possible to describe the pattern of relationships among world societies as a coherent, interrelated system composed of a center (or core) and an exploited periphery. These theorists intend to develop a systematic, historically grounded account of the evolution of the world-system during the last five centuries, particularly the emergence and spread of capitalism. They emphasize the importance of economic and political competition among nation-states and hypothesize that there are cycles in which particular core states rise to preeminence and then decline. On the other hand, they do not necessarily agree on the particular interpretation of these events. What world-system theory incorporates from the *Annales* school is a general conception of recent world history, part of Braudel's analytic framework (the three dimensions just discussed), and an intellectual agenda in regard to what events in the modern era need explaining.

## The Dependency Approach

The school of thought that has the most direct link with world-system theory is the dependency approach. Indeed, world-system theory is a direct outgrowth of it. Many of those who started as dependency theorists have come to be identified with world-system theory. Here I will rely primarily on the work of Andre Gunder Frank (1966, 1967, 1978b, 1980), who now identifies himself with the world-system perspective, although there are many different explanations of dependency (the approach never became a unified theory).

Dependency thinking represents a systematic attempt to replace modernization theory with an alternative view. The central concern of this school has been to account for what many observers feel is the limited progress peripheral countries have made in achieving economic development and general modernization. For critics of modernization theory such as Frank, the key to an understanding of the plight of peripheral countries is to examine the nature of their relationships with the wealthy capitalist countries. This view is strongly influenced by Lenin's theory of imperialism, but it attempts to go beyond Lenin by specifying the nature of imperialism more completely and by accounting for changes that have occurred since Lenin wrote at the beginning of the century.

In Frank's version of dependency, the relationship between the advanced capitalist countries and the periphery is exploitative. The rich countries have devised a system of trade and investment that benefits their corporations at the expense of the periphery. In the recent past, says Frank, this exploitation has taken two general forms. In the first form, which is the older of the two and dates from the colonial period, peripheral countries function primarily as sources of raw materials and agricultural commodities for the wealthy countries and serve as markets for the core's manufactured goods. The operation of the world market for raw materials and agricultural exports is shaped by the large corporations and financial institutions of the wealthy capitalist nations, which are the primary buyers. As a consequence, these markets are plagued by chronic overproduction and low prices.

At the same time, to operate their export sectors, install a modern infrastructure, and so on, the peripheral countries must buy advanced manufactured goods. The corporations of the core countries are in a position to charge relatively high prices for these goods. As a result, peripheral countries receive low prices for what they export and are charged high prices for what they import. The outcome of this pattern of trade is that peripheral countries can never earn enough from their exports to cover the costs of their imports and then to invest in a broad-based program of industrialization. (Indeed, many dependency theorists have argued that the situation of peripheral countries has progressively deteriorated because of "declining terms of trade." In this view, the prices of peripheral countries' exports have been declining relative to the prices these countries pay for imports. They are consequently earning less and less from the same volume of exports.)

Rather than help these countries to break out of this pattern, the wealthy capitalist countries and their corporations further reinforce it. They will only provide the peripheral societies with loans and aid to invest in the raw materials and agricultural production that the wealthy countries want to buy. Thus, aid and investment lead to further specialization in agricultural and raw material production for export rather than to balanced economic development. Expansion of the export sector only makes peripheral countries more dependent on the wealthy nations for markets, investment capital, technical assistance, and consumer goods. The overall result is that most of the wealth generated by the export sector ultimately ends up in the hands of foreign corporations. They get cheap production inputs from the periphery and high prices for the goods they sell in the periphery. Payments to peripheral farmers, miners, and the like in the export sector have to be low because prices for what is produced are low. Outside of the export sector there is little investment capital to improve the productivity of the workers, and production techniques remain backward. Hence, most of the people of these peripheral countries (except for the large landowners and merchants who participate in the export system) continue to be poor. These countries are locked into a pattern of development in which only the export sector modernizes, and even that sector's expansion only increases the country's dependence.

In the second form of exploitation, part of the labor force in some peripheral societies is used in low-wage industrial work to produce goods for the world market. Modernization theorists would see such industrialization as evidence that peripheral countries are beginning to go through their own "industrial revolution." In fact, says Frank, this industrialization is just another form of exploitation leading to only limited, unbalanced economic development.

Frank argues that the primary direct beneficiaries of peripheral industrialization are the owners of the plants, who increase their profits by paying low wages. (The consumers in the wealthy nations also obtain cheaper manufactured goods.) The low wages also make possible the production of goods at low prices using less sophisticated and expensive production equipment, which thereby decreases initial capital investment costs and increases the rate of return on investment. The new industrial plants exist primarily to exploit the availability of workers who have no choice but to work for abysmally low wages.

In the case of plants owned by foreign corporations, most of the profits are returned to them rather than being invested in the peripheral country. Even locally (or governmentally) owned plants do not provide the capital for further industrialization because much of the profit goes back to foreign financial institutions to pay off loans made to construct the new plants. What remains tends to be spent by the peripheral upper class on conspicuous consumption. There is little incentive for this class to invest in industrial production for the local market because low wages and the limited numbers of workers involved in export production mean that purchasing power in the domestic market is very limited.

The export industries are rarely purchasers of much from the domestic economy except, perhaps, raw materials. They rely primarily on the import of machinery and subcomponents from foreign suppliers. Their operation consequently does not provide a market for local suppliers. As a result, the new plants are mostly isolated "islands" of modern productive technology that are tied for markets and machinery to the large foreign corporations, banks, and foreign consumers. These industries do not stimulate further domestic industrialization. (Peripheral industrialization will be discussed in more detail in Chapter 4.)

Thus, says Frank, peripheral countries' increasing trade with and investment from the wealthy capitalist countries have not led to the economic development predicted by modernization theory. Rather, the peripheral countries have been locked into those economic activities that employ highly exploited, low-wage labor to produce cheap goods for the corporations and consumers in the wealthy countries. The peripheral countries remain poor, while the wealthy capitalist countries and their corporations benefit. Frank calls this process the "development of underdevelopment" (1966).

Frank provides but one account of the nature and causes of the economic dependency of the periphery. There are many others. Nevertheless, the overall conclusion of all these theorists is essentially the same. In their view, the poverty of the periphery can be explained by the exploitation of the region by the corporations of advanced capitalist countries. By one means or another, the benefits of modern, export-oriented activities in the periphery have not gone to the people of the periphery. These activities have not aided in the creation of balanced, modern economies that would provide the basis for the long-term improvement of economic conditions and living standards in the periphery.

IMPLICATIONS FOR WORLD-SYSTEM THEORY. Dependency theory began as an attempt to account for contemporary conditions in the periphery and quickly led its practitioners to extend the historical and theoretical scope of their work to answer questions left unanswered by their initial formulations. At the same time, dependency theory was subjected to severe criticism by both Marxian and modernization theorists, which raised further questions about it.

World-system theory is a direct outgrowth of the search for answers to those questions. At the very heart of world-system theory is the question of the relationship of the core to the periphery. Like dependency theorists, world-system theorists see that relationship as basically exploitative. But world-system theorists attempt to trace the nature of this exploitation to events previous to the twentieth century and relate it to the historical development of capitalism. They also do not accept the claims of dependency theorists uncritically. For example, world-system theorists raise questions about whether all peripheral countries are permanently locked into a dependent relationship with the advanced capitalist countries, as most dependency theorists claim. World-system theorists also try to create a more general theoretical model of the nature of peripheral exploitation.

## Summary and Conclusion

World-system theory was initially formulated by Wallerstein (1974a). Since then, it has become a major subfield within U.S. sociology. Despite considerable diversity and controversy within the field, scholars working in world-system analysis share a common general approach and view of the world that clearly distinguish their work from the modernization approach and owe much to previous theories.

World-system theorists' approach to the study of social change represents a direct critique of modernization theory in particular and its structural-functionalist underpinnings in general. Most importantly, world-system theorists reject the modernization theory claim that the problems of the periphery are the result of historical backwardness or traditionalism. Rather, they argue that the conditions of the periphery must be understood as a result of the system of exploitation proposed by Lenin and further explicated by dependency theorists. In its rejection of ahistorical, abstract theorizing, world-system theory also represents something of a return to a form of historical sociology that had been a major concern of nineteenth-century social theorists and a continuing concern of historians such as Braudel. Like them, world-system theorists seek to understand the fundamental nature of the history of the modern era, particularly the rise of capitalism as the central defining development of this era. World-system theory also incorporates and attempts to reinvigorate the comparative analysis of societies—another minor tradition in an often parochial U.S. sociology.

At the same time, world-system theory is part of a more general 1970s shift in U.S. sociology toward the revival of sociological work in the Marxist tradition. With Marx, world-system theorists view capitalism as both the engine of historical change in the modern era and the source of the exploitation and inequalities that characterize it. They also share a generally Marxist model of society, which focuses on class conflict. Like most other U.S. sociologists working in this tradition today, world-system theorists are not attempting to create an orthodox, or classical, Marxist sociology. Rather, Marx is a starting point for a new theoretical approach.

Finally, world-system theorists reject what they regard as the narrow specialization of the traditional division of the U.S. social sciences into separate disciplines. They are trying to create an approach that crosses the traditional boundary lines among history, economics, political science, anthropology, and sociology (Chirot, 1977: 6–11; Thompson, 1983b; Wallerstein, 1979a: 133–137, 1983a).

This approach to social change is joined to a particular view of the nature of the modern world and how it has been changing in the last several centuries. Central to this vision is Braudel's claim that the major events and trends in the modern era are traceable to a *global* system of political-economy (the world-system). Consequently, change in societies can best be explained by understanding the influence of this world-system on events within them. Internal structures and power relationships are significantly shaped by each society's position in and relationship to the world-system.

It is to the nature of that world-system that we now turn in the next few chapters.

# World-System Structure

$\mathbf{T}$he specific claims of world-system theory can be separated (some-what artificially) into statements about system "structure" and system "dynamics." The former comprises the defining characteristics of the system, its components, and the relationships among those components. The latter concerns the processes of change to and within the structure.

This chapter will examine the general nature of world-system structure. The first concern will be to identify its most general features. As have other theorists before them, those working within world-system theory see the modern era as one in which a new type of social system emerged. They have sought to specify its central characteristics and what sets it apart from past social systems. The second concern will be to determine the nature of the system's most important component parts and how world-system theorists define them. The discussion will conclude with an examination of the claims these theorists make about the processes and relationships among those components—that is, about how the system works.

## General Features

The most basic claim made by world-system theorists is that an identifiable social system exists that extends beyond the boundaries of individual societies or nations. These theorists argue that it is a mistake to view the world as a set of independent societies that can be analyzed by focusing solely on events internal to them. Rather, these theorists claim that the social structure of individual societies has to be understood within the context created by a larger system. That system is the set of relatively stable economic and political relationships that has characterized a major portion of the globe since the sixteenth century. Initially, the system was limited to Europe and South America in the sixteenth century. Since that time, it has expanded to incorporate all or almost all areas of the world (Hopkins, 1982a; Wallerstein, 1984b; Chase-Dunn, 1984). This world-system has several key characteristics.

The economic organization of the world-system consists of a single, worldwide division of labor that unifies the multiple cultural systems of the world's peoples into a single, integrated economic system (Wallerstein, 1979a: 5). By claiming that there is a single division of labor, world-system theorists are rejecting the more conventional approach, which has viewed the world-economy as composed of isolated and independent national economies that just happen to trade with one another. Wallerstein explains what he means by this single, integrated world-economy as follows:

> The concept "world-economy" assumes that there exists an "economy" . . . if but only if . . . there is an ongoing, extensive and relatively complete social division of labor with an integrated set of production processes which relate to each other through a "market" which has been "instituted" or "created" in some complex way (Wallerstein, 1984b: 59).

Wallerstein has also attempted to specify what he means by a "relatively complete social division of labor." Such a division exists when there is an "economic grid which is substantially interdependent" (Wallerstein, 1979a: 14). In turn, such interdependence exists when the exchange of goods in the system consists of those considered "essential" to the various trading partners. In other words, the trading partners could not continue the economic activities they consider central to their well-being without continuing the exchange. Economic activities in each part of a true world-economy depend on and make possible the activities in the other parts (Wallerstein, 1979: 14).

The result is an economic system that includes a number of cultural areas, states, or societies but constitutes a single economy based on a complex division of labor. Each part or area has acquired a specialized role producing goods that it trades to others to obtain what it needs. Thus, the world-economy is tied together by a complex network of global economic exchange (Wallerstein, 1984b: 60–61, 1979a: 5, 14–15).

By itself, the existence of geographically extensive economies with integrated, interdependent divisions of labor is not unique to the modern era. Ancient empires, such as Rome and China, created such economies. Wallerstein characterizes such empires as world-systems within their political boundaries. (Trade existed between the empires, but the limited nature of that trade does not fit Wallerstein's definition of an integrated division of labor.) But he argues that these economic systems were not world-economies; they were world-empires, with economic and political organization quite different from the modern world-system (Wallerstein, 1979a: 5). Hence, the particular nature of the political-economy of the world-system of the modern era sets it apart from its historical predecessors. It is a *capitalist* economy organized into an *interstate system*.

## CAPITALISM

World-system theorists regard capitalism as a global system for organizing economic activities. Owners of the means of production (individuals, private corporations, or state organizations) seek to "obtain a maximum price and profit for market sales" (Thompson, 1983b: 12) as a means to accumulate ever more capital (Wallerstein, 1984b: 60). Following Marx, world-system theorists argue that this capital accumulation is based on the central economic relationship in a capitalist mode of production: the exploitation of labor by capitalists. Owners of the means of production extract as much of the results of production from the workers as possible. This surplus value remains in the owners' hands, thereby leading to extreme economic inequality in the world-economy.

The existence of this economic exploitation is not unique to the modern era. Rather, the way in which exploitation occurs and who benefits from it distinguish the modern world-system from its predecessors. In world-empires accumulation of surplus occurred through the direct expropriation of wealth from the rural peasantry using political coercion (taxes, tribute, state-sanctioned systems of slavery) and state regulation, licensing, and taxation of others (urban artisans and merchants). Wealth was accumulated at the political center by those (usually a hereditary aristocracy) who controlled the state machinery. This political elite sought to increase its wealth by rising in the political hierarchy and increasing state power to obtain control over more land and peasants. (The elite had little interest in improving the productivity of economic enterprises themselves.)

In contrast, under capitalism economic power rests in the hands of those who own the means of production. The state's role consists of enforcing the social relations of production between owners and workers. It does so by protecting property rights and enforcing the terms of exchange among participants in the economy. The state also creates conditions favorable to operation of productive enterprises. Success goes to those who use the surplus generated by labor exploitation for capital accumulation, which improves the competitive position of one owner of the means of production over others (Wallerstein, 1974a: 15–16, 347–348).

Note that this definition of a capitalist world-system is more general and less restrictive in its requirements than the definition proposed by Marx to characterize the economic systems of the countries of Western Europe. At the level of the world-economy, all Wallerstein requires of the system to make it capitalist is that it be based on (1) profit-maximizing and the search for competitive advantage through efficiency, (2) the quest for continual capital accumulation, and (3) the exploitation of labor by the owners of the means of production (Wallerstein, 1984b: 60–61, 1979a: 16–17).

World-system theorists view capitalism as a feature of an *entire* world-system. They emphasize that the institutions of society are organized to meet the needs of this global system. The particular structure and internal institutional arrangements of a society cannot be fully understood unless one takes into account that society's position in and relationship to the world system (Chase-Dunn, 1981; Hopkins, Wallerstein et al., 1982b: 51–52). (This assertion has been called the "holistic assumption" in world-system theory [Hall, 1984].) For example, world-system theorists emphasize that the particular method of labor exploitation and extraction of surplus extant in a given part of the system is the result of the requirements of the world-system of capitalism as a whole. (As we will see, this particular claim has created quite a controversy among Marxists.)

THE INTERSTATE SYSTEM

The other basic defining feature of the modern world-system is its historically unique system of political organization. No single political entity (state) has ever obtained exclusive authority over the geographic area encompassed by the world-economy. Rather, the world-system's political organization is that of an interstate system of competing, sovereign "nation-states." Although these states vary considerably in their relative power, none of the stronger ones has been strong enough to destroy the others. The existence of multiple strong states has also prevented any one of them from seizing control of the territory of all the weak states. Such an attempt has always been blocked by the other strong states (Chase-Dunn, 1984: 76; Wallerstein, 1984b: 60). This fragmented political organization is opposite the situation that prevailed prior to the modern era. Previously, geographically extensive economies either simply disintegrated or ended up under the control of a single state, thereby creating world-empires (Wallerstein, 1979a: 5).

World-system theorists argue that the system of interstate competition and capitalism reinforce one another. Each is necessary for the existence of the other. Capitalism could not exist if there were a single world state. Such a state could use its coercive powers to destroy the independence of the capitalist class. On the other hand, competition among the capitalists of different nation-states has given no one state a permanent economic advantage on which to base the conquest of the others. Hence, the interstate system has persisted (Chase-Dunn, 1981). (We will discuss this argument in more detail in Chapter 6.)

## Components of the System

The economic and political relationships within the world-system take place among certain key components: economic zones, nation-states, social classes, and status groups. Before we discuss those relationships, it is necessary to define those components.

### ECONOMIC ZONES

The production processes in the world division of labor can be divided into three general categories: "core," "peripheral," and "semi-peripheral." Each type has tended to predominate in particular geographic areas under the control of particular states or systems of political administration (for example, colonies of other states). World-system theorists consequently speak of geographical areas and states as being in the core, periphery, and semi-periphery.

The economically and politically dominant states in the world-system are those in the core, which "consists of those states in which the agro-industrial production is the most efficient and where the complexity of economic activities and the level of capital accumulation is the greatest" (Thompson, 1983b: 12). Within the world division of labor, core states specialize in the production of the most "advanced" goods, which involves the use of the most sophisticated technologies and highly mechanized methods of production ("capital-intensive" production). At least until recently, this meant that core states specialized in the production of sophisticated manufactured goods. Core states are the most militarily powerful and administratively well organized of those in the world-system (Hopkins, 1982a: 12–13). For most of the history of the world-system, the core consisted of a limited number of states located in Western Europe. During this century, first the United States and then (in the 1970s) Japan joined the core.

At the other extreme in the world-system are those states and colonies in the periphery. Economic activities in the periphery are relatively less technologically sophisticated and more "labor intensive" than those in the core. (Labor-intensive activities are those involving the use of workers employing relatively little machinery.) For most of the modern era, production for export was concentrated on raw materials and agricultural commodities. Peripheral states (where they have existed) are militarily and organizationally weak (Hopkins, 1982a: 12–13). Throughout most of world-system history, parts of South America, Central America, Africa, and Asia have been in the periphery.

Between these two extremes are those states in the semi-periphery. They have some economic activities similar to those of the core ("core-like") and some more typical of the periphery ("peripheral-like"). Consequently, the extent of development of capital-intensive industry is somewhere in between those of the core and the periphery. Semi-peripheral state machineries are stronger and more autonomous from core influence than are those of the periphery. They play a crucial role as "intermediaries" in the world-system (Wallerstein, 1984b: 61; Thompson, 1983b: 12; Hopkins, Wallerstein et al., 1982b: 47). Brazil and Argentina are examples of present-day, semi-peripheral countries.

## NATION-STATES

The basic unit of political organization in the modern era is the nation-state. Beginning in the core, states slowly evolved into this new kind of political organization. (Modern, independent state organizations in the periphery generally emerged even later and still display only some of the characteristics of core nation-states.) A central defining feature of such political entities is that the state claims to govern a population group ("nation" or "people") that shares a common identity based on such factors as language, cultural practices, common institutions, shared historical experiences, and shared interests (in relation to other nations). As it developed during the last few centuries, the nation-state

> created the idea of the "citizen"—the individual who recognized the state as his legal home. It created the idea of a uniform system of law throughout a country . . . of legal equality, where all citizens have the same status before the law . . . of a state that exists to serve those citizens . . . of loyalty to a larger group than clan or caste . . . of common languages and common education systems, and common legal systems within clearly defined state boundaries . . . of state tariffs at those boundaries [and of] state debts and state banks managing state-wide currencies (Tivey, 1981: 13).

At least in the core, as state legitimacy came increasingly to rest on the notion that the state was the representative of the nation, states were obliged to extend greater political rights to citizens in terms of participation in and benefits obtained from state operations (Marshall, 1950).

This modern conception of the state is quite different from that of the hereditary rulers of ancient world-empires (and the feudal nobility that governed Europe prior to 1500). They considered the state as their "property" (conferred by the gods, tradition, and/or war) to do with as they pleased for their own personal benefit (Lenski and Lenski, 1978: 198–199). World-empires consisted of often disparate cultural groups that retained their identity. They viewed themselves (and were viewed by their rulers) as conquered subjects of an oppressive elite.

World-system theorists also emphasize another characteristic of nation-states. They have become large, centralized, and powerful organizations. Such powerful states stand in great contrast to the weak, decentralized political organization of feudal Europe.

World-empires were also relatively centralized and powerful. But the kind of power nation-states exercise is different from that exercised by those earlier states. Michael Mann, although not a world-system theorist, provides a useful way of describing the nature of this difference by distinguishing between "despotic" and "infrastructural" power. Despotic power refers to the "range of actions which the [political] elite is empowered to undertake without routine, institutionalized negotiation with civil society groups" (1986b: 113). It is arbitrary power. Infrastructural power refers to the ability of the state to "penetrate civil society and to implement logistically political decisions throughout the realm" (1986b: 113). Infrastructural power thus refers to the state's ability to carry out policies and control events in society. The most successful (core) modern nation-states have a high level of infrastructural power. Most have much less despotic power.

Hopkins and Wallerstein (et al.) refer to the greater effectiveness that the core nation-states came to display as "state strength." They define state strength as the "ability to make policies prevail against internal resistance and external opposition . . . [but it does] . . . not mean either the arbitrariness of the power of the leadership or the extent of bureaucratization" (1982b: 61). State strength is important because it determines the ability of government to act in ways favorable to the capitalist class. Wallerstein argues that there are five crucial actions a strong state is able to take: intervene in the world-market to help domestic producers; compete militarily with other states; perform state tasks efficiently (so that the state does not drain excessive resources from the capitalist class); organize the state administrative apparatus to function effectively; and establish a stable arrangement of political alliances with (but not despotic domination of) elements within the capitalist class (Wallerstein, 1980: 113).

## SOCIAL CLASSES

Relationships within the modern world-system develop, in part, along class lines. Following Marx, world-system theorists conceive of social classes as social groupings defined by their relationship to the means of production. Thus, the basic distinction in the class system of the capitalist world-system is between those who own the means of production and those who are denied ownership. In contrast, the most basic distinction in a world-empire is between those who control the state machinery and those who do not. Because these theorists view capitalism as a world-system, they consider social classes as worldwide strata that are not limited to particular national societies: "The world class structure is composed of capitalists . . . and propertyless workers. This class system also includes small commodity producers who control their own means of production but who do not employ the labor of others, and a growing middle class of skilled and/or professionally certified workers" (Chase-Dunn, 1983: 73; also see Hopkins, 1982b).

Note that this categorization specifically acknowledges the existence of middle classes. Wallerstein and his associates also distinguish between kinds of propertyless workers ("proletarians" in Marx's terminology) in a way Marx did not. They argue that some workers' households support themselves entirely, throughout the lifetimes of their members, by their work for capitalists. They call such households "lifetime" or "full" proletarians. Other households do not receive enough from their work for capitalists to support all their members for the duration of their lives. These households supplement what they receive from capitalists with independent commodity production (for example, part-time farming). Such households are "part-lifetime proletarians" or "semi-proletarians" (Hopkins, Wallerstein et al., 1982b: 68–69). This is an important (and controversial) modification of Marx's view of the class system under capitalism.

## STATUS GROUPS

Class is not the only social cleavage in the world-system. Borrowing from the work of Max Weber, Wallerstein argues that the system is divided up into "status groups," which consist of social groupings whose solidarity derives from cultural identification. The basis of that identification can be such factors as religion, language, race, or ethnicity. As previously discussed, status groups in the modern era have tended to become organized into nations or peoples governed by a single state. As a consequence, the global class system is cross-cut by status groups, especially nations. This has significant implications for political and economic relationships in the system. Most class struggles and conflicts actually occur within nations, even though the capitalist world-system is the objective basis of the classes and their interests. Nationalism has prevented global class solidarity of both the capitalist class and the proletariat. In addition, relationships among nations and other status groups in the world-system are as important as those among social classes (Wallerstein, 1984c: 34–35).

## Processes and Relationships Within the System

The central claims of world-system theory consist of statements about the basic political and economic processes and relationships generated by a capitalist world-economy organized within the political framework of the interstate system. This section's discussion will begin with an examination of the basic economic processes and relationships of the world-system. The section will then examine the political processes and relationships that create the context in which those economic patterns operate and that make them possible.

ECONOMIC PROCESSES

A global system of capitalism has certain basic economic processes whose fundamental imperative is capital accumulation for the owners of the means of production. Capitalist entrepreneurs and organizations compete with one another to maximize profits and are therefore endlessly driven to obtain more surplus by intensifying the exploitation of workers, recruiting larger number of workers into the capitalist labor process, obtaining new markets, and eliminating competitors. As a consequence, the capitalist class is innovative in its search for labor efficiency and expansionist in its search for exploitable labor and new markets. The search for efficiency also puts a premium on and provides a motivation for seeking new technologies and productive techniques. This drive for endless capital accumulation is the underlying economic motive force that drives all other processes and relationships within the system (Wallerstein, 1984b: 62–63; Chase-Dunn, 1983: 76; Hopkins, 1982a: 14–15).

*Interzonal Economic Relationships.* In the world-system view of modern history a central economic relationship exists between the core and the periphery. Peripheral societies specialize in the production and export of labor-intensive, low-technology goods desired by the core and the semi-periphery. In return, the core produces capital-

FIGURE 2.1 Relationships in the Capitalist World-Economy

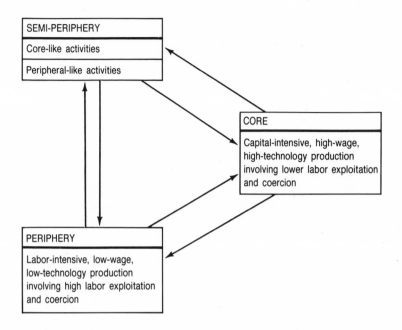

intensive, high-technology goods, some of which it exports to the periphery and the semi-periphery. The semi-periphery exports peripheral-like goods to the core and core-like goods to the periphery. In return, it receives goods produced with labor-intensive, low-technology methods from the periphery and capital-intensive, high-technology methods from the core (see Figure 2.1).

World-system theorists have a view of the nature of this trading relationship that in some respects is quite similar to dependency theory (but see Chapters 5 and 6 for how it may differ). World-system theorists regard the economic relationship between the core and periphery as fundamentally exploitative. Trade and other forms of economic relationships between the core and the periphery benefit core capitalists at the expense of the periphery. The periphery receives less from the core for its economic activities than the core receives from the periphery for its activities. In other words, most of the wealth (surplus value) generated in the periphery flows to the core (Wallerstein, 1984b: 61; Hopkins, Wallerstein et al., 1982b: 46–47; Hopkins, 1982a: 21).

The underlying reason most of the surplus value generated in the periphery ends up in the hands of core capitalists has been a matter of some theoretical uncertainty among both world-system and dependency theorists. Most world-system theorists accept the conclusions of Arrighi Emmanuel (1972), who maintains that the basis of peripheral exploitation is "unequal exchange." Emmanuel's theory is an attempt to apply Marxian economic theory to international exchange. His argument, which rests on the fact that the level of compensation for workers in the periphery is lower than that for workers in the core, is that the process of exchange of low-wage products from the periphery for high-wage products from the core is inherently unequal. The core receives inexpensive goods from the periphery because of the low wages paid in producing those goods. If the core had to produce those goods itself, they would be much more expensive because of the higher wage rate in the core. (A fuller presentation of his somewhat involved argument is beyond the scope of the present discussion; world-system theorists rarely do more than cite Emmanuel's conclusions and do not discuss the theory itself.)

For example, Samir Amin illustrates Emmanuel's argument using core-periphery trade. Peripheral exports of products from its "modern" sector amounted to $26 billion in 1966. He argues that the same goods produced in the core would have cost $34 billion. The difference between what the core actually pays and what it would have to pay ($8 billion) is what the core gains in the exchange of those goods (1976: 143).

Conversely, the periphery buys relatively expensive core goods produced by high-wage labor. If the periphery could produce them itself, they would be cheaper. Emmanuel attempts to demonstrate that as a result, when peripheral goods are exchanged for those of the core, much of the surplus value produced by workers in the periphery ends up in the hands of the producers of high-wage goods in the core. A substantial portion of the value of the labor of the periphery consequently is transferred to core capitalists as a result of the exchange. (Emmanuel's formulation has been a controversial one. Some of the debate about the theory of unequal exchange will be reviewed in Chapter 6.)

In practice, while citing Emmanuel, most world-system theorists focus on specific mechanisms by which surplus value created by low-wage labor in the periphery has been transferred to the core without attempting to rigorously prove or demonstrate the mechanisms' consistency with Emmanuel's formulation of unequal exchange (Bernstein, 1982: 235). To avoid conceptual confusion, the term *unequal exchange* will be used here only when referring to Emmanuel's argument. For the general process of the transfer of surplus to the core we will employ the term *peripheral exploitation.*

What is the significance of peripheral exploitation in the operation of the world-system? Christopher Chase-Dunn provides a concise summary:

> It has probably never been the case . . . that more surplus product was extracted from the periphery than was produced in the core. Most of surplus value accumulated in the core is produced by core workers using relatively more productive technology. Nevertheless, the surplus product extracted from the periphery has played a crucial role in allowing the relatively peaceful process of expanded reproduction in the core to proceed. This has occurred in three ways: (1) by reducing the level of conflict and competition among core capitalists within core states, (2) by allowing adjustments in power relations among core states to be settled without destroying the interstate system, and (3) by promoting relative harmony between capital and labor in the core (1983: 75).

Why does the additional surplus value have these effects? First, the extra wealth obtained in the periphery by core capitalists gives them an additional means of earning surplus value that does not require them to compete as much for the control of core markets. Second, the competition among core states for territory and economic advantage has been partially diverted from the core in its attempt to gain control of areas in the periphery. Hence, success for a core state need not require the destruction of its competitors. The periphery provides another outlet for core states' expansionism. Third, as Lenin argues, the additional surplus obtained from the periphery provides core capitalists with the means to satisfy some of the demands of the workers in the core without reducing the rate of profit as much. That at least reduces class conflict in the core. In addition, the production of increased surplus from the periphery (by increasing the scope of labor exploitation) has played a critical role in helping end periods of economic stagnation in the world-economy that could lead to class conflict.

For the periphery, exploitation by the core has been the fundamental factor shaping its development in the modern era. As a result, the periphery has not been able to accumulate the capital necessary for successful economic modernization. The failure of most of the periphery to achieve rapid, self-sustaining economic growth is attributable to its economic exploitation by the core. The capital needed for investment has flowed into the hands of core capitalists, and what investment there has been in the periphery has gone to enterprises oriented toward meeting core needs (Frank, 1984; Wallerstein, 1984b: 61). At the same time, the internal requirements of maintaining a system of intense labor exploitation at low levels of compensation have shaped the nature of peripheral class relations, political conflict, and the general features of most other institutional arrangements.

Within the world-economy the semi-periphery occupies a critical position as an intermediary between the core and the periphery. Semi-peripheral states function as regional trading and financial centers. As such, they are centers for the collection of surplus for transmission to the core and the administration of core investment in the periphery.

The semi-periphery also has a dual role in international exchange. The core is able to exploit those portions of semi-peripheral economies that are engaged in low-wage, peripheral-like production. Simultaneously, to some extent, their core-like economic activities also allow semi-peripheral countries to engage in an exploitative exchange with the periphery.

An additional defining feature of the semi-periphery is the nature of its core-like activities. They are concentrated in the "declining" sectors of economic activity in the core—that is, those sectors that are facing a falling rate of profit caused by high wages and the equalizing of the comparative costs of production among producers. No one producer can sell at a price that will yield an increasing share of the market and a high rate of profit. Each one has similar nonwage costs of production and is under pressure to increase (or at least maintain) wage rates. (The steel and auto industries are contemporary examples of this situation.)

The only way out of this situation from the point of view of the core capitalists involved is to shift their investment to new activities in which the rate of profit is higher. (In our example, steel or auto corporations might try to buy into the electronics industry.) In such a situation, the semi-periphery can profitably engage in the declining core activity because of comparably lower wages. That core producers are moving out of the activity provides an opening for alternative producers with a wage-cost advantage. (Currently, steel is increasingly being produced by such semi-peripheral countries as Brazil.) The constant movement of core capital to new, higher profit activities thus creates a structural position in the world-economy for those who can produce profitably in older activities employing low-wage labor. That is the niche of the semi-periphery in the world-economy (Wallerstein, 1979a: 70–71). (As we will see in Chapter 5, this situation also provides the opportunity for peripheral countries to move into the semi-periphery and semi-peripheral countries to try moving into the core.)

The attempt to engage in core-like activities in turn creates another defining feature of the semi-peripheral zone. To protect internal markets for their new core-like activities, semi-peripheral states have to restrict imports from the core. Consequently, semi-peripheral states tend to employ protectionist trade barriers (Wallerstein, 1979a: 72).

*Interclass Economic Relationships.* When they turn to economic relations between the social classes, world-system theorists employ a modified Marxian model. The defining feature of these relationships is the exploitation of workers by the capitalist class to acquire the surplus value produced by the workers. Unlike Marx, world-system theorists argue that the intensity and nature of that exploitation vary between types of proletarians and the different parts of the world-economy, depending on the particular system of "labor control" (method of organizing work). Systems of labor control vary along a continuum in terms of the degree of coercion employed.

At one extreme are those workers whose labor is extracted through some form of direct coercion. The most extreme form of such coercion is slavery. Other, less extreme forms would include serfdom (in which the worker is tied to the land for life and owes obedience to the landowner), sharecropping, and plantation systems operated by wage laborers. In all these systems workers are subject to control through means that are ultimately backed by state-sanctioned or imposed force, which enables owners to obtain worker labor at extremely low levels of compensation.

In most cases workers are compensated so poorly that their households are members of the semi-proletarian class. As such, they are "superexploited" workers: They do not receive enough compensation for their labor from the capitalist class to support their households at a level sufficient to "reproduce" their labor. Household members have to engage in other subsistence labor, at least for some period of their lives. This can occur in a number of ways. For example, the worker can engage in part-time farming while also employed, or most members of the household could remain in the home village engaged in subsistence agriculture while one worker goes to work on a seasonal basis on a plantation.

In any case capitalists get more than just the surplus directly generated by the workers whom they employ; they also receive part of the surplus generated by the households engaged in subsistence activities because these activities in effect subsidize the production activities of the capitalist class. (Part of a product's true value is the cost of reproducing the labor of the worker, according to the Marxist conception.) Super-exploitation and semi-proletarian households predominate in peripheral societies, are less common in semi-peripheral societies, and are least common in core societies (Hopkins, Wallerstein et al., 1982b: 69–70; Wallerstein, 1984b: 64; Wallerstein, 1979a: 126–127).

At the other extreme from direct coercion is economic coercion. Workers are free to sell their labor to any employer for any price they can obtain. They are coerced in the classical Marxian sense in that they do not own the means of production and consequently must work for the capitalist class. World-system theorists agree with Marx that under conditions of free wage labor, the capitalist class must compensate workers enough to reproduce their labor. Superexploitation cannot occur, and compensation levels must be higher. Indeed, world-system theorists argue that the growing political power of the workers in the core has meant generally rising wage levels, at least since the middle of the nineteenth century. Free wage laborers (and their families) are full proletarians. The largest proportion of full proletarian households is always in the core, and the smallest is found in the periphery. The proportion in the semi-periphery is somewhere in between peripheral and core levels (Hopkins, Wallerstein et al., 1982b: 69–70).

## POLITICAL RELATIONSHIPS

The economic relationships within the world-system would not be possible without the political processes and relationships that develop alongside of them. The economic relationships are politically enforced.

*Interstate Political Relationships.* Relationships within the interstate system are inherently competitive and unequal. States are locked in an intense competition to maximize their power in relation to one another. Each state constantly strives to increase its resources (military power, wealth, and so on) relative to the others in order to increase its autonomy from and/or influence over the other nation-states (and, frequently, to increase the territory under its control). State support for the national capitalist class (rather than the world capitalist class as a whole) is simply part of that strategy.

A central goal of international competition is for each state to obtain the best possible conditions and opportunities for its national capitalists. A successful national capitalist class contributes to state power by providing the necessary economic resources for state activities. World-system theorists point out that states in which the struggle for power resulted in a politically powerful capitalist class were the states that succeeded best in the quest for national power. The political power of the capitalist class reinforces this tendency for the state to support the national capitalist class. As a consequence of this interstate competition, the world-system has been characterized by repeated wars and shifting military alliances (Wallerstein, 1984b: 62; Hopkins, 1982a: 23–28; McMichael, 1985; Chase-Dunn, 1981).

The exploitative economic relationship between the core and the periphery requires a particular political relationship between them.

The periphery has to be forced to participate in the world-economy on terms favorable to core capitalists. Core states are able to dominate the periphery because of their greater economic resources, more powerful militaries, and the greater strength of their government apparatus.

Core domination of the periphery has taken several basic forms historically. The most obvious form has been the forceable seizure of areas in the periphery by specific core powers, which have turned those areas into directly controlled colonies. In other periods or other parts of the periphery, different core states have developed spheres of influence in which they have created client states. These peripheral states have done the bidding of and maintained close economic ties with their "patron" core power. In other cases peripheral states have not been the clients of any particular core power. Under those circumstances one or more of those powers have acted to make sure that these states adopted policies consistent with the maintenance of the basic pattern of peripheral exploitation. Competition among core powers for influence and/or direct control over peripheral states has been one of the major sources of core political and military competition and conflict throughout the history of the world-system (Thompson, 1983a; Frank, 1984).

In their relationships with the core and the periphery, semi-peripheral states function to prevent the political polarization of the world-system. Because they enjoy greater wealth, exercise more international power, and benefit from exploiting and dominating peripheral areas in their region, semi-peripheral states are not likely to ally themselves with the periphery against the core or to see their interests as similar to those of the peripheral states. Indeed, the semi-periphery's exploitation of the periphery is likely to generate resentment among those states. The semi-periphery's capitalist classes also have a vested interest in existing economic arrangements between the core and periphery because of their role as financial and trading intermediaries in the system of peripheral exploitation. Core states have frequently found it convenient to ally themselves with semi-peripheral states, allowing them to function as regional powers enforcing the existing system of economic and political relationships in their region.

Nevertheless, the interests of semi-peripheral states are not identical to those of the core. These states attempt to maintain their (partial) autonomy from the core and seek to minimize core exploitation, which constantly threatens to force them into peripheral status. They also may aspire to core status. That quest requires that they pursue policies that will protect and enlarge their core-like activities and state power at the expense of the interests of core capitalists and states. Thus, semi-peripheral states have to engage in a difficult balancing act. They are forced to acknowledge the greater power of the core and often receive benefits for cooperating with it. Yet, they simultaneously seek to maintain their freedom of action to pursue policies that will strengthen their position in the world-system (Wallerstein, 1979a: 69, 83–92, 95–108).

*Social Classes and Political Relationships.* The central class-based political relationship in the world-system is between the state and the capitalist class. The exact nature of this relationship remains to be worked out in world-system theory. In general, world-system theorists argue that the state follows policies that favor the interests of the capitalist class. Along with Marx, world-system theorists argue that the resources that the capitalist class commands because of its control over the means of production gives this class the greatest political influence in society. Nevertheless, the state is not a passive "tool" or agent of particular capitalists; state leaders do pursue their own interests. But it may be in their interests to support the interests of their national capitalist class (Rubinson, 1978; Block, 1978; Chase-Dunn, 1983, 1984).

What does the state do for its national capitalist class? Wallerstein (1984b: 64–65) suggests three primary state activities that serve the interests of the capitalist class. First, the state regulates the relationship between the capitalist class and the working class. Worker opposition to the exploitation of labor has to be controlled and the property rights of the capitalist class protected. The state intervenes to "limit and moderate the economic demands of . . . national work forces" (1984b: 65). Second, the state uses its power to shape world economic relationships to favor the interests of its capitalists; this includes seeking economically advantageous relationships within the core and enforcing the system of peripheral exploitation. Wallerstein emphasizes that the system of international economic relationships that characterize the world-economy has always reflected the active intervention of the states (especially those of the core) in the world-system. Third, core states use their power to bring new geographical areas into the world-system as part of the periphery. This assistance helps enable the capitalist class to incorporate new markets, new sources of exploitable labor, and new sources of raw materials. The intervention of core states in the periphery has been the means by which the capitalist world-economy has expanded during the modern era.

As we will discuss in the next chapter, the power of the capitalist class was not fully developed at the beginning of the modern era. Rather, that power emerged as part of the general process by which nation-states evolved in the core. There has always been a struggle for power among state leaders, the capitalist class, the working class, and other groups (the feudal aristocracy, peasants, various middle classes).

Wallerstein argues that the outcome of that struggle led to different political relationships in the core than in the periphery. In the core the capitalist class became the politically dominant class. Yet, at the same time, as workers in the core became fully proletarianized, state leaders found it their interest (primarily as means of securing mass support and legitimacy) to allow workers political rights. These concessions made it possible for workers to organize and make demands on the state and on the capitalist class, and some of the political rights granted (such as equality under the law or the right to sell one's labor) were necessary to the creation of a workforce of full proletarians. (Of course, the growing wealth of the core made it easier to give into these demands.) As a result, core states have generally become less repressive, and their workers have been in a position to demand progressively higher wage levels (Wallerstein, 1984b: 69; Hopkins, Wallerstein et al., 1982b: 69–70; Chase-Dunn, 1983: 73).

In contrast, the form of coercive exploitation that exists in the periphery requires a high level of state repression. In general, peripheral regions were brought into the world-system using some degree of force. The political systems created after inclusion had to use repression from the very beginning in order to create systems of coerced labor control (Hopkins, Wallerstein et al., 1982b: 70; Hopkins and Wallerstein, 1987: 777–779).

## Summary and Conclusion

The basic characteristics of world-system structure have persisted during the five centuries of its existence and clearly differentiate the modern era from the period in which the most powerful and successful systems of political-economy were world-empires. These structural characteristics have generated patterns of political and economic relationships that have provided the basic framework in which the historical events of the modern era have unfolded. Knowing about these general features of the system allows one to make sense of specific historical periods. That task of historical analysis has been a major focus of the work of world-system theorists. The next two chapters will examine those efforts.

# World-System Structure: The Early Centuries

This chapter will examine the operation of the world-system at three different points in its history to illustrate the general processes and relationships discussed in the last chapter. The description of the early part of the modern era will also provide a summary of the crucial changes that brought the world-system into being. Finally, the discussion will demonstrate that despite the vast changes in the modern era, the basic structure of the world-system has remained remarkably stable throughout its history.

The analysis of each period will focus on the features of world-system structure described in the last chapter. Specifically, the following topics will provide the framework for the discussion: (1) the composition of the core, periphery, and semi-periphery, (2) the relationships within the interstate system, (3) the division of labor in the world-economy and the mechanisms of peripheral exploitation, (4) the central features of the class structure in each zone, and (5) the nature of state structures and internal political relationships in each area of the system.

## The World in 1400

The last chapter pointed out that the world-system that came into being in the sixteenth century represented a new kind of political-economy.[1] To understand just how new it was requires some familiarity with the world just prior to the modern era. In 1400 the most advanced societies were the world-empires discussed in the last chapter. Other

TABLE 3.1
The Main Societal Types in Existence Prior to 1000 B.C.

| Societal Type | Initial Appearance | Major Technological Developments | Key Social Characteristics |
|---|---|---|---|
| Hunting and gathering | 35000–50000 B.C. | Spear, bow and arrow, specialized implements | Often nomadic bands organized by strong kin ties with limited systematic inequalities of wealth and power |
| Simple horticulture | 7000 B.C. | Cultivation of crops with hand tools; craft specialization; domestic livestock | Settled villages with limited intervillage political organization; some stable inequalities of wealth and power; intervillage trade; some warfare |
| Advanced horticulture | 4000 B.C. | Copper and bronze tools and weapons; irrigation; horse use and chariots; trading ships (sails) | Small "tributary empires" dominated by a warrior priestly class that used its power to extract wealth and labor from peasants; small "urban" centers with political, military, ceremonial, craft production, and trade functions; class systems, slavery, and organized war; long-distance trade in luxury goods |
| Simple agrarian | 3000 B.C. | Agriculture (animal-drawn plow); improved ships and wheeled vehicles | Empires with centralized state, bureaucratic administration, and standing armies; monetary, tax, and legal systems; state functions to extract wealth from peasantry; "true" cities; extreme inequality and exploitation |

*Source:* Based on Lenski and Lenski (1978: 88–192).

societies existed as well, and these were based on different levels of technological complexity. Table 3.1 summarizes these societal types.

The world-empires shared a basic level of technology, usually called "advanced agrarian," which appeared around 1000 B.C. It included the intense cultivation of crops using animal-drawn plows, the use of iron tools and weapons, and the sophisticated, highly specialized craft production of both necessities and luxury goods. Where rainfall was adequate or large-scale irrigation was possible, agricultural productivity was high enough to support large, densely settled populations. Simple machinery, based on cranks and pulleys, was invented. Construction techniques, mobilizing large numbers of workers, enabled the creation of monumental public works such as fortresses, temples, canals, irrigation systems, and road networks. By using wind-powered and oar-driven ships, communities were able to transport some bulky goods over moderately long distances (such as across the Mediterranean Sea). Land transportation, by animal-drawn wagons or pack animals, was much less efficient and limited the quantity of goods that could be moved overland.

Centralized state apparatuses, with bureaucratic systems of administration and large standing armies, provided the organizational basis for extensive empires. Within the boundaries of these empires, there was a significant degree of geographically based economic specialization and internal trade. Cities (containing perhaps 5 percent of the total population) functioned as centers of political administration, residences for the political elite, military fortresses, ceremonial centers, locations for specialized craft production, and the home of merchants engaged in trade. (As we have seen, Wallerstein considers these empires more or less self-contained world-systems. State power served the purpose of controlling large populations of peasant producers whose labor was exploited to benefit the hereditary political elite.)

In A.D. 1400 the advanced agrarian societies consisted of a chain of intensely cultivated regions under the control of a number of states, which stretched in an arc from Western Europe through the Near East and India to China. These societies were separated by wide areas inhospitable to intense agricultural production. (See Map 3.1.) Many of these advanced agrarian areas were only tenuously linked to one another by overland trade routes over which a limited number of travelers and goods moved slowly and perilously. Where relatively short sea routes existed, trade was more substantial.

Between the agrarian settlements, the land, which consisted mostly of desert, open grasslands, or mountains, was primarily inhabited by bands of pastoral nomads. Outside the arc of agrarian societies, a variety of societies at varying levels of technological and political development existed.

Northern Africa was dotted with trading cities separated by vast areas populated by nomadic herders. These cities were linked by trade to each other and to the agrarian areas of the Near East and Europe. East Africa was filled with open grasslands populated by village-dwelling herders and horticulturalists. Much of the area was organized into small states that maintained some trading relationships with the Near East and Asia. Village horticulturalists and some hunting and gathering groups settled the central tropical rain forest. Nomadic cattle-raising societies and hunters and gatherers inhabited arid southwestern Africa.

North and South America were the only areas completely isolated from contact with the world-empires of the agrarian regions. In 1400

MAP 3.1  World-empires and advanced agrarian areas in 1400

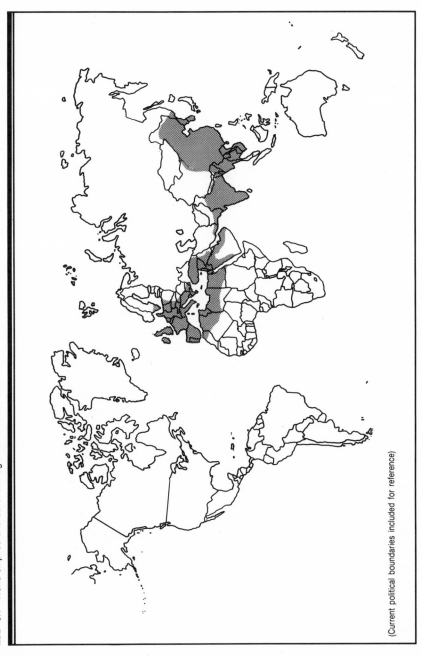

(Current political boundaries included for reference)

there were two well-defined areas of horticulturally based civilizations in the Americas—the central Andes and the central highlands and adjacent coastal areas of Central America—and they were in a period of political fragmentation and warfare, although both would soon be dominated by relatively centralized states. East of the Andes most of the population lived in scattered horticultural villages or in hunting and gathering bands. Most of North America was sparsely settled by linguistically distinct cultural groups living in horticultural villages.

In many ways, Europe was the least economically advanced and most politically disorganized agrarian area in 1400. Following the collapse of the western half of the Roman Empire in the fifth century, Europe had entered a period of extreme political and economic frag-mentation. Each locality was basically self-sufficient and politically autonomous; urbanization was extremely limited. The situation did begin to change about A.D. 1000. Regional trade, craft production, and small trading cities revived. Technological improvements in agriculture increased both productivity and the amount of land that could be put under cultivation. Innovations (often based on concepts originated in other agrarian areas) in nonagricultural technology followed. These changes provided the means and the incentive for efforts at political consolidation. By 1300 the population had grown substantially, craft activity was flourishing, the maritime city-states of Italy were com-mercially and militarily strong, the independent trading cities of northern Europe were prospering, and still-fragile kingdoms were slowly emerging in England, France, and Spain (Wolf, 1982: 101–108; White, 1962).

These advances were interrupted by the so-called crisis of feudalism. The crisis had a number of symptoms. During the fourteenth and early fifteenth centuries there were incessant wars, peasant revolts, and struggles for power between the kings and the nobility and among the emerging kingdoms. These events were accompanied by economic decline, famine, bubonic plague, and population decline (Wolf, 1982: 108; Wallerstein, 1974a: 19–33).

The apparent backwardness and crisis in Western Europe actually created conditions favorable to a fundamental transformation that broke the basic pattern of agrarian world-empires and gave rise to a new societal pattern. Indeed, the political fragmentation created an intensely competitive environment that encouraged innovation. Each state was struggling for economic and military advantage. Because of the relative weakness of European states, the merchant classes of the cities had a greater degree of autonomy to pursue their economic interests; if a local ruler made unacceptable demands, the merchant class could always move to a more accommodating political jurisdiction. Merchants and craft manufacturers also provided an important source of revenues for the developing states, which in turn gave them the political leverage to make demands on ruling elites for assistance. In a few of the stronger kingdoms, the power of the feudal aristocracy came under increasing challenge from the kings and the merchant classes of the towns (Chirot, 1986: 14–19; Wallerstein, 1974a: 19–33).

## The World-System in 1560

Wallerstein argues that the modern world-system was created during the "long sixteenth century" (1450–1620) in response to the crisis of feudalism.[2] He contends that three key, mutually reinforcing developments provided a solution to the crisis. The first was the geographical expansion of the Western European economic system. In the fifteenth century the region needed additional sources of food, raw materials, fuel, and bullion. Groups and states that obtained them stood to profit enormously and were motivated to search outside of the region for them. That quest led to the conquest of Central America and South America to obtain bullion; the creation of more extensive, maritime-based trading links with Asia; and the evolution of new patterns of trade with Eastern Europe that provided additional sources of food and raw materials (Wallerstein, 1974a: 38–63).

This expansion of long-distance trade provided the basis for the second fundamental development: a new division of labor within the expanded trading area that created the core, periphery, and semi-periphery. Core exploitation of peripheral and semi-peripheral areas benefited a rising merchant class and encouraged the expansion of manufacturing and trading activities in Western Europe organized along capitalist lines (Wallerstein, 1974a: 67–129).

The third crucial development was the interstate system. A long struggle for the domination of Europe by several kingdoms continued without a clear winner. The states themselves began to take on some of the characteristics of modern nation-states. Within those states a struggle for power occurred among kings, merchants, and the feudal aristocracy (Wallerstein, 1974a: 133–162, 221–297).

By the middle of the sixteenth century the crude outlines of the modern world-system had emerged. Although the struggle for advantage by the various groups and states in the system was by no means resolved, one can speak of the existence of a world-system of capitalism during this period.

COMPOSITION OF THE WORLD-SYSTEM

The world-system in the sixteenth century was still fairly limited in its geographic scope. It included all of Europe not under the control of the Ottoman Empire and the Spanish and Portuguese colonial empires in the New World. Portugal had also opened up direct sea routes to Asia and had some trading outposts there, Spain had claimed the Philippines, and there were a few trading outposts along the coast of Africa. The core was essentially limited to the nascent nation-states of Spain (Spanish Hapsburg Empire), Portugal, France, and England. Most of the rest of northern and Central Europe, along with Italy, made up the semi-periphery. The periphery consisted of Eastern Europe (to the borders of the kingdom of Poland, the Baltic states, and the Austrian Hapsburg state), along with the colonial empires in Central and South America. (See Map 3.2.)

## THE INTERSTATE SYSTEM

The failure of any one state to impose its will over most of the others in Europe occurred in the context of almost continual wars aimed at achieving that dominance. The primary contender for continental supremacy, the Spanish branch of the Hapsburg dynasty, controlled not only Spanish America but also Holland, Belgium, and parts of Italy. (The Hapsburg dynasty had been split in two in 1556. The northern, or Austrian, branch controlled areas in present-day Germany and Austria. The two branches remained very closely allied during the rest of the century.) Wallerstein attributes the failure of the Spanish Hapsburgs to achieve control of Europe to a number of things: no encouragement of domestic agriculture and manufacturing, an overextended and inadequate system of state administration, reliance on foreign borrowing to finance the state and imports, the costs of constant war, and a parasitical court bureaucracy (Wallerstein, 1974a: 165–221).

In its unsuccessful bid for dominance, the Spanish Hapsburg state became embroiled in a succession of wars that involved most of the core and semi-periphery. The Protestant Reformation involved the core powers in repeated wars in such areas as politically fragmented Germany. France fought the Hapsburgs unsuccessfully for the control of Italy in the decades before 1560 and several decades later was torn by a religiously based civil war. England, still just a minor core power at the time, began to challenge the Spanish for control of trade with the New World. During the last decades of the century, the increasingly economically successful Dutch broke away from Spanish Hapsburg rule to create an independent state. Both the Austrian and Spanish Hapsburgs also faced constant military pressure and frequent war with the expanding agrarian state of the Ottoman Empire. (At the time, that empire controlled most of the Middle East, Turkey, North Africa, and south-central Europe all the way to what is now eastern Austria.) One of

MAP 3.2  The world-system in 1560

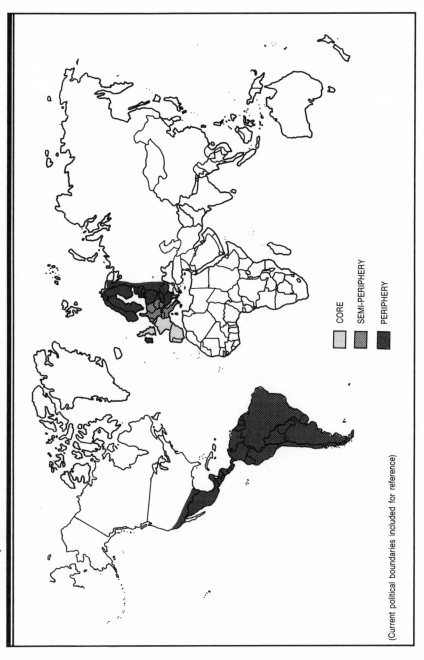

CORE

SEMI-PERIPHERY

PERIPHERY

(Current political boundaries included for reference)

the Hapsburg's greatest military successes was to halt Ottoman expansion.

Out of this seemingly endless European conflict came a pattern that assured that no one state could conquer the continent. When one state became a serious threat to the survival of others, those states formed alliances to counterbalance the threat. This system of constantly shifting alliances gradually evolved into an interstate diplomatic and military policy aimed at maintaining the "balance of power." When one state threatened that balance, the other states joined together to restore it.

Spanish and Portuguese conquest and the creation of colonial empires in the Americas provided direct core control of that part of the periphery. The European periphery was ruled by weak independent states, such as the kingdom of Poland. In the semi-periphery, the once powerful northern Italian city-states had become caught in the conflict between the Hapsburg dynasty and France. By the middle of the sixteenth century, the Spanish Hapsburgs directly ruled the southern half of Italy and some areas in the north. The remainder of Italy was organized into small states mostly in the sphere of influence of the Spanish Hapsburgs. Venice was the largest and most independent of these states, but it was clearly a second-class naval power in decline. The Austrian branch of the Hapsburg dynasty ruled in parts of southern Germany and most of present-day Austria. The rest of Germany was divided into small states and city-states. These states and the Hapsburg possessions nominally made up the Holy Roman Empire, ruled by the Hapsburgs. In fact, the "empire" was a loose confederation of states in which the Austrian Hapsburg state functioned essentially as the dominant regional power, in alliance with the Spanish Hapsburgs. During the sixteenth century the kingdom of Sweden also grew in political, economic, and military power. By the middle of the century, it was marginally integrated into the world-economy as part of the periphery; later, it emerged as a regional power.

European naval technology was slightly superior to the Asiatic. The Portuguese were consequently able to assure their right to trade at Asiatic ports and establish some trading outposts. But unlike South America, the strong agrarian empires of Asia (especially the Chinese) were more than a match for the Europeans in land warfare. As a result, the Portuguese were not in a position to demand more than trading rights.

## THE WORLD DIVISION OF LABOR

The economic organization of the just-emerging world-system already showed a clear geographic division of labor that enabled the core to benefit disproportionately from its trade with the periphery. The periphery was expanding its export activities, producing goods desired by core merchants and states. The Spanish-controlled colonies in Central and South America produced massive quantities of gold and silver bullion, all of which ended up in the hands of the Spanish (albeit temporarily). The Spanish acquisition of South American gold took the form of military conquest of the existing horticultural states and the forceful expropriation of existing gold and silver stocks. Once the immediate spoils of conquest were exhausted, Spanish-operated mines, using forced labor, maintained the flow of bullion to the home country.

The Eastern European periphery was in the process of specializing in the production of grain and other raw materials for export to Western Europe. To take advantage of the expanding Western European market and keep the profits from it for themselves, the large landowners sought to maximize grain production at low cost by minimizing labor costs. They did so by reimposing a system of serfdom on their peasants. A pattern of exchange emerged in which the European periphery specialized in the export of goods produced by poorly compensated, coerced labor. Faced with competition from core goods, urban craft production was not very successful in Eastern Europe.

At the same time, core merchants developed a system of trade in which they paid for grain and raw materials with textiles, luxury goods (including Asian spices), and bullion, thus ensuring core control of trade. By 1560 this trade, by ship through the Baltic, was dominated by Dutch traders. The volume of trade within Western Europe and with the periphery and semi-periphery and Asia soared. The bullion collected from Spanish America contributed to this trade expansion. In the hands of the Spanish state and aristocracy, it was spent on war; the support of a large, inefficient state bureaucracy; and lavish consumption by the aristocracy. Spanish agriculture and domestic craft manufacturing were allowed to languish. As a consequence, most of Spain's new wealth ultimately flowed out of Spain to pay for goods and grain produced elsewhere in Europe and to pay off loans obtained from European bankers to finance the Spanish state. The infusion of bullion into the hands of European merchants and bankers provided increased financial resources for investment and helped finance the trade with Eastern Europe and Asia. Trade within Western Europe and with the Eastern European periphery stimulated craft manufacturing, especially in textiles. The increasing demand for food to support growing urban populations and for wool to sustain the textile industry encouraged the commercialization of Western European agriculture. Fields formerly in subsistence production for feudal estates were consolidated into pastureland for wool production. Similarly, those estates converting to commercial grain production found a system of paid labor and/or tenant farming more efficient. The growth of commercial markets for agricultural products encouraged efficiency through the adoption of more sophisticated techniques in agriculture.

Thus, Western Europe in 1560, which had emerged as the center of a new, geographically extensive economic system, specialized in trade, finance, and craft manufacturing. It now had access to needed food supplies and raw materials from the European periphery at low cost. Its merchants, bankers, and commercial fleets controlled the trade within the system. Agrarian feudalism was being displaced by commercialized, capitalistic economic relationships: private property, saleable land and labor, and the quest for maximum profit. Growing economic opportunities and intense competition put a premium on efficiency and innovation in craft manufacturing, agriculture, and marine technology. Overall, Western Europe enjoyed a small but significant edge over the rest of Europe in technology, available capital, and craft manufacturing.

The portions of Europe that constituted the semi-periphery in this century occupied an "intermediate" position in the new global division of labor. They maintained some major trading and manufacturing centers. For example, Italian bankers, merchants, and traders still dominated Mediterranean trade, but that trade was declining in importance relative to trade in the Atlantic and the Baltic. The merchants and bankers of some German cities were likewise involved in the trading system with the Eastern European periphery. In general, semi-peripheral craft manufacturing was less advanced than that of the core states. Italian textile production remained specialized in the older types of manufacturing of high-quality luxury fabrics, which were not price competitive with the new forms of textile production in northwestern Europe. During this period Italian manufactures were in decline and losing out in the competition for the European market. At the same time, semi-peripheral areas also engaged in more peripheral-like activities: the production of raw materials (silver, copper, timber) and agricultural commodities for the core.

Asia remained outside of the world-economy despite trade with Europe (dominated by Portuguese traders). Europeans could not directly expropriate wealth, as they did in South America, because they lacked the military means to subordinate the Asian states. Nor were they in a position to determine the nature of their trading relationship with the Asians. European manufactures such as textiles were neither superior to nor cheaper than Asian goods. All that Europeans could consequently offer for Asian goods was bullion, at a price dictated by Asian merchants, which meant a drain of bullion for the Europeans. Trade was therefore limited to the import of small amounts of Asian luxury goods. The Portuguese merely participated in a preexisting pattern of Asiatic trade among autonomous agrarian states.

European penetration of Africa was limited to a number of Portuguese coastal trading posts and naval resupply stations. Originally trade consisted of the exchange of European manufactures for spices, gold, timber, and ivory. By the middle of the sixteenth century, the Portuguese had initiated commerce in slaves, mostly to provide labor in their rapidly developing sugar plantations on islands off Africa and in Brazil.

## CLASS RELATIONSHIPS

The basic pattern of class relationships described in the last chapter had just begun to emerge in the world-system in the middle of the sixteenth century. A class of merchant capitalists had become more important in the core. They controlled the trading and financial institutions that operated the system of international exchange, invested in craft manufactures, and created the market mechanisms for an increasingly commercialized agriculture. Their wealth, numbers, and economic importance had been steadily increasing during the century, while in both urban and rural areas of the core, workers were increasingly employed as wage laborers.

Nonetheless, the bulk of the population still consisted of peasants, and the traditional landed aristocracy remained wealthy and powerful, although it was hard-pressed for money to participate as consumers in an increasingly cash-based economy (in a state of rapid price inflation, in part due to the influx of bullion). As a result, feudal bonds and obligations between peasants and the nobility loosened. The relationship between lord and peasant became a contractual one based on tenancy and cash payments; peasants were less likely to be permanently bound to the land. Reorganization and commercialization of agriculture reinforced this trend further by reducing the need for peasant labor on many estates. While significant remnants of feudal classes and class relationships remained, the basic trend in the core class system was toward a system of exploitation of relatively free workers by a capitalist class that owned the means of production.

In contrast, in the periphery increasing numbers of workers were being brought into production processes oriented toward export to the core under conditions of direct coercion and extreme exploitation. In Spanish America, bullion was produced by the forced labor of the native Indian population. Others were put to work on Spanish-owned lands to produce food for the mines and colonial towns. The system used to coerce Indian labor changed several times during the sixteenth century. Gradually, after the middle of the sixteenth century, the system of forced labor in agriculture gave way to the hacienda system. Peasants on large, Spanish-owned estates were given access to land in return for shares of the crop, cash payments, and fixed labor obligations to the landowner. The peasant share of production was so low that it guaranteed permanent indebtedness, which bound the family to the land and the landowner, forced the household to support itself through subsistence activities, and provided additional goods and services to the landowner. Peasants on the haciendas were reduced to a condition of near serfdom, while peasants who were allowed to remain in traditional villages became subsistence producers. They provided a pool of seasonal labor and sometimes were required to supply labor for the mines and pay various taxes.

Overall, the Spanish conquest of horticultural empires of Central and South America destroyed the preexisting economic and social organization of those societies. In its place, the Spanish created a new colonial system in which government and landownership were exclusively in Spanish hands. Spanish administrators, mine owners and landowners, and urban merchants constituted a tiny, privileged upper class. Much of the rest of the urban population consisted of artisans, petty merchants, colonial state clericals, and the like of Spanish descent. The Indian population was an exploited labor force that was drafted, using various methods of coercion, to labor in the mines and on the large estates under conditions of extreme brutality and virtually no compensation for their labor. Extreme exploitation (combined with European diseases, and economic and social disruption) decimated the Indian population during the sixteenth and seventeenth centuries.

In the Eastern European periphery, grain production for export was carried out on large estates where the landed aristocracy imposed a new system of serfdom. (Prior to the sixteenth century the system of feudal serfdom had been weakening.) In this so-called second system of serfdom, peasants were bound to the land, and the landowner received most of the production. Wallerstein (1974a) regards this revived serfdom as a form of capitalist labor control. Production was for sale on the world market (rather than to maintain a relatively self-sufficient, manorial economy). Revival of feudal bonds to the land meant the landowner could force peasants to work for less than they would have received as individual landholders or as free wage laborers. Arrangements were such that the peasants supported themselves with their own labor and also worked in the production of crops for export.

The result was a class system composed of a tiny group of wealthy landowners and a great mass of impoverished peasants bound to the land by law and custom. The failure of domestic manufactures to develop (because of foreign imports and the lack of a large domestic market), the political dominance of the landed aristocracy (at the expense of the towns), and foreign control of international trade all kept the merchant class and urban artisan class small and relatively impoverished.

Class relationships in the semi-periphery were rendered more complex than in the periphery by that zone's intermediate position in the world-system. The situation of the Italian city-states (such as Venice) was illustrative of the situation in the middle of the sixteenth century. The capitalist merchant class was larger and wealthier than that of the periphery. Core-like craft manufactures supported a small class of urban artisans and workers who were still organized more as feudal guilds than those in the core. The growing importance of food production for domestic consumption and export and the export of raw materials increased the importance of the large estates and their hereditary owners. The economy was gradually becoming more agrarian, and much of the rural population was bound in relative servitude on the great estates through various forms of tenant farming.

## STATE DEVELOPMENT

Nation-states were forming within the core and were arising out of a triangular power struggle among the monarchy, the landed aristocracy, and the growing merchant class. Certain patterns characterized those states that were ultimately to be the most successful (England, Holland, and France). The monarchies persisted in their attempts to create strong, centralized states with absolute, despotic power. But the continued power of the aristocracy, the growing power of the merchant class, and the emerging interstate system (with its need for resources to sustain almost endless war) thwarted monarchial aims. At various times, the monarchies had to enlist the support (through various concessions) of either the aristocracy or the merchant class in order to increase state power, which was achieved at the expense of the other class. Both the aristocracy and the merchant class also sought to reduce each other's power by using state power.

> For the . . . [merchant class] . . . the strong state . . . was a prime customer, a guardian against local and international brigandage, a mode of social legitimation, and a preemptive protection against the creation of strong state barriers elsewhere. For the . . . [aristocracy] . . . the strong state represented a brake on these same capitalist strata, an upholder of status conventions, a maintainer of order, and a promoter of luxury (Wallerstein, 1974a: 355).

Gradually, as the struggle for power continued, state strategies shifted toward more reliance on the merchant class because it had more resources to which the monarchy had access through taxation or loans. This access was especially critical if warmaking capacity was to be maintained. Slowly, the power and the privileges of the aristocracy were reduced, thereby increasing both state power and that of the merchant class, which began, in turn, to win major concessions from the state to support its economic activities. The merchants then supported the creation of a centralized state in opposition to the aristocracy. The demands of the merchant class for policies supporting its activities, plus the requirements of improving warmaking capacity, pushed the core states in the direction of increasing their "infrastructural" power. Indeed, core states (especially England and Holland) began to recognize that entrepreneurial activities were in the direct interest of the state and sought to sponsor and protect them. Nevertheless, in the middle of the sixteenth century this process was still in its early stages; its outcome became clear only in subsequent centuries.

The states of the European periphery remained relatively weak. The growing wealth and power of the landed aristocracy limited the concentration of power in the hands of central political leadership, and state lawmaking authority, where it existed, was employed to increase the privileges of the aristocracy and ratify the increasing bondage and exploitation of the peasantry. The small local merchant class remained weak and subordinate to the aristocracy. State policy favored the import-export trade with the core and not local manufactures.

In the American periphery, the interests of the Spanish and Portuguese monarchies were twofold. First, they sought to limit the autonomy, authority, and independent resources of the colonial authorities in order to maintain control over their empires. (In this attempt they were only partially successful, as the colonial authorities sought to maintain their autonomy.) Second, they sought to create systems of colonial administration that would maximize revenues from the colonies. For example, the Spanish state demanded one-fifth of all the bullion produced in the Americas. In their attempts to maximize output of the mines, the Spanish authorities also carefully regulated the laws governing land-ownership and the employment of native labor.

In the semi-periphery the larger states (such as the Austrian Hapsburgs) attempted to emulate the centralizing tendencies of the core states. They had some success, but less than that of the core monarchies. The power of the aristocracy remained stronger, that of the merchant class remained weaker, and aristocratic privileges were a significant block to the centralizing tendencies of these states. The merchant class, on the other hand, was less able to extract favorable policies from the state and had more difficulty avoiding state control of its activities when that regulation either served the short-term interests of the state or protected the interests of the aristocracy.

## The World-System in 1763

The nascent capitalist world-system of the sixteenth century had become a somewhat geographically larger and a much-better-established system by the middle of the eighteenth century.[3] The trends of the sixteenth century had resulted in the creation of what is often called merchant capitalism. Capitalist economic relationships were more firmly entrenched, the power of the merchant capitalist class was greater, state development had proceeded further, and the relative power and position of states in the interstate system had changed. The central features of world-system structure were more easily discernible.

COMPOSITION OF THE WORLD-SYSTEM

The core consisted of Great Britain, France, and the Netherlands. Spain was rapidly losing its struggle to remain in the core. As of the middle of the eighteenth century, it could be regarded only as a marginal core power. Portugal had already declined unambiguously into the semi-periphery, which continued to include politically fragmented western Germany and the much larger Hapsburg Empire—southern Germany, Austria, and Hungary (gained at the expense of the Ottoman Empire). The semi-periphery also included the much weakened northern Italian states (but just barely), southern Italy, and the expanding state of Prussia (located in eastern Germany and what is now western Poland). The somewhat diminished kingdom of Sweden (present-day Sweden and Finland) was on the borderline between periphery and semi-periphery.

The seventeenth century world-system had expanded geographically. More areas had been added to the periphery. The weakness and internal turmoil of the Mughal Empire in India had allowed the British to seize effective control of the province of Bengal. The Dutch retained control of the East Indies (present-day Indonesia), which they had acquired in the seventeenth century. But most of Asia still had not been integrated into the world-economy. Nevertheless, significant European settlement on the coast of North America (mostly British controlled) had occurred, West Africa was dotted with more European trading posts, Poland remained in the periphery, and the expanding Russian Empire of Eastern Europe was being integrated into the world-economy. Even the once powerful Ottoman Empire was in the initial stages of being incorporated into the periphery. (See Map 3.3.)

## THE INTERSTATE SYSTEM

The chronic economic and military competition and conflict within the core during the seventeenth and early eighteenth centuries had resulted in major changes in the interstate systsem by 1763. The two dominant core powers, France and Great Britain, had fought several wars (and would fight more until 1815) motivated by a desire to control more European territory as well as overseas colonial possessions and trading rights. Although as of 1763 France had surrendered its North American colonies to the British state and its trading operations in India to the British East India Company, it retained its land-based military power in Europe. Spain had experienced a fairly steady decline in its military and economic power since the early seventeenth century but still kept its American colonies and continued to be a minor player in the system of international alliances. Semi-peripheral Portugal retained Brazil and some other possessions but was a virtual client state of the British. Holland had briefly been the most powerful core state and the most important trading and financial center in seventeenth-century Europe, but by the middle of the eighteenth century, it had lost out to Britain as a naval power and was no longer preeminent in commerce and finance. Holland had become a minor core power, frequently allied with Great Britain. In Central Europe two militarily powerful states, Prussia and the Austrian Hapsburg Empire, competed for control over a semi-peripheral Germany fragmented into small kingdoms and city-states. To the east the Russian monarchy presided over a growing empire that had expanded westward to Poland and the Baltic and southward against the declining Ottoman Empire. In Africa the European demand for slaves contributed to the development of a system of kingdoms whose primary purpose was to capture slaves and enrich a small warrior elite.

## THE WORLD DIVISION OF LABOR

By the mid-eighteenth century the world division of labor had changed significantly, even as its basic structural features had remained the same. The relative importance of the international trade in luxury goods and bullion had declined; bulk imports of raw materials and agricultural commodities from the non-European periphery had become more important. (There was a long period of relative stagnation in world-system trade in the seventeenth century. During the eighteenth century total trading volume began to rise again.) Emphasis increased

MAP 3.3  The world-system in 1763

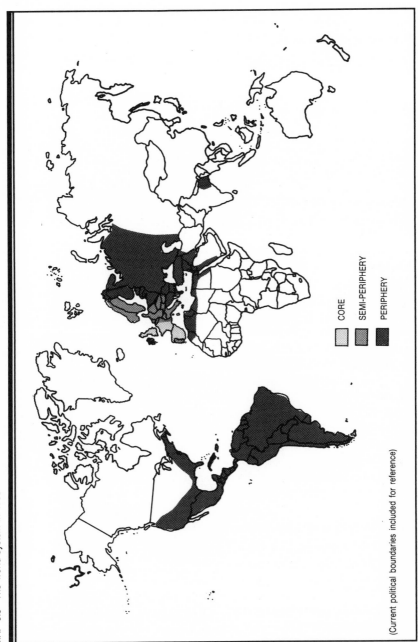

CORE

SEMI-PERIPHERY

PERIPHERY

(Current political boundaries included for reference)

on goods manufactured in the core for domestic consumption and export.

Central to the new system of international trade were the European-owned, slave-operated sugar plantations in the Caribbean periphery, which exported sugar to Europe. In turn, the plantations imported manufactures from the core and food from the core and North America. To sustain itself, the sugar economy needed a steady supply of African slaves (survival rates were low in the Caribbean), who were supplied primarily by the British. Slave traders bought cheap textiles, rum (made with sugar), and guns to sell to African kingdoms in return for slaves.

Less important patterns of trade included the shipment of food, tobacco, and raw materials from the North American British colonies. In turn, these colonies bought British manufactures and luxury goods (tea, for example) and acquired slaves from Africa. The rapid development of their own maritime commerce by the merchants of New England and the Middle Atlantic colonies gave those areas a semi-peripheral role in the world-economy.

British manufacturers and merchants also benefited from treaties that had led to the opening up of Spain, Portugal, and their colonies to British goods. Bullion produced in the South and Central American colonies and some agricultural commodities paid for these British goods. Spain and Portugal were thus functioning as conveyor belts of the wealth of their colonies to other core countries—a typical semi-peripheral role. The British used the bullion they obtained to become involved in the Asian trade (buying teas, spices, and luxury goods). Britain also dominated the exploitation of the North Atlantic fisheries. After 1763, control of Bengal by the British East India Company led to the brutal, forced expropriation of the wealth of that area of India. Thus, Britain was the most important entrepôt for goods produced in colonial areas and Asia, which it then reexported to the rest of Europe.

Eastern Europe continued in its peripheral role as a supplier of food and raw materials in return for bullion, manufactures, and luxury goods. (But economic stagnation and the decline in the grain trade during the seventeenth century had meant some greater reliance on domestic manufactures, which were often produced on the large estates.) Grain and raw materials from Russia were just beginning to become a regular part of this Baltic trade. Britain, a heavy exporter of grain as late as the early seventeenth century, increasingly relied on its ability to pay bullion for grain so that its agriculture could specialize in the production of wool for textiles. Holland remained important in the Baltic trade but was losing out to the British (as it already had in the Atlantic).

Semi-peripheral Europe also remained an important supplier of raw materials and agricultural products to the core. The position of the northern Italian cities as centers of trade and manufactures had continued to decline. They were of primary importance as trading centers in their immediate regions. The kingdom of Sweden had enjoyed a brief period of expanding manufacturing and trade several decades earlier, but its economic position had subsequently deteriorated. The Hapsburg Empire in Central Europe was predominantly agricultural, but some of its western provinces and its capital city of Vienna produced limited manufactures. Vienna was a significant trading and financial hub for Central and Eastern Europe. Some of the German cities remained minor craft manufacturing and regional trading centers. Prussia participated in the Baltic grain trade, and its strong state had made major efforts to encourage the growth of domestic manufactures.

The trend toward increased core specialization in manufacturing continued. Both the range of goods and their volume increased. For example, in Great Britain textile manufacturing, shipbuilding, and the metallurgical industry had become major areas of specialization in the economy. British textile manufacturing was organized in the "putting out" system in which textile merchants contracted with independent, individual weavers to produce handmade cloth. These merchants provided the materials and bought the product at a (low) fixed price.

This system of exchange continued the core's exploitation of the periphery. The extreme exploitation of African slave labor on the plantations of the New World generated a surplus that ultimately ended up in the hands of European merchants. The European slave traders acquired the labor of African slaves for the price of a few guns and trade goods and then sold the slaves at immense profits to the plantations. The profits of the plantations went to the European owners, the shippers and wholesalers of sugar, and the slave traders.

At the same time, the ongoing ability to extract bullion cheaply in the Americas through the extreme exploitation of coerced labor provided the core with bullion to pay for those things it could not pay for through the export of its manufactures (especially in Asia). The ruthless exploitation of the laborers in the mines and the slaves on the plantations was accompanied by a whole system of exploitation in the rest of the economy:

> Mineowners sold to merchants who extracted high prices for European manufactured goods. Mineowners then pressed upon hacienda owners or managers to supply them with foodstuffs and raw materials at low prices. Hacienda owners and managers pressed upon the native communities, drawing their members either into dependent serf-tenancy on

the estates or seasonal employment at low wages. Within this hierarchy, the emerging Indian communities came to occupy the lowest rung (Wolf, 1982: 145).

The second serfdom in Eastern Europe continued to enrich a small group of large landowners at the expense of the serfs. (Russian agriculture also consisted of large estates operated by serf labor.) But the exchange of low-wage grain for high-wage core products meant that the bulk of the surplus produced still ended up in the core.

British policies of direct expropriation of the wealth of Bengal (the "rape of Bengal") amounted to a systematic looting of the province. The result was economic disruption, declining agriculture and craft manufacturing, deteriorating average living standards, and recurrent famines during the next four decades in that Indian province. The African slave trade enriched the British slave traders and a small warrior elite of the coastal African kingdoms at a terrible cost to Africa. In the eighteenth century alone, an estimated 6 million Africans were captured and sold into slavery. The social and economic life of the tribal groups in the interior was shattered.

Core exploitation of the periphery primarily benefited the merchant class of the core that operated the trading system and also provided some of the stimulus to the demand for core manufacturing: ships and naval stores, guns and rum for the slave trade, tools and equipment for peripheral plantations and mines, and textiles. Additionally, there is evidence that some of the profits amassed by the merchant class ultimately provided part of the pool of capital necessary for investment in manufacturing in the core.

CLASS RELATIONSHIPS

Extreme political and economic inequality existed in all parts of the world-system at the time. The mass of the population had no political power and was impoverished and exploited. Nonetheless, the relative degree and type of exploitation and poverty still differed in the three zones of the world-system.

In the core most of the rural population was relatively free to sell its labor and was not tied permanently to the land of a particular landowner. Some of the rural population were "yeoman" small land-owners and independent craftspeople; many more were tenant farmers, day laborers, or servants. The putting-out system in Britain had also created a large number of relatively impoverished, village-based craft workers. In addition to this relatively poor majority, there were growing groups of somewhat better off urban craftspeople and petty merchants.

Nevertheless, most of the urban population was made up of poorly paid laborers working for wages. The capitalist merchant class had increased significantly, both in size and wealth. The landed aristocracy remained wealthy and in possession of some of its special privileges and much of its social prestige, but its economic position and its political position had declined relative to those of the merchant class. The extent of that decline varied among countries. (The British aristocracy maintained its position in part through the method of intermarriage with the merchant class. Established merchant class families could also gradually assimilate themselves into the aristocracy by purchasing estates and being elevated into the aristocracy by royal decree.)

In the periphery almost all of the population was impoverished. Workers in capitalist enterprises oriented toward export usually survived under conditions of coerced labor and extreme exploitation; they were tied to the land as formal serfs (Europe), as permanent near-serf tenants on estates (haciendas in South America), or as actual plantation slaves (the sugar plantations).

In the European periphery the landed aristocracy continued to be the dominant class, and the merchant class continued to be small and weak. European-origin owners of large estates or (especially in Brazil) slave-based plantations and mines constituted the upper class in Spanish and Portuguese America. The urban merchants, artisans, and petty merchants composed a tiny middle class. The European planter class dominated in the sugar-producing Caribbean and the southern colonies of British America. In British Bengal the East India Company pursued a set of policies in which British officials dominated the higher levels of government administration and commercial activities but encouraged the creation of a new native landowning class and a class of native lower-level functionaries and soldiers. This structure partially displaced the previously dominant ruling and landowning class of what had been a typical agrarian social structure.

In the semi-periphery the landed aristocracy remained more important and wealthier than the relatively smaller merchant class. The urban artisans and petty merchants were only somewhat larger in number than in the periphery. In the countryside, the peasantry still labored for the landed aristocracy, mostly as tenants, under conditions that were much more feudal than in the core.

STATE DEVELOPMENT

In the core the process of creating true nation-states was well under way, and state structures were much larger and organizationally complex.

Systems of bureaucratic administration, standing armies, rationalized legal systems, and the like had substantially increased the administrative effectiveness of core states and their ability to mobilize resources. The concept of the state representing a particular people or nation was gaining intellectual currency. Political philosophers of the period (such as John Locke, Charles-Louis Montesquieu, Jean-Jacques Rousseau) had begun to popularize such ideas as social contract, natural rights, and popular sovereignty. These principles increasingly encouraged the belief that the state served the people and that there were such things as citizen rights. On the other hand, continued claims by kings that the state existed to serve the royal house had provided the justification for the growth of absolutist regimes in France and Spain. (Even absolutist kings often portrayed themselves as the protectors of a particular nation and justified policies in terms of national interest.) Increased state strength was employed by a centralized state bureaucracy to reinforce the despotic power of the monarchy.

To some degree, the power of the merchant class relative to both the aristocracy and the monarchy had increased in all core countries, which meant that state policy more clearly reflected merchant concerns. The prevailing economic approach of core states was mercantilism. This approach entailed heavy tariffs to protect industry, state support of export activities, and attempts to create protected sources of supply and markets in the periphery through the control of colonial empires.

Nevertheless, the power of the merchant class varied from country to country. In Great Britain and the Netherlands the merchant class had the most political influence and the power of the monarchy was restrained. In Holland the Dutch state had been, almost from its inception, essentially an oligarchy of the merchant class. In Great Britain the struggle between Parliament and the king had been resolved in favor of Parliament, thus ending a period of internal instability. In the early years of the eighteenth century, politics in the English Parliament reflected the clash of interests between those oriented toward domestic, mostly agricultural interests (the smaller landholders of the rural aristocracy) and those oriented toward imperial, maritime, and trading interests (the merchant class, allied with the larger land-holders and the state bureaucracy). The merchants and large landowners initially formed an alliance because of the latter's interest in state-subsidized exports of grain to Europe in the pre-1750 period. As the market for British manufactures increased rapidly after 1750, they also benefited from the sale of timber, the production of wool, and the leasing of land for mining, quarrying, ironworks, and limekilns. Gradually, those who favored the overseas trading strategy gained the upper hand, and a growing upper-class consensus on state strategy provided political stability and allowed prime ministers the latitude to pursue aggressive foreign policies in support of Britain's overseas interests.

In France the influence of the merchant class was much more limited relative to that of British merchants. The monarchy had continued to centralize power in its hands, both at the expense of the aristocracy and the merchant class. In return for acquiescing to the despotic power of the monarchy, the aristocracy had obtained protection of its special privileges, which helped aristocrats maintain their incomes and estates. (For example, they enjoyed exemption from royal taxation.) Reflecting both dynastic interests and geography, state power was more oriented toward territorial ambitions in Europe than toward furthering trading and manufacturing exports or expanding the colonial system. Nevertheless, the French state was strongly mercantilist. It subsidized and protected domestic manufactures and supported trading and colonization in both North America and Asia until defeated in its overseas efforts by the British in 1763. The important financial role of the merchant class in supporting the state also gave that class some ability to make political demands on the monarchy.

Wallerstein argues that despite the greater despotic power of the French state, England was the stronger state in the eighteenth century. It proved more capable of mobilizing financial resources and implementing both domestic and foreign policy. Its upper class was more unified politically, and that unity provided strong support for state policy (Wallerstein, 1980: 245–289).

In Spain the state was even more rigid and the aristocracy retained more influence. Yet, even Spain, despite its history of neglect of commercial and manufacturing activities, attempted economic reforms to encourage domestic manufacturing and further the interests of its merchants in international trade. But these belated reforms proved insufficient to reverse Spanish economic decline.

In the European periphery the territorially large Polish state remained extremely weak and dominated by the landed aristocracy. It was so weak in fact that by the end of the century, Poland would be completely dismembered and annexed by the Prussian, Russian, and Austrian Hapsburg states. The Russian Empire, on the other hand, was a militarily expansionist, despotic state and in the middle of the seventeenth century was just beginning to play a real role in the interstate system. Political power was completely centralized in the hands of the monarchy because the aristocracy had lost control over state affairs and had become obligated to provide service to the state. In return for that service, the state conferred rank, social privileges, and rights to great estates. But despite its growing military power, the Russian state remained administratively weak and inefficient; it had a backward economy and few economic resources; and manufactures, which were limited, consisted of state-sponsored enterprises oriented mostly toward military production. Finally, everywhere in peripheral Europe the urban merchant classes remained politically weak, and their interests were subordinated to other groups.

In the Spanish and Portuguese Americas the system of direct colonial rule continued, with the major political tension between the large landowners and the colonial administration. The former wished to pursue their interests without the intervention and taxation of the latter. British colonies in America were also subject to direct administration, and the British government tried to tie the colonies into a protected trade zone with the home country in a way that benefited British manufacturing.

In the semi-periphery the two major powers, Prussia and Hapsburg Austria, were attempting to create states more or less on the model of French absolutism. In Prussia a powerful monarchy created a highly centralized bureaucratic state designed to mobilize resources for war, which allowed Prussia to play a military role disproportionately greater than its size and level of economic development would have otherwise allowed. The landed aristocracy, in return for the protection of its estates was recruited into state service in the bureaucracy and the military. Prussia aggressively encouraged domestic manufactures through subsidies and tariff protection in an attempt to create the economic base needed to support the state.

The Austrian Hapsburg monarchy had also tried to centralize state power and create an effective administrative apparatus, but it faced enormous difficulties ruling a polyglot empire of numerous linguistic and cultural groups with different legal and governmental traditions. Various reforms were attempted, but they met with limited success. The system of administration improved but remained relatively inefficient. In the various regions of the empire, local interests, usually the landed aristocracy, were able to retain substantial special privileges and thwart the reforms proclaimed in Vienna.

The remainder of the semi-periphery was ruled by small states in Germany and Italy. The northern Italian states were relatively weak and inefficiently governed, and the landed aristocracy retained very substantial power and the ability to protect its interests. In fact, continued decline in the Italian states' manufactures and trade had increased the importance of the landed aristocracy engaged in agricultural exports, which used its power to intensify the coercion of the peasantry. Various great merchant families also retained significant influence in places such as Venice, although their importance had declined relative to the landed aristocracy. A similar situation prevailed in Germany, but merchant interests remained more powerful in some states.

## The World-System in 1900

In the century and a half preceding 1900, the Industrial Revolution had transformed the economy, and thus the society, culture, and politics, of the core.[4] Although most theorists consider these changes to have shaped the modern world, world-system theorists interpret the Industrial Revolution as a continuation of a process begun in the sixteenth century. In this view, despite the massive changes accompanying the Industrial Revolution, the basic framework of the world-system persisted.

### COMPOSITION OF THE WORLD-SYSTEM

As of 1900 Great Britain, France, Germany, and the United States were the four main core powers. Belgium, the Netherlands, Switzerland, Sweden, and Denmark constituted the minor core powers, and Austria-Hungary, Russia, Spain, Italy, and Japan made up the significant semi-periphery. The southern part of southeastern Europe was peripheral, and the rest of the world was in most cases incorporated into the world-system as part of the periphery. (See Map 3.4.)

### THE INTERSTATE SYSTEM

Application of industrial technology to weaponry gave the core countries an overwhelming military advantage over other countries. Core countries also had the economic power to build large military establishments and to move large military forces over long distances.

In the middle decades of the nineteenth century Great Britain had been dominant economically, had enjoyed unchallenged naval superiority, and had acquired a very large colonial empire, including India and about half of Africa. But by 1900 its economic and military advantage over the rest of the core had begun to diminish, and the United States, a semi-peripheral country in 1850, was on the verge of passing Great Britain in industrial production and was flexing its growing naval strength. It had just defeated Spain and seized most of the remnants of Spain's colonial empire (Cuba and the Philippines). Nevertheless, the United States was still a net debtor nation (to the British) and was only a secondary naval power. Germany, which had not even been a unified state in 1850, was unified and industrialized by 1900, and this economic success, along with a powerful army and expanding naval power, made Germany the chief apparent rival to Great Britain. (Germany had only a small colonial empire in the periphery.) France

MAP 3.4  The world-system in 1900

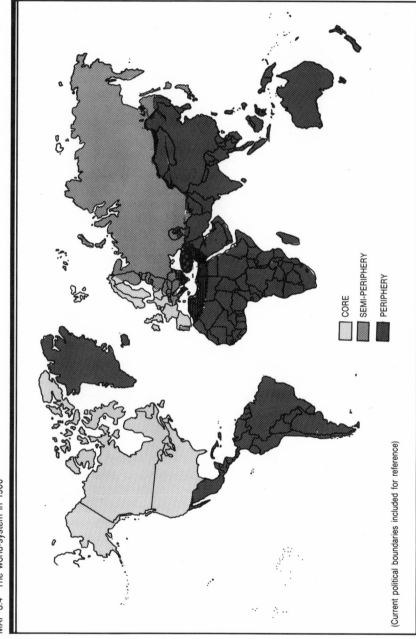

CORE

SEMI-PERIPHERY

PERIPHERY

(Current political boundaries included for reference)

was somewhat less industrialized than Great Britain and Germany, but it had a significant military establishment and substantial colonial empire in Africa and Southeast Asia. Although because of its defeat and loss of territory to Germany in the 1870s, France was implacably hostile to the Germans, the long conflict and competition between France and Great Britain had receded.

During the nineteenth century Britain had used its economic and military power to create a system of alliances that minimized wars among the core powers, but in the last decades of the century, that system had begun to break down. In its place, the more usual pattern of shifting alliances among core powers to maintain the balance of power had reasserted itself. The alliance system had been increasingly oriented toward containing the growing power of the German state.

In the periphery the system of European colonial empires had reached its zenith. The last decades of the nineteenth century had witnessed a frantic scramble to carve up much of the periphery outside of Latin America into colonies. In those cases in which states remained formally independent there, the Europeans had either turned them into client states or were in the process of competing with one another to do so. With the exception of Ethiopia, all of Africa had been divided up into European colonies. France and Britain had the largest African empires. The Ottoman Empire, although independent, was militarily weak, economically stagnant, and administratively disorganized and was the object of attempts by England and Germany to turn it into a client state. India was a British colony. China was controlled by a disintegrating agrarian state that had been forced to accept humiliating economic concessions, trade enclaves, and political intervention by the core powers. Most of Southeast Asia was under the colonial administration of France. Canada, Australia, and New Zealand were prosperous, European-settled British colonies specializing in agricultural exports. Almost all of Latin America consisted of weak, independent states. Great Britain intervened repeatedly in the internal affairs of these states, and British investors dominated foreign investment in their economies. U.S. political and economic influence in the region was growing rapidly. Russia and Austria-Hungary competed for influence over the weak, nationalist states of southeastern Europe.

The semi-periphery was divided into states that were either rising or declining in power in the interstate system. Spain was extremely weak and still declining. Its humiliating defeat by the United States and the loss of Cuba and the Philippines at the turn of the century had signaled its final elimination as a European power. Austria-Hungary controlled much of Central Europe but was also a declining power. It was weakened by internal strife resulting from the rising nationalism of its subject ethnic groups and its limited industrialization. Italy was politically unified and had begun to industrialize, but it was still backward by core standards. Russia, despite its peripheral economy, had been a major secondary European power throughout the nineteenth century because of its large population, vast resources, and relatively centralized state. It had been late to begin industrialization, but its state-sponsored industrialization during the 1890s had been extraordinarily rapid. Japan, despite a medium-sized population and almost no natural resources, was a rising semi-peripheral power. It had systematically and rapidly industrialized during the last half of the nineteenth century, and its modernized military establishment proved capable of defeating the Russians in 1905.

THE WORLD DIVISION OF LABOR

The world division of labor had become even more sharply differentiated by 1900. Improvements in transportation and communication technology lowered their cost and increased their speed. Efficient transportation of bulky goods by land and sea over ever longer distances made possible a vast increase in the volume of trade and the creation of national and international markets for a wider range of products. In the wake of the Industrial Revolution, the core had increasingly specialized in industrial manufacturing. The periphery concentrated almost exclusively on the export of raw materials and agricultural commodities to the core. Core manufactured goods could be produced so cheaply with industrial technology that they displaced much of the craft production of the periphery. For example, British-produced textiles virtually destroyed handicraft textile production in India. (Later, British-owned mills were built in India.) In fact, the peripheral societies generally had no choice but to allow the entry of core goods as they were not in a position to erect trade barriers. Even in the relatively independent states of Latin America, those social elements connected with export activities to the core had a vested interest in allowing unrestricted trade with the core.

In the periphery the export sector consisted primarily of large plantations, tenant-operated estates, mines, and those support activities necessary for financing, transporting, and marketing the production for export. Most typically, each peripheral country specialized in the production of one or just a few things for export. In some cases, especially in the colonial areas, Europeans operated massive industrial-style plantation systems. Large-scale mining was also usually directly owned and administered by Europeans. On the other hand, by 1900 much of the actual production (especially in agricultural commodities) took place in native-owned enterprises, large or small. In those cases, Europeans concentrated their ownership in import-export trading, banks, shipping firms, and other support facilities. For instance, the British owned the entire Argentinian railroad system.

This division of labor perpetuated the system of peripheral exploitation and uneven development in the world-system. Simply put, the periphery produced cheap raw materials and agricultural commodities in exchange for core-produced manufactured goods. Prices for peripheral exports were low because producers invested relatively little in equipment and relied mostly on very cheap, unskilled labor. As a result, production costs were minimized and production was easily expanded. If prices rose because of high demand, more producers could easily enter the market or existing producers could expand production because capital investment costs were modest and workers did not require much training. The increase in supply would then depress prices.

In practice, however, although long-term average prices were low, peripheral export prices tended to swing widely, thereby creating boom and bust cycles for various raw materials and agricultural commodities. Conversely, prices of core goods were less variable and subject to fewer downward pressures because production required large investments in production equipment and more skilled and expensive labor. As a result, sources of supply were more limited and harder to expand. The trading relationship between the core and periphery created pressures that reduced the prices for peripheral goods and required low peripheral production costs. In turn, cost constraints helped to maintain the long-term pattern of peripheral production using low-wage labor and the exchange of the resulting commodities for core goods produced by high-wage labor.

This basic process of core-peripheral exchange was reinforced in several ways. First, peripheral areas within colonial empires were frequently limited to buying from the "mother country" and therefore could not shop around for cheaper suppliers. At the same time, colonies could export only to or through the core capitalists of their colonial masters, which limited access to export markets. Second, core financial institutions provided most of the capital for peripheral production, and thus much of the profit generated by peripheral production flowed back to the core as interest payments on capital investment loans. Third, core exporting firms and shippers charged high prices for their services to import and export to the periphery. This depressed prices for goods produced in the periphery (to compensate for high handling charges) and increased the cost of goods imported into the periphery (with the "middlemen" getting most of the profit). In short, these arrangements further assured that most of the surplus produced by the exploitation of the periphery ended up in the hands of core capitalists.

As in previous centuries, the periphery was consigned to a limited form of economic development directed toward meeting the needs of the core. Export-oriented, labor-intensive, highly exploitative production expanded but did not lead to the economic development of the rest of the periphery's economies, which lacked the capital to invest in industrial production or domestic agriculture. Most international investment capital was controlled by core capitalists. As of 1913, Great Britain, France, Germany, and the United States provided 85 percent of the funds available for international investment (Chirot, 1977: 31). Core investors had no interest in general peripheral economic development and obviously were not going to invest in enterprises that would compete with their own. The expansion of the export sector did not stimulate the rest of the economy; this sector did not produce goods used in domestic production or create a significant demand for goods or services (other than labor) produced elsewhere in the economy. Infrastructure, such as ports or railroads, was oriented toward serving the export sector rather than the general needs of the economy. Because the workers' wages in the export sector were insufficient to meet even their subsistence needs, the growth of that sector created little demand for domestically produced manufactures. At the same time, core capitalists and/or the domestic elite kept the country open to the import of production equipment and consumer goods, which made it difficult to start domestic industries. Finally, because of the frequent boom-and-bust cycle of export industries, they were not a reliable source of income with which to support diversified investment in the economy.

In contrast to the limited development of the periphery, the capitalist core had undergone rapid industrialization during the nineteenth century, and the advantage enjoyed by the core was now immense. For example, as of 1900, per capita income (in 1965 dollars) averaged about $1,300 in the core; in the periphery the average was about $100 (Chirot, 1977: 28). The core, comprising about 15 percent of the world's population, was producing 80 percent of the manufactured goods (Chirot, 1977: 24).

The Industrial Revolution was made possible by industry's increasing ability to efficiently harness more energy per worker, using first water wheels and then fossil fuels to power machinery. Production in the core thus became much more capital intensive. The first application of industrial technology in manufacturing occurred in textiles during the late eighteenth and early nineteenth centuries. Use of steam engines for ships, railroads, and manufacturing processes and the invention of large-scale steel production set off a second wave of industrialization in the mid-nineteenth century. By 1900 electrical generation, the invention of the internal combustion engine, and the manufacture of chemicals were further revolutionizing core economic activities. The resulting increase in the productive capacity of the core increased its total wealth many times over (Lenski and Lenski, 1987: 257–260).

Increases in collective wealth on such an unprecedented scale had immense direct implications for these societies. At least some of the new wealth had reached all segments of core societies by 1900. General living standards rose, health conditions improved, and life expectancy increased. Population rose rapidly at first, but the rate of increase slowed as family limitation practices spread (Lenski and Lenski, 1987: 270, 276–278).

Industrial technology gave rise to the factory system and to the rapid shift of the labor force out of agriculture and into the factory and service occupations required by the industrial organization of the economy (Lenski and Lenski, 1987: 279–281). Production was predominantly urban based and urbanization was rapid. By 1900 about half of the core's population lived in cities and towns. Analysts have long considered urbanization one of the basic processes that transformed core societies in the nineteenth century. For instance, the requirements of a population living primarily in densely packed urban areas stimulated the growth of governmental service activities (water supply, police). The small, close-knit, culturally homogeneous rural village was replaced by urban social structures consisting of systems of subcultures (such as ethnic groups), localized neighborhood communities, and complex intimate social networks (Fischer, 1984; Laumann, 1966; Shannon, 1983: 62–87).

In the core, capitalist economic relationships permeated every aspect of economic activity. Almost all of the male labor force either worked for wages or engaged in commercial agriculture. Industrial and commercial activity was increasingly concentrated in a smaller number of large, publicly held, joint-stock corporations. The first of the large, bureaucratically administered modern corporations had emerged. Capitalism had become "corporate capitalism."

The semi-peripheral states had also undergone some industrialization, but it was oriented mostly toward meeting domestic, especially military, needs. State involvement in fostering and subsidizing industrialization and protecting domestic firms from core competition was marked in the case of Japan and Russia. (Indeed, state-owned enterprises were common in Russia and were employed temporarily in Japan to get certain industries started.) All of the semi-periphery also engaged in substantial peripheral-like production. Russia relied heavily on grain exports. The eastern, essentially peripheral regions of the Austro-Hungarian Empire also continued the basic pattern of export-oriented agricultural production on large estates. (Russia and Austro-Hungary had, however, abolished serfdom.)

At least some of the semi-periphery continued to function as regional trading and financial centers. Industrial, financial, and commercial activities were conducted in the northern cities of Italy. (Southern Italy was still essentially a peripheral area.) Vienna, the capital of the Austro-Hungarian Empire, remained the center of that country's industrial activity and the focal point of a regional trading and financial network. It served not just the eastern periphery of the empire but also the independent peripheral states in southeastern Europe (such as Serbia and Bulgaria).

Russia and Japan had yet to become important regional financial and trading centers. Russia had only recently begun rapid industrialization, and Moscow and Petrograd were oriented toward serving the vast peripheral hinterland of Russia itself. Japan was faced by the essentially closed system of European colonies in Asia. The core also dominated the China trade through a system of European-controlled trading cities. (That closure was a major source of Japanese frustration and would eventually lead it to embark on a policy of military expansionism to break the stranglehold of the Europeans.) Japan was somewhat anomalous. Because it lacked raw materials for export, had a large population, and possessed little agricultural land, Japan had moved relatively quickly toward an emphasis on the export of cheap, light manufactured goods (such as textiles) produced by low-wage labor. (This strategy was a harbinger of the sort of peripheral industrialization discussed in the next chapter.)

Economically, Spain continued its decline and failed to industrialize. With the loss of most of its colonies, little remained of its function as the trading and commercial headquarters of a colonial empire. It appeared to be descending to peripheral status.

## CLASS RELATIONSHIPS

In the core the class system had for the most part assumed its modern, complex form. A dominant capitalist class had almost completely supplanted and/or merged with (as in England) the landed aristocracy; the middle class had grown; and most of the rest of the population was made of wage laborers (the majority of whom were full proletarians). Nevertheless, as of 1900, the transformation of the class system was still under way, and the proportion of the population in the various social classes was shifting rapidly.

According to Chirot, several distinct classes existed in the core during this period. At the bottom of the class system were farm laborers and tenants, who made up about 14 percent of the population. (Some of these probably qualified as semi-proletarians.) Slightly more prosperous farm owners and managers made up another 17 percent of the population. Urban, working-class manual and semi-skilled workers and their families constituted 48 percent of the population. The lower middle class (mostly clerical and sales workers) and middle class (managerial and professional workers) accounted for the other 21 percent. At the top of the class system, major capitalists (less than 1 percent of the population) owned about 33 percent of all the wealth and received about 15 percent of all the national income (Chirot, 1977: 60–61).

A major change in the system of labor control had occurred by 1900 in the periphery. Slavery had been all but completely abolished, as had most kinds of formal serfdom. In their places, the large plantations and estates relied on various forms of sharecropping, cash-rent tenancy, and/or (often part-time) wage labor. Mines and infrastructure facilities (such as railroads) also employed wage labor. Despite this apparently greater freedom of peripheral workers to arrange their own employment, in practice the actual power of landlords and other employers over them was still almost unlimited. Levels of compensation for workers in the export sector remained at or below that necessary for the long-term reproduction of their labor power (the system of superexploitation discussed in Chapter 2).

The remainder of the labor force was engaged mostly in traditional agricultural pursuits, whose technology of production was primarily preindustrial. Yet, even in this sector, the effect of integration with the world-economy was apparent. In those societies in which forms of communal, village ownership of land had previously prevailed, land tenure rules had been converted to more closely fit the capitalist pattern of individual, private ownership. In the process many peasants had lost their land to native or European landowners. These landless peasants provided full or part-time labor in the export sector. Even in cases in which peasants had retained their land, the introduction of European-style systems of government administration resulted in the introduction of systems of taxation involving cash payment. Consequently, even these peasants had to produce goods they could sell to pay taxes. The displacement of village craft production by European-produced goods further increased the need for production for the market. In many cases, peasants obtained needed cash by working on a seasonal basis as wage labor in the export sector. Overall, despite the surface appearance of the apparently traditional rural villages, even rural areas were integrated into the new system of economic organization. Village life was a mixture of traditional pursuits and capitalist exchange relationships.

Rural production essentially subsidized the export sector. Food production in the villages made it possible for superexploitation to occur in export enterprises. Seasonal workers could return to the village when there was no wage labor available, and peasant families could send some of the members to work in the export sector for a few years at very low wages.

Overall, peripheral systems of stratification were more variable than those of the core. Despite that variability, Chirot (1977, 1986) suggests that a typical pattern of stratification was discernible by the early twentieth century. At the top of the stratification hierarchy was a tiny elite. In some cases in colonial areas all or part of this elite was composed of Europeans. In all cases this elite either owned or was the primary operator or beneficiary of the export sector of the economy. As the export sector of the economy expanded, a new upper middle class emerged consisting of Westernized intellectuals, civil servants, white-collar employees (in the export sector), and larger merchants. In many cases there remained a small "old" upper middle class of smaller landlords and/or officials of traditional institutions (for example, the clergy). There was a lower middle class, often divided into two groups: a "new" lower middle class of clerical workers and an "old" lower middle class of artisans, small merchants, and landowning peasants. These intermediary groups totaled less than 10 percent of the population. The export sector also created a small working class of superexploited wage laborers.

Despite the growth of the middle classes, the overwhelming majority of the population still consisted of impoverished peasants, but even this group had become more heterogeneous as the economy had become more integrated into the world-system. Some were peasant landholders; others were tenants on large estates, plantation workers, or landless agricultural laborers. The degree of economic inequality in these peripheral systems was extremely high. Almost all of the wealth and the vast bulk of the income of the society ended up in the hands of the upper class.

Semi-peripheral class systems were similar in many ways to those in the periphery (especially in Russia, which had only recently emerged from peripheral status). They retained significant peasant classes, and the landowning class was still quite important. Nevertheless, a capitalist class associated with commerce and industry had grown in size and wealth, and core-like industries supported a growing urban working class employed as wage laborers (some of whom were full proletarians).

The "new" middle classes, while still very small, were larger than those in the periphery.

## STATE DEVELOPMENT

Core states were now fully developed nation-states. Compared to other states, the governments of the core were strong, centralized bureaucracies with access to the resources of wealthy economies. The infrastructural power of the state to intervene in and regulate society was considerable. For example, central banks and other financial agencies gave core states substantially greater ability to regulate internal economic activities.

Nineteenth-century internal political conflict had yielded substantially increased citizen rights, which in principle constrained the despotic powers of the state. Citizens were subject to a system of universal laws that applied equally (in principle) to all. State legitimacy was based on the notion of a state serving the interests of the nation as a whole. Core states were representative democracies, and legislative bodies elected by the vote of the entire adult male population were the rule and had the most formal authority over government policymaking. Core states also had more direct responsibility for the social and economic welfare of their citizens. (For example, Germany put into place a system of state-funded retirement for workers.) Relative cultural homogeneity, the growth of universal citizen rights, and mass political participation all contributed to rising nationalist feelings in core populations. These developments in turn gave these states a high degree of mass legitimacy and support. Consequently, they were able to mobilize their populations effectively in times of war (as World War I was soon to demonstrate).

Although virtually universal male suffrage was now the rule in these states, the capitalist class clearly exercised the most political influence over state policy, while the landowning classes possessed only a shadow of their former influence. State leaders generally identified national interests with the interests of national corporations, especially regarding trade and foreign investment. With suffrage, the middle classes acquired some political influence and did occasionally challenge the interests of the capitalist class in the name of social reform. On the other hand, the middle classes were highly nationalistic and supported national competition with the other core states and expansionist policies in the periphery. The working class was beginning to play a political role, and working-class political parties, although with limited influence, were appearing in many core states. More prosperous farmers played a role similar to that of the middle classes, whereas farm laborers and tenants were politically irrelevant.

In the periphery political structures consisted either of colonial administrations or weak independent states. European administrators answerable only to the state leaders of the home country governed the colonies; lower-level administrative positions were filled mostly by Europeans; and natives occupied only the lowest positions in the government apparatus, if they were employed at all. Colonial governments displayed some of the trappings of the nation-state: centralized state bureaucracies, universal legal codes, and at least some rudimentary service agencies (for example, postal service, some transport facilities, limited educational systems). The government's primary concern was to maintain order (in the face of potential native revolt) and ensure smooth operation of export-oriented economic activities.

The independent states of the periphery were developing at least the outward appearances of core-like nation-states. State apparatuses were weak and displayed low levels of administrative effectiveness. Some of these states even attempted to function as representative democracies but were extremely unstable and frequently slid into dictatorial rule. At least in Latin America, the politically dominant class, whose members engaged in export activities, favored export-oriented state policies: openness to core imports, encouragement of core investors, and state intervention to allow them to maintain systems of coercive exploitation of their workers or tenants. These elites considered openness to core imports a precondition to obtain access to core markets for their exports. They also wished to obtain access to luxury goods, core capital, core investment in export-oriented infrastructure (such as railroads), and core production equipment. In some cases, land-owning-class domination was reinforced or replaced by the direct intervention of core states, which supported repressive client states in return for policies favorable to European trading and investment interests.

Semi-peripheral states were much stronger than those in the periphery and more repressive than those in the core. In most a relatively centralized state bureaucracy attempted to increase state power in the interstate system by means of state-sponsored industrialization. This meant circumscribing the privileges and sacrificing the economic interests of a landholding aristocracy engaged in peripheral-like export production. For example, all of these states began by eliminating serfdom and other vestiges of feudal relationships between the peasantry and the aristocracy. At the same time, consumption levels of the new working and middle classes had to be kept low to maximize saving and investment for industrialization. Heavy taxation of the peasanty also provided much of the income for high levels of state expenditures. Only a repressive state apparatus was capable of pursuing such policies.

The emerging class of industrialists stood to gain from these policies and was enlisted by the state as a junior partner in the industrialization effort. The capitalist class cooperated with state policies in return for state subsidies, repression of the workers, and other special privileges.

## Summary and Conclusion

According to world-system theory a capitalist world-economy and a system of competitive nation-states began to emerge in the sixteenth century. Since then this system of political-economy has had relatively stable general features and has constituted the basic framework in which the events of the modern era have unfolded. In each period since the sixteenth century, a particular pattern of international exploitation and nation-state conflict has reproduced itself. The principle "players" in this international drama have changed, the techniques of exploitation have differed in their details, the level of technology has risen, and economic production has increased tremendously. In many respects the world appears to have been transformed in the last five centuries, yet the basic economic and political processes and relationships of the past centuries are strikingly similar in their fundamentals to those of our own century.

# The Contemporary
# World-System

**A** s we saw in the last chapter, world-system theorists maintain that the underlying structure of the system has remained essentially the same throughout its five-hundred-year history. Is that still true? The twentieth century has seen a succession of dramatic economic and political events: two large-scale wars among the core powers (World Wars I and II); numerous smaller wars; significant changes in the relative power of the core states; periods of extreme economic crisis and periods of major economic expansion; and unrest, wars of independence, and destruction of the old colonial empires in the periphery. Most dramatic of all, almost one-third of the world's population is governed by Marxist states officially hostile to capitalism. The world of 1900, apparently so stable, seems to have come unraveled.

Yet most world-system theorists, while acknowledging that the world-system has come under increasing challenge, argue that underneath all these changes, one can still discern the elements of the same basic structure that appeared in the sixteenth century. This chapter will attempt to demonstrate that claim. The discussion will be organized around the same topics addressed in the last chapter. We will examine each of the zones of the world-economy outside of the major Communist states, beginning with the core. The chapter will conclude with a presentation of world-system theorists' attempts to analyze the role of Communist states in the twentieth century.

## The Core

The combined wealth, technological expertise, and military power of the core continue to exceed those of the rest of the world.[1] The core is still the location of the most technologically advanced, capital-intensive, high-wage production. The core retains its capitalist system of political-economy and is still organized into a system of competitive nation-states. Changes in the core have occurred within the context of an ongoing, not a fundamentally transformed, world-system.

## CORE PARTICIPATION IN THE INTERSTATE SYSTEM

The relative power of the European core states has shifted. Great Britain, the dominant power of the nineteenth century, has just barely been able to retain its status as a major core power. It has been weakened by industrial decline, exhausted by two world wars, and stripped of its colonial empire. It faces an uncertain future. After World War II, Germany was divided by the victorious core allies and the Soviet Union into two countries. West Germany, the larger of the two, recovered to become the most economically successful country in Europe. East Germany is part of a system of Eastern European client states of the Soviet Union. France remains one of the three most powerful European states. Most of the rest of the European states outside of the Soviet orbit consist of minor core powers. (See Map 4.1.) (Ireland and Spain, however, are on the borderline between the semi-periphery and the core. Greece and Portugal clearly are in the semi-peripheral category.)

The most important development in the core has been the emergence of the United States as the overwhelmingly dominant core country. (As we will see in Chapter 5, such dominance by one core state—called a period of "hegemony"—has characterized the world-system before.) At the end of World War II the United States enjoyed a temporary monopoly over nuclear weapons, possessed the largest and most efficient economy, and displayed a new willingness to assume the role of leader and protector of the world-system. As a means of protecting Western Europe from the Soviet Union and of reviving capitalism in the core, the United States helped to facilitate the economic recovery of Western Europe. As the ability and willingness of the European core states to project their power into the periphery waned after 1945, the United States increased its military, economic, and political involvement there. In the more recent past, the U.S. economic position has eroded, and that has weakened its overall position of dominance in the world-system. Nevertheless, the United States is still the most powerful core state.

By the 1970s formerly semi-peripheral Japan had also become a full-fledged member of the core. After Japan's devastating defeat in World War II, the United States (through military occupation) worked to create an economically prosperous and politically stable Japan capable of allying itself with the United States. Japan was quickly restored to

MAP 4.1   The core, 1975–1983

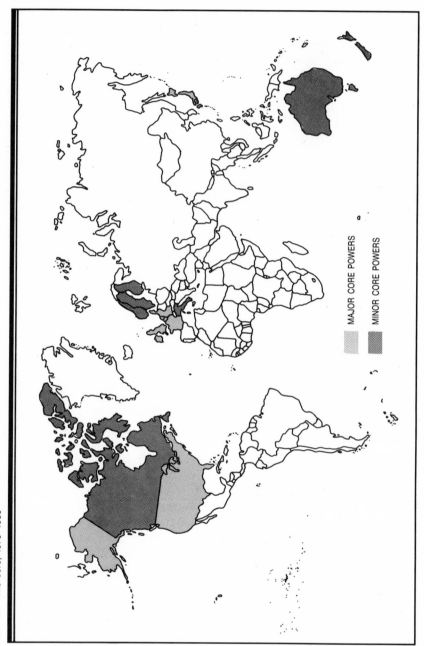

MAJOR CORE POWERS

MINOR CORE POWERS

political independence and given the freedom to adopt policies necessary to rebuild its economy. The Japanese took advantage of an expanding world-economy and relatively open trading opportunities to create a highly efficient, export-oriented manufacturing sector. By the 1980s Japan had one of the largest and most productive economies in the core and was beginning to emerge as a world financial center. But it did not seek to become a major military power, and it continued to be closely allied to and militarily dependent upon the United States.

The post-1945 period was also one of those rare times when peace and stability characterized intercore relations. (As we will see in the next chapter, such periods occur when one power becomes dominant in the core.) The United States used its economic and military power to unite the core in an alliance against the Soviet Union and at the same time encouraged its allies to reduce trade barriers within the core and establish institutions to implement common economic policies and assure core financial stability. Nevertheless, economic competition and disagreement over economic policy and other international issues continued and became increasingly explicit after 1970. Thus, the basic pattern of intercore capitalist competition remained, although muted. The common military alliance against the Soviet Union and the military strength of the United States just served to limit the amount of open political conflict among the allied core states.

## THE CORE IN THE WORLD DIVISION OF LABOR

The core states also continued to be the location of the most advanced forms of industrial production, the highest per capita income, and the greatest increases in per capita wealth in the world. The core, with 16 percent of the world population, accounts for 60 percent of total world economic activity. (The Soviet Union and its allied states account for another 25 percent of gross national product [GNP] and 9 percent of the population [Chirot, 1986: 232].)

Lower trade barriers, international financial stability, U.S. assistance to Europe (in the 1950s), and domestic economic policies designed to stimulate consumer demand all contributed to rapid economic growth in the core during the 1950s and 1960s. Although the British economy lagged behind most others, the entire core experienced substantial economic expansion and a rising standard of living. In the process U.S. economic dominance soon eroded, the economies of Europe expanded and modernized, and Japanese export industries catapulted that country into membership in the core. Despite these changes, the United States remained the financial center of the capitalist system, and its industry continued to enjoy a technological advantage in some manufacturing sectors.

The 1970s began a period of slower economic growth, increasing financial instability, and greater economic competition within the core. High inflation and escalating energy prices disrupted core economies. The competitive position of U.S. manufacturing continued to deteriorate. Financial speculation and the growth of massive debts, both in the periphery and the United States (in the 1980s), threatened the stability of core financial institutions. Intense competition among core manufacturers for a slowly growing world market threatened to generate trade wars. Relatively high levels of unemployment plagued most of the core during the 1980s. No serious depression occurred, but general economic conditions remained unsettled. In short, the stability and prosperity of the Pax Americana in the 1950s and 1960s was replaced by the more normal pattern of competition and uncertainty.

There were some significant shifts in the relative importance of various core industrial activities. Under conditions of intense intercore competition, many of the traditional mass-manufacturing industries (such as steel, autos, and textiles) encountered slowed markets and declining profit rates. Production moved to semi-peripheral (or even peripheral) countries to take advantage of low wage rates. At the same time, newer industries (such as the high-tech manufacture of electronics) assumed growing importance in the core. (The migration of mature industries to the semi-periphery is a normal process in the world-system.)

Within the context of a basically capitalist mode of production, core internal economic organization took the form of increasing domination of the economies by ever-larger, bureaucratically administered corporations whose financing shifted away from new stock issues and toward financial institutions. Although fewer corporations were directly controlled by particular upper-class families, ownership of these corporations remained ultimately in the hands of the capitalist class. Corporate managers, sitting atop complex systems of bureaucratic administration, enjoyed considerable latitude in the day-to-day operation of large firms. Some sociological observers argue that the increasing power of top managers indicates a fundamental shift in the effective control over corporations to the corporate leadership. But most neo-Marxist scholars (including world-system theorists) reject that assertion and maintain instead that the behavior of top managers is constrained by market conditions and by pressures from financial institutions and the stock market to profit-maximize in standard capitalist fashion.

In addition, a few large corporations (oligopolies) increasingly dominated the markets, many corporations acquired divisions in several different markets ("conglomerate" firms), and "multinational" corporations (operating in a number of countries) appeared to be creating a situation in which a few corporations ("world-oligopolies") dominated world markets. Thus, the general tendency toward greater economic concentration continued in the capitalist world-economy (Eitzen, 1988: 407–437; Mintz and Schwartz, 1981a, 1981b; Chirot, 1977: 190).

To world-system theorists these changes simply represent the normal operation of the system. The relative economic position of the core states constantly changes in response to the demands of competition and innovation. What constitutes the most advanced form of production may change, but the core is still the location of that production. The organization of capitalist enterprises continues to evolve in the direction of larger, more bureaucratically administered firms (Chase-Dunn, 1984).

CLASS RELATIONSHIPS IN THE CORE

Internally, the core states experienced significant but gradual and evolutionary change in their class systems during the twentieth century. Continued alteration in the distribution of jobs contributed to a modest increase in the size of the middle classes. In the United States, for example, the proportion of the population in the middle classes increased to about one-third (but that trend may be reversing). The percentage of workers who were extremely poor farm laborers and small farmers declined, as did the proportion of workers employed in factories. On the other hand, the proportion of workers in clerical and service jobs increased. Until recently, however, the distribution of income changed only slightly (toward greater equality), and the distribution of wealth changed very little. Thus, the basic pattern of a high degree of economic inequality remained, and the capitalist class retained its dominance (Szymanski, 1983: 76–119; Eitzen, 1988: 255–295; Chirot, 1977: 189–191).

Wallerstein sees these changes as continuations of certain basic tendencies in the system. The proportion of full proletarians continues to increase, while political pressures for more income equality and the bureaucratization of the state and private business firms lead to rising wage levels and the growth of the middle classes (Wallerstein, 1984b: 67–68).

CORE STATE DEVELOPMENT

The capitalist class still exercises a disproportionate influence in the core. But both Marxists and world-system theorists disagree about why this is so. World-system theorists do agree that the long-term interests of the capitalist class still determine most core state policies. On the other hand, the demand made by the lower social classes for greater political influence does force core state leaders to accommodate these demands in order to maintain political stability, but leaders try to do so without fundamentally altering the state's role in promoting the process of capital accumulation (Block, 1978; Hopkins, 1982a: 27–28).

Thus, the process of incorporating more of the population into the political process, a feature of nineteenth-century state development, is also at work in this century. Most core working classes are now more politically active than they were in 1900. Working-class political parties, with mildly "socialist" political platforms, are part of electoral politics in most core states, except for the United States, and these parties have with some success obtained increased state intervention in the economy, more social welfare programs, and more protection of worker rights. In exchange, workers accept the basic system of capitalist political-economy, support the anti-Soviet alliance, and generally advocate "national" (corporate capitalist) economic goals in relations with other states (Chirot, 1977: 193; Marger, 1987: 41).

The middle classes in the core are a major factor in electoral politics, support a number of voluntary organizations that represent their interests, and as a result exert pressure on core states for specific policies that benefit them. These classes often support specific "reform" measures, including some opposed by the capitalist class. Although the middle classes have usually been indifferent or passively supportive of state foreign policies, they have occasionally opposed military adventures in the periphery when those operations dragged on without resolution (for example, French involvement in Algeria and U.S. involvement in Vietnam). Nevertheless, the middle classes generally limit their demands to specific policies or reforms and continue to support the existing system of political-economy (Chirot, 1977: 191; Marger, 1987: 227–253).

Finally, the size and importance of core state bureaucracies have grown tremendously in response to the increased social welfare and regulatory role of core states. The size of the U.S. government also reflects the creation of large, permanent military, intelligence, and foreign service establishments after 1945. To some degree, these large state bureaucracies are political forces in their own right, with particular interests in the formation of state policy that may not always be consistent with the immediate policy demands of the capitalist class. Yet, overall, these bureaucracies are constrained to follow a basic policy direction consistent with the long-term interests of the capitalist class (Chirot, 1977: 193–200; Block, 1978; Marger, 1987: 115–164).

## The Periphery

The periphery has experienced tremendous political turmoil and socioeconomic change during this century.[2] The world of colonial empires and generally passive client states has been destroyed. Many peripheral countries aspire to modern, core-like economies and act accordingly. At the same time, vocal opposition to core power is expressed almost everywhere. Despite the dramatic quality of these changes, world-system theorists maintain that the nature of the periphery and its relationship with the core are still unchanged in their essentials. (Map 4.2 indicates the current membership of the periphery.)

PERIPHERAL PARTICIPATION IN THE INTERSTATE SYSTEM

Although opposition to European rule was evident in the periphery early in this century, colonial administrators were generally able to repress independence movements in the pre–World War II period. But after 1945, despite overwhelming conventional European military superiority, the nationalist movements mobilized sustained mass opposition to colonial rule by means of mass protests, strikes, sabotage, and, if necessary, guerrilla warfare. In some cases the military capacity of these movements was increased by aid from the Soviet Union.

As a result, the costs of retaining colonies became unacceptably high for the core powers. The colonial powers faced damage to their enterprises, the disruption of commercial and trading relationships, and the administrative and police expenses required to deal with unrest. In cases of wars of independence, the colonizers were confronted with the prospect of having to fight almost endless, small, but expensive wars of attrition against guerrilla movements. These costs were particularly unattractive in the post-1945 period because they threatened to retard economic recovery from World War II, and the war-weary European public was especially unwilling to support counterinsurgency.

Nevertheless, the core powers only surrendered control grudgingly. Britain, France, and Portugal all became embroiled in one or more colonial wars. Even when war did not break out, most areas witnessed a period of protest and unrest before independence was granted.

Once independence in the periphery was recognized as unavoidable, most core powers (with the support of the United States) attempted to minimize the extent of the change from the colonial to the post-colonial period. They sought to install governments that would maintain friendly political ties with their former rulers and continue the existing pattern of trade and investment. A particular concern was to prevent radical political elements from gaining power. The core powers hoped that the peaceful turnover of power to moderate nationalist groups would forestall Marxist-inspired revolutionary movements, which threatened to wreak havoc with existing economic arrangements and align themselves with the Soviet Union.

Although the former colonies became independent states, the resulting relationship between the core and periphery, known as the "neoco-

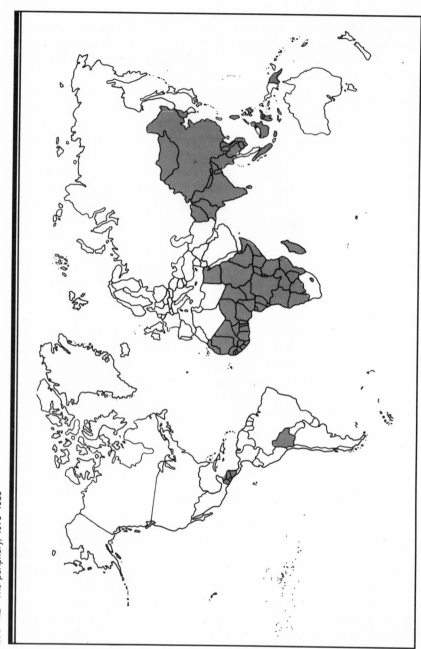

MAP 4.2 The periphery, 1975–1983

lonial" system, was much the same as it had been before independence. Traditional export activities continued, as did core involvement in peripheral economies. The periphery cooperated with and obeyed the rules established by core-dominated financial institutions such as the World Bank. Private ownership of productive facilities and basically capitalist economic relationships remained. The new states maintained diplomatic relationships with the core, avoided close ties with the Soviet Union, and kept radical social and political change at bay.

As the European states reduced their military presence and granted independence, the United States took on more responsibility for maintaining and defending the neocolonial system. European states (and investors) continued to play a role in their former colonies, sometimes a substantial one, but the United States was the primary defender and "policeman" of the periphery for the core.

The United States played this role in several ways. In some cases the United States was able to bring into or maintain in power native political elites that were willing to function as its direct "clients." These elites obtained economic aid and military assistance in order to maintain themselves in power (and, frequently, enrich themselves) and in return agreed to be official (anti-Soviet) U.S. allies. They minimized restrictions on foreign investment and emphasized capitalist-oriented economic modernization. Quite frequently these elites were allied domestically with conservative landowning, merchant, or other business interests.

Initially, the number of such client states (or near clients) was quite large. In the 1950s they included most of the states of Central America, many in South America, Turkey, Iraq, Iran, Saudi Arabia, Taiwan, South Korea, the Philippines, and South Vietnam. The vast bulk of U.S. military and economic aid went to these states during the 1950s and 1960s (Chirot, 1977: 164–165). In addition, with U.S. acquiescence or assistance, a few former French and British colonies (especially the smaller states in Africa) remained as effective clients of their former colonial rulers.

Despite these core efforts, the number of true client states was sharply reduced by the 1980s. Some were lost to military coups that replaced the existing leadership with more independent and nationalistic leaderships (for example, Iraq). Other client states collapsed in the face of mass unrest (for example, Iran and Nicaragua). Some succumbed to Marxist-oriented revolutions (for example, Cuba). A larger number of states remained relatively closely tied to the core but were no longer true clients (for example, Thailand).

The result was a less obvious form of neocolonialism. An increasing number of states were governed by overtly nationalist, independent elites that were often openly hostile to the neocolonial system and as a result attempted to avoid direct military or diplomatic alignment with the United States (or the Soviet Union). They also attempted to devise programs of economic development that were less dependent on direct core investment and frequently involved substantial direct state ownership and/or economic planning and state partnership with private investors. Many also attempted to regulate their trading and investment relationships with the core.

In general, the United States has had little choice but to tolerate these changes, although this tolerance has been neither unlimited nor unconditional. In return for not attempting to punish these states, the United States has expected them to abide by some policy guidelines, such as (1) core property is not to be expropriated without acceptable compensation; (2) trade with the core must continue, although some tariffs or other restrictions are allowed; (3) strong military, economic, or diplomatic dependence on the Soviet Union must be avoided; (4) participation in the system of international finance and currency arrangements (for example, repayment of loans) must be continued; and (5) "extreme" radical domestic policies intended to establish a revolutionary socialist state must not be actually implemented. In short, the periphery could be somewhat independent of the core, as long as that independence did not involve alliance with the Soviet Union or radical "withdrawal" from the capitalist world-economy. If peripheral states followed such a moderate course and maintained normal diplomatic relations with the core (unlike Iran, for example), they could expect some very modest foreign aid from the core (designed to encourage friendly relationships and counterbalance any Soviet aid). They could also enjoy access to core loans, technology, and markets (Feinberg, 1983).

The U.S. reaction to regimes that violated one or more of the preceding guidelines has been a combined attempt to punish the offending countries, force them to change their policies, and/or make examples of them to discourage other states from following in their footsteps. "Punishment" has included denial of access to core markets, technology, and credit; attempts at subversion or disruption of the government; and, occasionally, direct military intervention. In some cases, these actions did result in a regime change or policy change (as in Iran in 1953, Guatemala in 1954, and Grenada in 1982), but in many more cases, they increased domestic economic difficulties for the peripheral state and encouraged it to turn more frequently toward the Soviet Union for assistance (Feinberg, 1983).

World-system theorists do not regard these changes as evidence that the world-system is breaking down, at least in the immediately fore-

seeable future. Periods of decolonization and reduced direct control
of the periphery are not new in the history of the world-system. Rather,
they have been typical of periods in which one core power is hegemonic—as was the case in the post-1945 period. Peripheral states are
able to maintain their formal independence, but their freedom of action
remains severely limited, they remain subordinate to the demands of
states in the core, they have only a very limited ability to pursue
policies counter to core interests, and they are extremely weak militarily
and economically. The periphery also lacks the resources to implement
many of the domestic policies that would lead to more rapid economic
development, and in any case, implementing policies opposed by the
core can have dire consequences in terms of economic and military
sanctions. Because the periphery needs core capital and technology,
these states have little or no choice but to continue participating in
the world-economy under conditions dictated by its requirements.
Hence, peripheral states have exchanged direct political and economic
control for a less obvious set of constraints.[3]

## The Periphery in the World Division of Labor

Although economic activities in the periphery and the nature of its
financial relationship with the core have been changing, the periphery
remains the primary location of coerced and highly exploited low-
wage labor. New mechanisms of peripheral exploitation reinforce the
unequal exchange of peripheral products produced by low-wage labor
for those of the core produced by high-wage labor. Consequently, the
core still obtains much of the surplus value created in the periphery.

The nineteenth-century pattern of raw materials and agricultural
exports remains an important aspect of peripheral participation in the
world-economy. In most of the periphery, those more traditional products
still constitute the bulk of their exports. (This is especially true in
Central America, the smaller South American countries, and sub-Saharan
Africa.) Most of the labor force is engaged in agriculture, both for
domestic consumption and export. As before, prices and demand for
these products in the world market are erratic and often low (Petras,
1984a, 1984c; Frank, 1981: 62–131).

Indeed, the situation of those countries most heavily involved in
traditional export activities deteriorated between the 1950s and the
1980s. Prices for many of their exports declined relative to prices of
industrial goods (World Bank, 1987: 17), and in the 1970s prices of
petroleum and petroleum-based inputs (such as fertilizer) greatly
exceeded these countries' ability to increase exports. In the more
densely settled countries, continued population growth, conversion of

agricultural land to export commodity production, weather calamities, poor agricultural policies, and environmental deterioration created difficulties in meeting domestic food needs. Economic mismanagement and expenditures for military equipment further worsened the economic situation (World Bank, 1987: 15–17; Frank, 1981: 62–131; Brown, 1987: 3–29).

At the same time, some of the periphery also constructed major industrial facilities, although industrialization remained quite limited in most countries. In the poorest peripheral countries (such as Pakistan), industry accounted for (on average) 17 percent of production in 1965 and 19 percent in 1985. In the slightly "more developed" periphery (such as Indonesia), industry's contribution to production rose from about 24 percent in 1965 to 32 percent in 1985 (World Bank, 1987: 206). (A very small number of countries actually established sufficient industry and increased the size of their economies enough to achieve semi-peripheral status.) In the beginning much of the newly developed industry produced consumer goods for the domestic market (so-called import-substitution industrialization). In the 1970s and 1980s more industrial production was oriented toward export, and state policies were focused on encouraging that kind of industrialization. But in the periphery (unlike the semi-periphery, as we will see) import-substitution industrial production remained predominant. Manufactured goods made up only about 5 percent of total peripheral exports in 1985 (World Bank, 1987: 49).

Some of this new industry was built and owned by core corporations, but an increasing proportion was owned by local capitalists, the government, or partnerships of the government and local or core corporations (Petras, 1984a, 1984c; Frank, 1981: 96–111). This change reflected a more general trend in the periphery-core relationship in which direct core investment and ownership became increasingly less important. This trend derived from peripheral government efforts to reduce foreign ownership in their economies by placing restrictions on it and from core concern about the safety of direct ownership in facilities located in the periphery. Core corporations were increasingly fearful of political instability and/or nationalization by peripheral governments. In fact, a few did seize some foreign-owned manufacturing, transportation, mining, or oil facilities (Petras, 1984a, 1984c; Frank, 1981: 133–156).

Finally, newly independent states throughout the periphery sought to stimulate rapid economic development through government action. Foreign aid and loans combined with limited national resources were used to build infrastructure (roads, ports, electrical grids), invest in "human capital" (education and health), and build or subsidize industrial facilities. At first, most of the loans and aid funds came from core governments or international development agencies (such as the World Bank) supported by core governments. But during the 1970s loans from core banks exceeded the amount of governmental assistance to the periphery (World Bank, 1987: 18; Frank, 1981: 133–156).

Overall, significant amounts of infrastructure were built. Health services improved enough to result in a major reduction in the death rate. (Rapid population growth also occurred because fertility fell only slightly.) Educational facilities expanded. Some countries reduced the amount of direct foreign control over their productive facilities. Some constructed significant manufacturing plants. (India produces almost as much steel as Great Britain, produces most of its own transportation equipment, has an electronics industry, and, in many respects, is approaching semi-peripheral status industrially.) Most of the periphery experienced very rapid urbanization, and the percentage of the labor force in agriculture declined (World Bank, 1984: 3–14).

These economic developments do not convince most world-system theorists that a basic change occurred in the periphery's role in the world division of labor, its economic relationship with the core, or its relative economic position in the world-economy. Traditional exports still comprise the largest percentage of the periphery's production, and the limited amount of manufactured goods produced for export are in labor-intensive (that is, low-wage) industries (for example, textiles and apparel manufacturing). Hence, peripheral industrialization is just a continuation of its role in low-wage production (Chase-Dunn, 1984; Caporaso, 1981).

Indeed, world-system theorists argue that the expansion of industry and the rapid increase in the urban workforce in the periphery are evidence of continuing or even intensifying exploitation there. Because of the prevailing poverty, lack of steady employment, and repressive state actions in urban centers, former peasants can be forced to work in industry at wages that make them semi-proletarians. As we have seen, Wallerstein regards an increase in the numbers of semi-proletarian workers as a process that increases exploitation. (Recall that semi-proletarians are superexploited workers.)

In addition, the majority of urban workers do not even work in the new industrial plants. They work in the "informal" sector, which consists of small production enterprises (such as sewing shops), scavengers, water carriers, one-vehicle taxi or bus operators, manual day-laborers, and various other service providers. Income levels in this sector are usually even lower than in the new industrial plants, and members of each household (often including children) must work to support the family (Bromley, 1978). This informal sector has several functions. It absorbs labor that cannot be employed in agriculture or large-scale manufacturing; subsidizes export manufacturing by providing the factories with production inputs at low prices and cheap goods and services to poorly paid workers; and helps make possible wages below that necessary for the subsistence of manufacturing workers' households. Workers in manufacturing enterprises supplement their inadequate wages by "moonlighting" in the informal sector or by having other family members work in that sector. Thus, the informal sector functions much like traditional agriculture, which also continues to make possible superexploitation by providing supplemental food or income produced by various family members (Portes and Walton, 1981: 67–106; Wallerstein, 1984b; Frank, 1981: 157–187; D. Smith, 1987; Portes, 1983). In short, the periphery remains the location of those activities that are (relative to the core) most exploitative (Chase-Dunn, 1984; Wallerstein, 1984b).

A number of other mechanisms also continue to make possible the transfer of peripheral wealth to the core. Because fewer peripheral enterprises are core owned, the export of profits from core-owned peripheral enterprises is a less important method of peripheral exploitation. But erratic, often low prices for agricultural products and raw materials limit the profitability of what remains the periphery's most important exports to the world market; thus, the core still gets cheap products produced by heavily exploited labor. The same problem also exists for peripheral industrial exports, such as textiles, apparel, and steel, in which there is a chronic problem of worldwide production overcapacity. Most peripheral exports continue to be shipped, insured, and wholesaled by core corporations (Frank, 1984).

Another mechanism of peripheral exploitation—"debt peonage"—has become more important. Lacking sufficient capital, peripheral governments and businesses borrowed massively from the core in the 1970s, usually at quite high interest rates. (Some peripheral countries borrowed simply to finance imports of increasingly expensive petroleum to keep their economies functioning.) Unfortunately, market demand and prices for most peripheral export production were much lower than expected; in fact, prices for traditional exports declined to the lowest level in the post-1945 period. Corruption, mismanagement, heavy military spending, and the like also led to misspending of the borrowed money. As a result, peripheral export earnings were not enough to cover import needs, make loan repayments, and generate capital for further economic development projects. Most of these countries ran continually high trade and international financial deficits during the late 1970s and 1980s. Further emergency borrowing to cover their payments and trade deficits simply increased debts.

By the 1980s a growing percentage of peripheral export earnings was going to pay foreign lenders, and an increasing percentage of borrowing was used to refinance existing debts. According to the World Bank, in 1985 all "low-income" countries (essentially the poorest two-thirds of the peripheral countries) employed 16 percent of their export incomes in debt service (World Bank, 1987: 28). Thus, a declining percentage of the proceeds from exports (and even additional loans) was available for further investment or for the importation of necessary production equipment or consumer goods. At the same time, core banks, concerned that the peripheral countries would not be able to repay them, drastically reduced the amount of new loans for investment in peripheral economies. Some increased assistance from international lending agencies helped peripheral countries avoid default, but this was not enough to resume capital investment at the rate necessary for sustained economic growth. Economies stagnated, and an increasing percentage of the surplus generated by their exports ended up in the hands of core financial institutions.

The situation worsened throughout the 1980s. To obtain more loans, many peripheral governments had to embark on policies of extreme economic austerity. They cut real wages; slowed down domestic economic activity, which was reliant on imported inputs; drastically reduced government budgets; and devalued their currencies (to discourage imports by making them more expensive and encourage exports by making them cheaper for core countries to buy). In turn, lower wages further decreased the domestic market for industry and consequently increased reliance on export activities. The early 1980s were marked by virtual economic depression in much of the periphery; only slow economic growth had resumed by the end of the decade. So desperate did the situation become that peripheral states were encouraged to sell off state-owned or privately owned enterprises to core investors (at distress prices) in partial settlement of their indebtedness (so-called debt-equity swaps).

In sum, debt repayment has become another means by which surplus produced in the periphery ends up in the core. Peripheral export earnings are paying off core loans, and in most countries foreign loans for investment in export-oriented production (traditional or industrial) have not generated enough new wealth for further development of their economies (Chase-Dunn, 1984; Magdoff and Sweezy, 1984; Magdoff, 1986; Frank, 1981: 132–156).

Finally, an additional drain of capital has been the result of the behavior of peripheral capitalists, who have invested a large amount of their wealth in the core. For example, one mid-1980s estimate put private investment of Latin American capitalists in the core at about

$180 billion—roughly equal to one-half of all Latin American external debt (Magdoff, 1986: 9).

As a result of these developments, general economic conditions in the periphery have shown only limited improvement, and balanced, self-sustaining economic growth seems to have eluded most countries. Uneven development in the world-economy continues, with the periphery remaining impoverished relative to the core. In terms of average levels of income, the periphery is absolutely impoverished and extremely poor relative to the core. Per capita GNP ranges from about $100 to $1,000 per year in the periphery compared to a range of about $4,000 to $16,000 per year in the core (World Bank, 1987: 202–203).

Moreover, there is no evidence that most peripheral countries are growing fast enough economically to catch up with the core. Only a handful of peripheral countries have achieved average rates of growth in per capita GNP that consistently equaled or exceeded those experienced in the core in the forty years following 1945. Most of these were either oil-producing countries with small populations or a few small countries that industrialized rapidly in the 1970s and 1980s. They account for a very small percentage of the population of the periphery. (But the People's Republic of China managed to average a rate of growth twice that of the core.) For the overwhelming bulk of the countries of the periphery, economic growth stayed slightly ahead of population growth, but per capita GNP grew at a rate barely equal to or less than that of the core. (Averages for growth in per capita GNP during 1945–1985 were typically less than 2 percent a year for the periphery and 2.4 percent in the core.) The poorest peripheral countries had the slowest rates of growth and were clearly falling behind the core (and semi-periphery) (World Bank, 1987: 202–203).

## CLASS RELATIONSHIPS IN THE PERIPHERY

In some ways the social classes and class relationships of the periphery bear a strong resemblance to those of 1900. Extreme economic exploitation guarantees a continued high degree of economic inequality. Most of the population remains utterly impoverished, and the export sector is still run by the dominant class. At the same time, political independence and changing economic activities have contributed to some changes in the class system: The composition of the dominant class has been altered in many countries, the middle classes are somewhat larger, the urban lower class is much larger, and the peasant class has become more differentiated. Amin (1980) estimates that in the 1970s about 2 percent of the peripheral population were upper-class capitalists and top bureaucrats, 8 percent were lower-level white-collar workers and small business owners, 10 percent were urban working class or unemployed, 5 percent were substantial landowners, 15 percent were "middle peasants," and 60 percent were impoverished peasants.

Thus, the overwhelming majority of the population consists of poor peasants. Relative to the situation in the core, the urban middle classes are still quite small. So, too, is the urban working class employed in large enterprises. In those countries that established large, export-oriented plantations in the nineteenth century and that have remained primarily agricultural exporters, the upper class is still mostly made up of large landowners and urban merchants (Thomas, 1984: 49–57).

The class system of the periphery continues to be characterized by extreme economic inequality. Amin also estimates that (1) the poorest 25 percent of the population receives 5 percent of the income, (2) the poorest 50 percent of the population receives 12 percent of the income, and (3) the poorest 75 percent of the population receives 35 percent of the income (1984: 17). Although actual data are sketchy, most world-system theorists would generally agree that such economic inequality probably has increased in the long term (Amin, 1984: 23). This implies that even the limited economic growth that has occurred has primarily benefited those in the upper parts of the class system and that average income figures do not adequately convey the true extent of peripheral poverty. The World Bank estimates that about one-third of the population in the periphery lives in "absolute" poverty. (Absolute poverty refers to a level of income below that necessary to maintain minimal health and "normal" levels of physical activity [World Bank, 1981: 18].)

There is also some evidence of change in these class systems. Europeans no longer constitute even a significant fraction of the economic or political elite in most peripheral countries. The peasant class has become more differentiated. At one extreme there are more landless peasants in utterly abject poverty, and at the other there is a small number of commercial farmers with medium-sized holdings. Nevertheless, almost all of the rural population continues to live in extreme poverty. Especially in the former colonies, independence and the creation of a new state bureaucracy have given rise to a state-dependent middle class whose members range from high-level technocrats to relatively low-level salaried employees. Except in the smallest and poorest countries of sub-Saharan Africa, growth of larger-scale, locally owned private enterprises has created an emerging capitalist class of business owners. In those countries with large-scale private industries, this "new" capitalist class includes quite wealthy industrialists—although many in this class may have their origins in the large landowner class.

Everywhere in the periphery massive urbanization has created a much larger urban lower class. Most typically, between one-fifth and one-third of the populations live in urban areas (World Bank, 1987: 286), and in some cases, even in quite poor countries, the urban population will quite quickly account for one-half of the total. The overwhelming majority (more than 80 percent) of the urban population is lower class, and most workers are employed in the informal sector. As we have already discussed, large enterprises (state or private) have provided regular employment for only a minority of these workers. In both sectors the workers are usually superexploited semi-proletarians. The extreme poverty of this rapidly growing class has spawned massive urban slums of wretched poverty, squalor, and degradation in every large city in the periphery (Amin, 1980; Portes and Walton, 1981: 67–106; D. Smith, 1987; D. Johnson, 1985). Thus, class relationships in the periphery remain those of extreme exploitation of the mass of the population by a small upper class. Most of the population survives under conditions of miserable poverty. Almost all of the surplus not appropriated by the core ends up in the hands of a small elite.

## PERIPHERAL STATE DEVELOPMENT

Despite considerable variation, the states of the periphery face a number of common problems and display a number of similar characteristics. They are relatively weak, both in relation to core states and in their ability to implement domestic policy. They are dominated by small elites intent on maintaining linkage to the world-economy. These elites stay in power and maintain the system of extreme economic exploitation only because of their willingness to use state power repressively. Despite that willingness, these leaders' hold on power is relatively precarious: Peripheral regimes are unstable. World-system theorists argue that all these characteristics can be explained by the requirements of and constraints imposed by the operation of the global system of political-economy.

World-system theorists generally see power over peripheral states (except for a few revolutionary states) as being concentrated in the hands of various groups that have an interest in maintaining their countries' participation in the world division of labor. The extreme exploitation that integration into the world-economy creates requires coercion enforced by a state apparatus. Hence, those local groups that benefit from that integration (and get a share of the surplus generated) use their resources to dominate a state that pursues policies favorable

Box 4.1   Peripheral Exploitation:
Its Effects on Sexual Inequality and Women's Fertility

Most of the work in world-system theory has focused on the consequences of peripheral exploitation for economic conditions, class relationships, and political structures. Much less attention has been paid to other possible social consequences. There is no good theoretical reason why that should be so. World-system theory explicitly claims that incorporation into the world-system has been the most important factor accounting for the social conditions in peripheral societies.

Recent research by a number of scholars is beginning to correct this lack of balanced consideration of the social consequences of peripheral exploitation by examining its effects on women in peripheral societies. A good example of this sort of analysis is provided in the research of Ward (1984, 1985; also see J. Smith et al., 1988). A brief summary of her argument reveals the potential usefulness of a world-system perspective in making sense of social conditions in the periphery.

Ward begins her analysis with an unexpected finding from the point of view of modernization theory. That theory associated core economic development with a steady decline in "fertility" (the number of children a women bears). This decline was part of the "demographic transition" in the core, in which both fertility and mortality (the death rate) declined to low levels during the nineteenth and twentieth centuries. In the modernization view, economic development in the periphery should have the same effect. So far, however, while mortality has declined, fertility has been very slow to follow (and population growth has consequently been very rapid). The question Ward addresses is why high fertility continues in the periphery.

The available evidence indicates that increasing participation in the world division of labor has directly led to lower economic and social status for peripheral women relative to men. The limited number of jobs in the formal sector of the urban economy has gone primarily to men. Similarly, men have been the primary workers in commerce, export agriculture, and other parts of the export economy, whereas women have been relegated to activities in the informal service sector of the urban economy and subsistence agriculture in the countryside. Thus, women's labor subsidizes the export-sector by making superexploitation of the (mostly male) workforce in that sector possible. This "women's work" is both more poorly compensated (involving either direct production of necessities or poorly paid services) and confers less social prestige than does the wage labor of the men in the export sector.

What does this have to do with women's fertility? Previous research indicates, and Ward's confirms, that women's fertility is higher when their socioeconomic status relative to men is lower. A number of reasons have been advanced for this relationship. At the most general level, a woman's lower status gives her less control of decisions relating to family size.

In addition, other consequences of participation in the world-economy tend to reinforce high fertility among peripheral women. Household subsistence activities necessary to compensate for low wages in the export sector increase the economic value of children, whose labor can be employed in those activities—having more children is a means to obtain more labor. The continued extreme economic inequality and limited prospects for mobility in the periphery also may contribute to high fertility. (The fertility decline in the core may be explained in part by couples choosing to have smaller families to take advantage of growing economic opportunities.) There does seem to be an empirical relationship between the degree of economic inequality and fertility levels. High inequality is associated with high fertility. In addition, extreme poverty in the periphery creates conditions in which infant and child mortality is very high, which encourages couples to have large numbers of children to assure that at least some of them survive. Thus, what appears to be a puzzle for modernization theory becomes comprehensible by applying world-system theory. Peripheral status in the world-system creates pressures for high fertility.

to them and enforces the system of economic exploitation (Duvall and Freeman, 1981).

The composition of these elite groups varies from society to society. For example, in the smaller, peripheral countries of Central and South America, where agricultural commodities are still the primary exports, a small group of large landowners holds predominant political power. They are allied with the military leadership (many of whom are drawn from the landowning class) and a small but growing group of urban businesspeople. Actual leadership of these states has fluctuated between dictators drawn from the officer corps and elected leaders drawn from or acceptable to the landowning class. (Especially in the past, many of these elites also relied on their client status with the United States to obtain assistance to stay in power.)

State policies have reflected this distribution of power. The state has acted to protect large landowners at the expense of the peasants, maintain a large military as a means of maintaining the loyalty of the officer corps and assure domestic control, and allow relatively open investment in the economy by foreigners (Thomas, 1984; Frank, 1981: 237–238).

In the numerous small, poor countries of sub-Saharan Africa, the pattern is different. Because a native class of large landowners or businesspeople did not emerge during the colonial period, most of the large export enterprises (such as mining) are in the hands of foreigners or, in a few cases since independence, of the state. Most other exports are derived from agricultural commodites produced by small farmers. As has already been mentioned, following independence in the 1950s and 1960s the reins of power were passed to leaders of moderate, urban-based nationalist movements and a small, mostly European-educated, civil service. This urban-based middle class of state bureaucrats used its power to orient policy toward modernization based on state activity.

Government policies have also reflected the need to maximize export earnings from agricultural and raw materials to pay for imports (to support urban consumption and the state). The regimes have tended to neglect the food-producing agricultural sector. In fact, many governments have controlled agricultural prices to keep urban food prices low, which has discouraged the expansion of food production at a time of rapid population growth.

For the urban middle class, the road to success is primarily through government employment, a fact that contributes to rampant corruption, nepotism, and overstaffing in state bureaucracies. Given the narrow (urban) political base of these regimes, the military has been in a position to play a major role in naming state leadership and has increasingly assumed power itself. In turn, the military has increased its claim on limited government revenues. Competition among leaders of different tribal groups has further contributed to political instability (Mugubane, 1985).

In the larger and/or more industrialized states of the periphery, the situation is made more complex by the growing role of an industrially based capitalist class and the decline in relative importance of the landowning class. The result has been an alliance among the industrial capitalist class, state technocrats committed to national power and industrialization, and the military—frequently in close cooperation with foreign multinationals and financial institutions. State policy reflects the interests of those groups and is similar to that of many semi-peripheral states (Thomas, 1984: 109–112; Duvall and Freeman, 1981).

Peripheral political elites rely heavily on repression and restrictions on mass political participation to stay in power. These peripheral states are, at best, elite-dominated systems of limited electoral democracy (as in India) and, more frequently, overtly authoritarian regimes. The state operates primarily to benefit the economically dominant classes and/or the leadership of the state and therefore forces a set of exploitative economic relationships on the mass of the population. More concretely, corruption, inefficiency, a perceived failure to assert national autonomy in relation to the core, and a general lack of success in raising living standards contribute to popular dissatisfaction with the government. Consequently, the impoverished, exploited rural masses and urban workers provide a fertile recruiting ground for revolutionary movements. Leadership for these movements is frequently drawn from young, middle-class intellectuals who are strongly nationalist, disaffected from the current regime, and attracted to various revolutionary and/or nationalist ideologies. Thus, regimes cannot count on mass support and are frequently faced with challenges to their rule; state repression is the most common response (Thomas, 1984: 96–98).

The repressive nature of the peripheral state also contributes to another one of its characteristics: instability. State leaders face the very real possibility of losing power as the result of popular rebellion. Not only does this popular unrest threaten stability; it ensures the military a central role in peripheral politics, which further destabilizes these regimes. In almost all these states, the army's primary role is to maintain the apparatus of repression; in fact, most regimes cannot survive without the support of the army. As a consequence, the military, which is highly politicized, is in a position to play "kingmaker" in the selection of the political leadership. When the military perceives civilian leadership as ineffective or policies as wrong, the temptation to remove the leadership becomes irresistible. Not surprisingly, many military leaders have political ambitions of their own and seize power directly as military dictators (Thomas, 1984: 82–112).

There are several other sources of peripheral state instability. Ethnic, religious, or tribal affiliations often weaken national identification and support for the central government (Chirot, 1977: 56–59). As we have seen, peripheral states have also been subject to the repeated intervention of the core powers in support of those political factions that favor core economic and geopolitical interests. The ability of the core to disrupt the economy, support subversive groups, or intervene militarily has been, and continues to be, a potential threat to the survival of any regime in the periphery.

As in the past, the periphery contains relatively weak states. In part that weakness is just a result of economic circumstances. These states often lack the economic resources, trained personnel, communications and transport infrastructure, and so on necessary for effective state functioning.

The administrative effectiveness of the state is further limited by corruption, low motivation, and incompetence. Given limited economic opportunities, many groups come to regard state employment as a means for personal enrichment or at least for minimal comfort and economic security. Corrupt regimes also often attract the support of core states, because such regimes make malleable clients. Core states can get peripheral governments to pursue desired policies by purchasing the friendship of a few officials.

From the point of view of the dominant class, government corruptibility may likewise be a convenient means of making state leaders more responsive to its interests. Given that the dominant class wants the state to enforce coercive exploitation, corruption and governmental ineffectiveness in delivering services to the masses are beside the point. Those in the upper class are likely to be satisfied as long as the police and military can maintain order and protect upper-class interests. A stronger, more effective state might, in fact, pose a threat to elite power and privilege. Of course, weak, ineffective states may have less success in maintaining social order during periods of unrest (Thomas, 1984: 67–81; Frank, 1981: 231–240).

World-system theorists regard the political structures of the periphery of the late twentieth century as a continuation of the pattern that has persisted throughout the modern era. Although the specific form this pattern has assumed may have changed, the basic political results have not. State structures function to maintain a system of coercive exploitation. Political structures are just strong enough to protect the economic activities integrating the society into the world division of labor and maintain a high degree of economic exploitation and labor coercion. At the same time, the states are not strong enough to resist core intervention when economic integration into the world-economy is threatened or to challenge the interests of the dominant classes.

## The Semi-Periphery

Rapid development of manufacturing activities in the periphery has made clear identification of membership in the semi-periphery somewhat difficult. Authors outside of world-system theory, such as Daniel Chirot (1977, 1986), argue that all but the poorest countries of the world are now semi-peripheral. Others, such as James Petras and Howard Brill (1986), argue that the world division of labor has become so complex that it no longer makes sense to divide the world into three distinct zones. Wallerstein himself is inconsistent in categorizing the semi-periphery (Arrighi and Drangel, 1986). Among world-system theorists, Giovanni Arrighi and Jessica Drangel (1986) make the most systematic attempt to resolve this issue, and we will rely on their categorization here. Map 4.3 summarizes their position. (They do recognize that there are borderline cases in which countries are between the semi-periphery and either the core or periphery.)

Compared to 1900, the total number of countries in the semi-periphery has increased, even though two major countries, Japan and Italy, have "ascended" from the semi-periphery to the core. (We will discuss the causes for "ascent" in the next chapter.) In spite of that numerical increase, in terms of population sizes relative to the other two zones, the size of the semi-periphery is about the same as it was before 1940 (Arrighi and Drangel, 1986).

### Semi-Peripheral Participation in the Interstate System

Semi-peripheral states continue to enjoy a greater degree of independence from the core than do those of the periphery. During the 1950s a number of them were closely allied with the United States and followed its lead in international affairs. Some (such as South Korea) were peripheral U.S. client states during that period. In the more recent past these states have been less likely to follow the U.S. policy lead. Nonetheless, the United States has continued to exert heavy pressure on them (similar to that put on peripheral states) to pursue domestic and international policies generally acceptable to it. Those states that have tried to ignore these pressures (Chile in the 1970s) have been subject to varying degrees of U.S. intervention (Feinberg, 1983).

The larger of these states have functioned as regional powers with substantial influence over the peripheral countries in their regions.

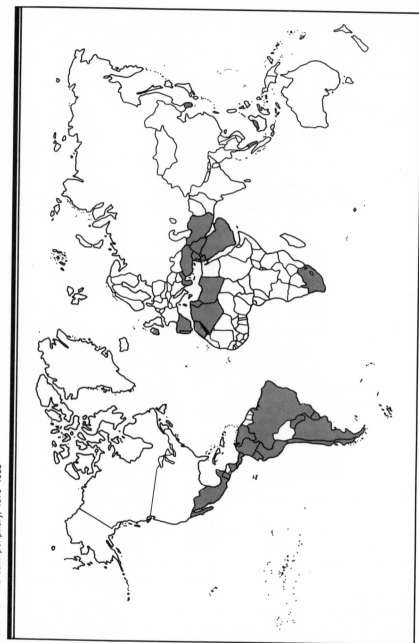

MAP 4.3  The semi-periphery, 1975–1983

Certainly, Brazil, Argentina, and Mexico have played major roles in Latin America. The so-called Pacific rim states (Malaysia, Taiwan, and South Korea, for example) have been taking a more active, cooperative role in dealing with problems of their region.

## THE SEMI-PERIPHERY IN THE WORLD DIVISION OF LABOR

The semi-periphery experienced significant industrialization after 1960. In the three decades since then average increases in per capita GNP for all of the semi-periphery approximated that of the core. (Growth was slightly lower than the core in 1960–1970, higher in 1970–1980, and lower in the 1980s.) Thus, in the aggregate the economic position of the semi-periphery relative to that of the core was stable. Per capita yearly incomes in these countries in 1986 ranged from about $1,000 to $4,000 per year (World Bank, 1987: 202–203), but the experience of specific countries in the semi-periphery varied widely.

The most successful states in the semi-periphery, the newly industrialized countries (NICs), have enjoyed economic growth rates higher than any other group of countries in the world-economy. The NICs include Brazil, South Korea, Taiwan, Hong Kong, Singapore, and Mexico before its economic difficulties in the 1980s. In the last decade both Thailand and Malaysia have also been industrializing rapidly and are now on the borderline between the periphery and semi-periphery.

The NICs have created rapidly growing, increasingly diversified industrial sectors. Diversification began with the expansion of light manufacturing facilities to produce consumer goods for the domestic market (import-substitution industrialization). After 1970 more investment went into heavy manufacturing (steel, autos), and a greater percentage of production was exported either to the core or the periphery (Petras and Brill, 1986; McMichael, 1982; Caporaso, 1981).

Most of this industrial development was not the result of direct core investment in productive facilities. As in the periphery, investment was undertaken by local capitalists and/or the state with (for the most part) capital obtained from private core lenders. In the more successful NICs (Taiwan, South Korea, Singapore) a significant portion was also generated through domestic accumulation of capital. In those countries total debt owed to foreign lenders was tightly controlled to keep it down to a level that export earnings could support. On the other hand, the two largest NICs, Brazil and Mexico, accumulated massive external debts that led to increasing financial crisis in the 1980s (McMichael, 1982; Crane, 1982; World Bank, 1987).

The emergence of the NICs suggests that raising a country's status in the world-economy is, in fact, possible. Currently, the most likely major candidates for "ascent" seem to be Taiwan and South Korea. (Thailand and Malaysia may be following the lead of their successful Asian neighbors.) Both countries have avoided debt peonage, and increases in average wage levels have created a real internal market of full proletarians. Brazil has been less successful. It suffers from a massive, crippling external debt problem that has been slowing economic growth and forcing the government to impose the kind of austerity measures previously discussed in relation to peripheral countries. Average wage rates for industrial workers and the standard of living of the urban and rural poor have been declining. Mexican development in the 1970s was based on exploiting its large oil reserves for export and domestic industrialization. The collapse of oil prices in the 1980s left Mexico in even worse shape than Brazil. Economic expansion halted, living standards deteriorated, and unemployment or underemployment characterized nearly half the labor force. Indeed, external debt as a percentage of GNP is higher in Brazil and Mexico than in any other countries in the world (World Bank, 1987; McMichael, 1982; Chirot, 1986: 254; Frank, 1981; 6–27).

Growth was slower and more uneven in the rest of the semi-periphery. Most countries experienced some industrialization, but a few (including heavily industrialized Argentina) experienced relative stagnation. Several (Turkey, Peru, Argentina, Chile) got trapped in the external borrowing cycle that led to debt crises of varying degrees. Economic expansion was greatest (as was foreign borrowing) in the 1970s. The slower growth of the world market and the intensifying debt crisis (which reduced the availability of new capital inflows) in the 1980s meant much slower growth for almost all of the semi-periphery and real economic crisis for several of the largest and many of the smallest semi-peripheral countries (World Bank, 1987: 18–22; Frank, 1981: 1–6).

Several final points about this semi-peripheral economic development need to be emphasized. First, not all exported production goes to the core. Semi-peripheral countries export to the periphery (and to each other) and in so doing act somewhat like core countries in their economic relationships with peripheral countries. Second, export of more traditionally peripheral-like products to the core remains important in the economies of most of the semi-periphery, although less important than before. Thus, elements of the economy (as we would expect) continue to function in a peripheral-like fashion. To the extent that their economies continue to rely on such traditional exports, semi-peripheral countries are in the same exploitative relationship with the core as are peripheral countries. Brazil faces many of the same dilemmas as a coffee producer that El Salvador does.

Third, even when manufactures are exported to the core, they remain of the sort that has always defined the semi-periphery's role in the world division of labor. The new industries of the semi-periphery are the old, declining industries of the core. By relying on the now easily transferred technology of traditional mass production using semiskilled labor, the semi-periphery can use the advantage of low wages to capture a segment of the world market. (Recall that semi-peripheral states have always followed this strategy in attempting to develop economically.) Fourth, the more successful semi-peripheral states continue to function as regional trading and financial centers.

Hence, world-system theorists view recent developments in the semi-periphery not as some sort of unprecedented economic breakthrough, but as extensions of the normal role of that zone in the world-economy (Arrighi and Drangel, 1986; Evans, 1979; McMichael, 1982). The greater power of semi-peripheral states allows them to pursue policies that prevent them from being forced into a peripheral economic relationship with the core. For example, they are able to take steps to protect and encourage domestic industry until it is capable of competing with core industry on the world market. As we will discuss in the next chapter, this is exactly what Taiwan and South Korea did during the early part of their industrialization. At the same time, however, resisting "peripheralization" is difficult. Although the long-term average position of the semi-periphery is stable relative to the core, the success of specific semi-peripheral states varies widely. A few states may be fairly successful, but most semi-peripheral states lack the means to achieve rates of economic growth and industrialization necessary to catch up to the core. Thus, ascent into the core is rare (Arrighi and Drangel, 1986).

## CLASS RELATIONSHIPS IN THE SEMI-PERIPHERY

As a result of the greater industrialization, urbanization, and per capita incomes of the semi-periphery, the zone's class systems are "intermediate" between those of the core and the periphery.[4] The rural peasant population is much smaller than in the periphery. Between one-half and two-thirds of the population are urban (World Bank, 1987: 264–266). The bulk of the peasantry faces conditions similar to those of the peripheral peasantry: extreme, often growing, poverty and landlessness. (Like the periphery, the semi-periphery contains a small but growing group of modest landowners engaged in commercial agriculture.) Exploitation of the peasantry and other workers engaged in peripheral-like activities is often as intense as in the periphery. Yet, the greater power and autonomy of the semi-peripheral state make modification of that exploitative relationship possible. Less of the surplus extracted from the workers goes to the landowning class or foreign investors. By various methods the state or native capitalists can appropriate part of the surplus. This surplus can in turn be applied to investment in core-like industrial activities. For example, both Taiwan and South Korea instituted land reform measures that reduced the privileges of large landowners and then used tax and agricultural policies to extract surplus from the peasants for the initial phase of industrialization.

The bulk of the rapidly growing urban population is lower class, and, as in the periphery, consists of two groups: those who work in the formal sector and those who work in the informal sector. The formal sector of the urban economy is larger than in peripheral countries. Exploitation of workers in these core-like manufacturing activities appears to be much greater than that of workers in the core, and industrial wage levels are much lower. On the other hand, many workers are better off than their counterparts in the periphery. At least some semi-peripheral countries contain workers who can be regarded as full proletarians.

Nevertheless, those in the informal sector constitute the overwhelming majority of the urban lower class. Employment in that sector appears to be increasing faster than in the formal sector. Although probably not as absolutely destitute as such workers in the periphery, most of these workers are semi-proletarian. Thus, even in most of the semi-periphery, large-scale industrial enterprises have not been absorbing the huge increase in the urban lower class (South Korea and Taiwan excepted).

The urban middle classes are significantly larger in the semi-periphery than in the periphery. Industrialization and the expansion of the state bureaucracy have led to a rapid growth in the absolute size of these classes. Despite their growth, they still remain a very small minority of the urban population. There is a substantial upper middle class of professionals and managers in private business firms, state enterprises, and the state bureaucracy. This class also includes a more traditional middle class of small business owners. In comparison to its counterpart in the core, this upper middle class is in a much more privileged position in society. Relative to the poverty of the majority of the population, members of this class are extremely affluent. In fact, Wallerstein argues that the level of compensation for this class is often higher than that of the core upper middle class (Wallerstein, 1979a: 102). In addition, the lower middle class, consisting of white-collar clericals, clerks, school teachers, and semi-professionals, has grown significantly.

The composition (if not the size) of the upper class has also been changing. Large landowners and merchants (typical elites in the traditional periphery) have declined in relative economic importance. In their place (but sometimes recruited from their ranks) has emerged a class of wealthy industrialists and financial investors.

This semi-peripheral class system is characterized by extreme economic inequality. Rising average per capita income has not been distributed equally, and in most cases the trend has been toward growing inequality. The increasing national income has gone to the new industrial capitalist class and urban middle class (Chirot, 1986: 255–256). After 1980 even workers in the formal sector of the urban economy typically experienced declines in their real (already very low) wages. Most of the available evidence suggests that conditions among workers in the urban informal structure and among the poorest elements of the peasantry either have not improved or have deteriorated. (But, in contrast, South Korea and Taiwan experienced declines in economic inequality [Crane, 1982]. As we will see in the next chapter, this difference may be related to their more successful strategies of ascent in the world-system.)

## SEMI-PERIPHERAL STATE DEVELOPMENT

Semi-peripheral states are clearly more powerful, are more administratively effective, and have more internal authority than do peripheral states. Yet, none of these states has maintained stable forms of representative democracy of the type found in the core. They have fluctuated between unstable (often upper-class-dominated) "democracies" and authoritarian states.

Most of these states are controlled by a sometimes uneasy alliance of rising industrial capitalists (with or without the support of the older landowner/merchant class), top state bureaucrats, and the military. These groups also maintain close relationships with core corporations. This alliance is more or less unified around one central goal: increasing national power through rapid industrialization. Each member of the alliance stands to benefit from such a policy and needs the other members to implement the rapid industrialization strategy (Duvall and Freeman, 1981; Evans, 1979).

Hence, semi-peripheral states have attempted to achieve rapid industrialization through heavy state involvement in the economy. The state determines the overall development strategy; obtains capital from the core—either as direct loans to the state or as the guarantor of loans made to domestic capitalists—and generates additional investment capital by keeping wages and domestic consumption low. The state builds needed industrial infrastructure such as roads and electrical systems. In cases in which local expertise or capital is judged inadequate, state enterprises or joint ventures between core multinational corporations and either the state or local capitalists are established. The state uses various forms of repression to maintain low wages, harsh working conditions, and squalid urban living conditions. This policy of repression accounts for the prominence of the military in the ruling coalition.

Initially, most states followed a policy of protecting domestic industries from foreign competition in order to create local industries to serve the national market. More recently, most have shifted to a strategy of encouraging export industries and have opened up their markets somewhat more to core imports and direct investment. The participation of and the need for close state coordination with core multinationals and financial institutions as partners in these industrialization efforts have made them virtual members of the ruling coalition (Evans, 1979; Duvall and Freeman, 1982).

As we have seen, this strategy has had only limited success in all but a few semi-peripheral countries. That limited success has been one source of semi-peripheral political conflict. Even when the result of these efforts has been considerable industrialization, political tensions have increased. Continued and often increasing economic inequality and stagnant or declining wages for most workers (except in South Korea and Taiwan) breed mass discontent. Harsh working conditions, suppression of labor unions, and political repression amplify this discontent (even in South Korea). Although the middle classes fare well in the more successful semi-peripheral countries, they are growing restless with their exclusion from political power and with the repressive nature of the state. The upper class is often split between the "old" landlord class and the "new" industrialists and investors. Ethnic, religious, and regional hostilities remain common and are quick to take on political or economic overtones under such conditions.

Such political conflict and discontent have generally led to even greater state repression. But in some of these countries, especially in South America during the 1980s, the lack of economic progress, corruption, and repression resulted in mass political unrest. In response, the military retreated from active, open involvement in the government and allowed some form of democracy as a way of restoring state legitimacy. Such "democratization" has happened before, yet if the past is any guide, these democratic governments will have difficulty correcting the sources of unrest without abandoning the goal of rapid capital accumulation and industrialization. When unrest flares up again or elected governments threaten to give in to mass demands, the result will be the intervention of the military to reimpose order through terror and repression.

Thus, the basic characteristics of semi-peripheral states have not really changed that much. They are relatively stronger and more centralized states than their peripheral counterparts. State power is mobilized to intervene in the economy to speed capital accumulation and protect domestic industry. The requirements of that strategy generate political tensions and mass unrest, which lead to state repression.

## Socialist States in the World-System

The twentieth century has been characterized by a number of anti-capitalist and anticore revolutions. As a result, about one-third of the world's population is now governed by socialist states that officially subscribe to a revolutionary, Leninist view of the world. The actual behavior of these states has only approximated that predicted by Marx and Lenin.

In some ways these new socialist states have behaved as various Marxist theorists expected. They abolished most forms of private ownership of the means of production and instituted centralized state control of the economy. They withdrew from normal participation in international trade and limited their economic relationships with capitalist countries. Starting with very limited industrial bases, they embarked on ambitious industrialization programs. They made progress in modernizing their economies and in providing social services to their populations. Their official political goals included social and political equality, the support of socialist revolutions in the rest of the world, and the eventual transition to fully Communist societies as envisioned by Marx.

In other ways these countries have fallen substantially short of achieving their original revolutionary goals. Socialist states have been authoritarian and repressive. Their centrally planned economies have been plagued by bureaucratic mismanagement and burdened by massive military expenditures. Special privileges for the ruling party bureaucrats have stood in stark contrast to the regimented and austere life led by the average citizen. Especially in the recent past, these states have become increasingly dependent on the importation of advanced technology and capital and have had to increase their economic ties with the core. Economic reforms have focused on the use of market mechanisms to increase efficiency and material incentives to increase worker productivity.

Marxist scholars have responded to these ambiguous results with a number of conflicting interpretations of the nature of socialist states.

Most of the debate has focused on the Soviet Union and its system of client states in Eastern Europe. Inevitably, world-system theorists have been drawn into the debate.

World-system theorists concentrate on two general issues in regard to the nature of the Soviet system. The first is the Soviet Union's relationship to the world capitalist system. Is the Soviet Union essentially separate and autonomous from the world-system? Or is it really part of the system? The second issue is the internal system of political-economy and class relations in the Soviet Union. How socialist (or capitalist) is the basic system of political-economy? Has a capitalist social class system reemerged? What are the roles of the state and the party leadership?

Chase-Dunn (1982a, 1982b, 1982c) advances an interpretation of the role of the Soviet Union in the world-system that is at least representative of the world-system theory position on these issues. (World-system theorists continue to disagree in major ways on this issue but generally seem to accept Chase-Dunn's overall conclusions.[5]) Chase-Dunn builds his theoretical argument on Wallerstein's position that there is but one world-system with a single general capitalist mode of production. Political and economic integration into the system requires that a country adopt a form of political-economy consistent with the general logic of global capitalism.

Chase-Dunn portrays the Soviet Union's position in the world-system as fairly typical of a semi-peripheral state attempting to achieve core status. Like other such states (only in more extreme form because of core hostility), the USSR initially limited economic links to the core so as to avoid involvement in the world-economy in a way that would perpetuate the country's semi-peripheral status. It created a protected national economy in which its less advanced and efficient industries could grow without core competition. At present, however, links to the world-economy are growing. In typical semi-peripheral fashion, the Soviet Union is an exporter of raw materials and petroleum (its biggest export) and in return seeks high-technology equipment, expertise, and credit from the core to modernize its industrial sector. Because of this increasing participation in the world division of labor, the Soviet economy is more subject to the direct discipline of world-market prices and demand, and thus its internal economic policies must become more overtly capitalist (for example, increased concern for the efficient allocation of capital, labor productivity, and market demand).

Chase-Dunn argues that participation in the competitive nation-state system has been an even more crucial factor in pushing the Soviet Union in a capitalist direction. The Soviet leadership quickly realized that state survival and military parity with the core powers were dependent upon rapid industrialization. To that end the Soviet state embarked on a policy of rapid, "forced-draft" industrialization in the 1930s: high capital accumulation obtained by limiting consumption, forced collectivization of agriculture to extract maximum surplus and necessary food production from the peasantry, and forms of coerced labor (including slavery). Although these policies were much more draconian and repressive than in other semi-peripheral countries that have tried to catch up with the core (such as Japan), the basic intent and direction of policy, argues Chase-Dunn, were the same.

If the relationship of the Soviet Union to the core is essentially one of a "rising" semi-peripheral state, what of its relationship to the periphery? Has it not been the sponsor of anticapitalist, anticore revolutionary movements and states? Is not the Soviet Union actively trying to destroy capitalism in the periphery? Chase-Dunn answers that such a view oversimplifies the Soviet role in the periphery. It is true that the Soviet Union has not acted like a core power in the periphery. Its relationships with peripheral countries have not been economically exploitative. (In fact, Soviet client states, both in the periphery and Eastern Europe, have been an economic burden on the Soviet state.) On several important occasions it has supported such revolutions, and that support has created problems for the core. Nevertheless, argues Chase-Dunn, the Soviet Union is not a revolutionary state seeking socialist revolution in the periphery. Rather, its actions are part of a more general policy toward the periphery that is politically opportunistic. The Soviet Union is primarily concerned with improving its competitive position relative to the core as part of a drive to become a great world power. Sometimes support of indigenous revolutionary movements in the periphery provides an opportunity to serve that end. Sometimes it does not. When it does not, Soviet support is not forthcoming. Moreover, even quite conservative regimes have been the recipients of Soviet support when such support provided a means of increasing Soviet influence in the periphery.

Chase-Dunn concedes that the effect of Soviet support for anticore movements and regimes has been to constrain the exercise of core power in the periphery. Yet, such support has not and does not represent an immediate threat to the overall operation of the world-system. The new revolutionary regimes ultimately also have had to come to terms with the reality of trying to survive within the context of the world-system.

Chase-Dunn also argues that there is evidence that the internal organization of Soviet society is essentially capitalist, with some socialist features. He points out that in world-system theory there are a number of ways in which a society can organize the accumulation of surplus value (for example, slavery or serfdom) and still be part of the capitalist world-economy:

> Soviet . . . juridicially collective forms of property and centrally determined investment decisions and income distributions may be a functional part of the capitalist system. . . . The forms of property and the organs of collective planning that have developed in the Soviet Union . . . simultaneously represent important experiments in the logic of socialist development and increasingly functional forms of the reproduction of capitalism as a system—indeed, perhaps the highest stage of capitalism (1982b: 35).

More specifically, Chase-Dunn acknowledges that centralized state planning of the economy does include consideration of "social needs" (the socialist basis for making economic decisions). Yet he argues that such considerations are secondary to the aims and needs of the state for rapid capital accumulation and state power, both internally and internationally. As a consequence, basically capitalist economic criteria form the basis for economic decisionmaking. The end result is state exploitation of the workers for the benefit of the state and, secondarily, for the benefit of a privileged class of state bureaucrats. The system is stable in part because of a massive repressive apparatus and the total exclusion of workers from economic and political decisionmaking. In addition, the state seeks mass support and legitimacy through appeals to nationalism, identification with socialist ideology, promises of economic improvements, provision of a wide range of basic social services, guarantees of employment, and limitations on income inequality among workers.

Political power is highly centralized in the state and party bureaucracy. The political elite in this dual bureaucratic structure increasingly functions as a ruling class. It is interested in preserving and passing on its special privileges and identifies its interests with those of the state.

A NOTE ON SOCIALIST STATES IN THE PERIPHERY. Outside the Soviet bloc, the remainder of the socialist states are in the periphery. With a population of more than 1 billion, China is clearly the most important of these poorer, less industrialized socialist states. After the success of the 1949 revolution, China was extremely hostile to the core and tried to industrialize completely outside of and independent of the world-system. China was briefly allied with and accepted aid from the Soviet Union in the 1950s, but it soon broke its ties with the Soviets and became embroiled in a border dispute with them. Despite repeated periods of political turmoil and domestic policy shifts, China achieved significant, but erratic, economic growth during the 1950s, 1960s and 1970s. In the 1970s China's concern about Soviet "expansionism" led it to establish relatively friendly ties with the United States. At the same time, China began modifying its commitment to a completely centralized, planned economy. The state replaced collective agriculture with a system of independent peasant producers; introduced market mechanisms for the sale of goods and the allocation of capital; permitted the establishment of small private enterprises; rapidly expanded trade with the core in agricultural commodities and labor-intensive manufactures such as textiles; and encouraged foreign loans, technology transfers, and either direct investment or joint ventures by core corporations (Selden, 1985; Frank, 1980).

From a world-system point of view, these events in China suggest that it is essentially reintegrating itself into the world-system as a peripheral country. Organization of the economy is increasingly consistent with the needs of integration into the capitalist world-economy, and foreign policy seems to reflect a desire to become a regional power in Asia. China has frequently found itself supporting repressive, conservative regimes and/or making alliances with the core against the Soviet Union (as in Afghanistan). The sheer size of China (despite the fact that it is one of the poorest countries) and its relatively strong, authoritarian state have enabled it to avoid the kinds of "full peripheralization" experienced by smaller states. The regime's ability to regulate economic activities with the core may put China in a position to pursue policies that will allow it to rise out of the periphery in the future (Frank, 1980: 235–249; Chase-Dunn, 1982b).

The remainder of the socialist states in the periphery are relatively poor and small, and their states are relatively weak, although fairly centralized, administratively effective, and internally autocratic.[6] Faced with the hostility and sanctions of the core, their options are limited. Attempts at withdrawal from the world-system have meant either acceptance of client state status with the Soviet Union (and the Soviet path toward development) or lack of access to capital and technology necessary for rapid industrialization. Very few states have chosen the latter option. The alternative, which an increasing number of these states seem to have adopted in the recent past, is to attempt limited integration into the world-economy as peripheral societies. To the extent that peripheral socialist countries pursue this strategy, world-system theorists would predict that they will develop more or less in the direction China has, although probably with less success.

**Summary and Conclusion**

World-system theorists believe that the basic structure of the world-system remains intact in the late twentieth century. As will be discussed in the next chapter, some of the events and trends of the twentieth century may presage eventual destruction of the world-system. Nevertheless, the process of breakdown is still in its early phase. The overall division of the world-system into core, periphery, and semi-periphery continues, despite the fact that some states have changed their position in the system and the specific economic activities of the periphery have undergone significant changes.

The overwhelming majority of the world's population still resides in the periphery. Core capitalists continue to exploit it, although the specific methods employed have been modified. Harsh exploitation, political and economic coercion, and mass poverty still characterize the region. Most of the periphery continues to lag behind the core in the rate of economic growth, and the economic gap between the two zones has continued to widen. Although the core faces real opposition from the peripheral states that replaced the colonial empires of 1900, core powers continue to intervene there. That intervention, or the threat of it, constrains the behavior of the relatively weak peripheral regimes. Those states still have little choice but to remain integrated into the world division of labor on terms dictated by the normal functioning of the world-economy and the power of core states.

The creation of large socialist states has represented a major challenge to the capitalist core in the twentieth century. Yet as the century draws to a close, the core appears not only to have contained that challenge but to have created conditions in which most socialist states have been partially reintegrated into the world-system. They have established systems of political-economy compatible with partial participation in the capitalist world-economy.

# World-System Dynamics

**A**lthough its basic structure has remained intact, some aspects of the world-system have varied over time. These changes constitute system "dynamics." The study of dynamics from a world-system perspective is an attempt to create a theory of modern history—that is, a historically specific account of social change in the modern era.

World-system theorists focus on three major issues in regard to dynamics. First, they seek to identify the system's basic tendencies to change (trends) in particular directions over time. Second, they identify certain cycles—those events that happen in repetitive patterns that are shaped by the system's structure. Third, they attempt to explain why not all countries retain the same position in the structure of the system. Some core states have changed position relative to each other. Other states have moved from one zone of the system to another. Some have risen in status (ascended), and some have fallen (descended).

As the next chapter will demonstrate, the study of system dynamics is still in its infancy. Alternative formulations of even the most fundamental issues abound. To simplify what would otherwise be a highly confusing discussion, the focus in this chapter will be on the work of Wallerstein and his close associates.

## Secular Trends

The central imperative of a capitalist economy is the constant effort to accumulate more capital. A primary means by which capitalists can do so is to increase the exploitation of workers. As we will shortly see, this drive to increase exploitation becomes particularly intense during the periods (inherent in a capitalist economy) of economic stagnation and declining rates of profit. During such periods (so far) capitalists find new means to increase both the scope and intensity of exploitation in order to restore profit rates. This tendency to steadily increase exploitation is *the* long-term trend in the modern era; without its continuation, the world-system could not have survived for five centuries. Economic stagnation and falling rates of profit would have led to social and political crisis, which in turn would have destroyed the system. This trend toward increasing exploitation has taken two forms: "broadening" and "deepening" (Hopkins, Wallerstein et al., 1982c: 123; Wallerstein, 1984b: 63).

BROADENING

Broadening refers to the spread of capitalist economic activities into new geographic areas. As we have seen, the world-system at first only occupied part of the globe. It gradually expanded until by the end of the nineteenth century the whole world was part of the system. This outward expansion was a fairly continual process, but one in which there were certain periods of rapid expansion: 1450–1520, 1620–1660, 1750–1815, and 1880–1900. The areas that were added entered the system as part of the periphery (Hopkins, Wallerstein et al., 1982b: 55; Stinchcombe, 1982).

Broadening occurred through the process of "incorporation," which had several features. First, a sector of the economy emerged that began to produce goods in demand in the world-economy. Second, workers in this new sector were transformed into "labor in relation to capital." Control over their labor power passed into the hands of those who accumulated the surplus generated by the workers' labor for capitalists. These workers were mostly superexploited semiproletarians. As we have seen, labor recruitment and discipline usually entailed some form of coercion. Third, the surplus generated in the new sector was siphoned off to core capitalists in some way. As a consequence, little or no capital was available to invest in the long-term, balanced development of the economy (Hopkins and Wallerstein, 1987; Hopkins, Wallerstein et al., 1982c: 126–129).

In the political sphere incorporation involved the creation of centralized administrative structures with the basic features of a modern (core) state. Such "state-like" structures (often colonial administrations) were just strong enough to assert exclusive territorial jurisdiction and assure the smooth extraction of economic surplus. At the same time, even when they became independent states, such political structures were weak relative to core states and consequently were not in a position to resist incorporation into the world-economy on terms dictated by core capitalists (Hopkins and Wallerstein, 1987; Hopkins, Wallerstein et al., 1982c: 132).


## DEEPENING

Deepening refers to the extension of capitalist economic relationships to more aspects of life within societies already in the world-system. Deepening has involved several related processes (Hopkins, Wallerstein et al., 1982a: 104–106, 1982b: 54–57).

First, it has entailed "commodification"—making more goods available to be bought, sold, and owned as property. According to Wallerstein, the two most important forms of commodification have been the commodification of land and labor because both increase the economic factors of production available for capitalist exploitation.

Second, deepening has involved "mechanization"—the use of more machinery to increase output per worker. This process reflects the constant drive on the part of capitalists to reduce labor costs in order to maximize profits and to accommodate the downward pressure on prices caused by competition from other capitalists. Thus, technological innovation increases in importance.

Third, deepening has included "contractualization"—the regulation of social and economic relationships by formal, precise, legal agreements. Commodification requires contractualization because the process of buying and selling property requires a set of uniform, enforceable rules (backed by the state) to assure that the terms of exchange will be honored by both parties. Otherwise, such exchanges would entail too much risk.

Fourth, deepening has involved increasing "interdependence"—the growth of a highly specialized division of labor involving the exchange of goods viewed as essential or necessary by the trading participants. Because workers, organizations, and geographic areas have become more specialized in their economic needs, they must trade with other producers. As a result, workers, communities, and countries have become progressively less self-sufficient and more dependent on exchange of their specialized products. Their participation in capitalist economic relationships in the world-economy has become more economically imperative.

Finally, deepening has entailed greater "polarization"—increasing dissimilarity between the core and periphery in terms of average levels of wealth and the behavior of state organizations. Unequal exchange and other forms of exploitation return most peripherally generated surplus to the core. In addition, as we have seen, wage-levels in the core are higher because more workers have had their labor completely commodified so that they are full proletarians whose wages are sufficient to reproduce their labor. Conversely, in the periphery, more of the labor force has been converted into superexploited semi-proletarians. Wallerstein argues that this conversion actually has led to lower real living standards than had prevailed before. The difference in the accumulated wealth and income levels between the core and the periphery has steadily increased.

In a parallel development, the political structures of the core have come to be characterized by relatively nonrepressive, "liberal," formally democratic regimes—another reason core workers have been successful in their demands for higher wages. Meanwhile, political organization of the periphery has changed in the direction of the more authoritarian regimes needed to enforce coercive forms of labor control. The result is that the difference in the degree of state repressiveness between the core and the periphery has increased: State repressiveness has polarized.

Neither broadening nor deepening has occurred at a steady pace. Rather, the rate has varied because periods of rapid increases in exploitation have corresponded to the pattern of economic cycles. The nature of this connection will become apparent once those cycles are explained.

## Economic Cycles

World-system theorists believe that the world-economy has gone and (and is still going) through times of rapid growth alternating with periods of stagnation. In addition to relatively brief cycles of prosperity followed by recession (business cycles), Wallerstein and his associates argue that there have been two main kinds of economic cycles in the history of the world-system: "Kondratieff (or long) waves" and "logistics."

### KONDRATIEFF WAVES

Kondratieff waves (or cycles) are named after the Russian economist who in the 1920s first proposed their existence. Each wave consists of a period of economic growth followed by a period of stagnation. On average, each full cycle of expansion and stagnation lasts between forty and sixty years. Wallerstein calls the growth period "phase A" and the stagnation period "phase B" (Wallerstein, 1984a). In the last century the pattern of Kondratieff waves has been as follows (Hopkins, Wallerstein et al., 1982a: 118):

| Phase A | 1850–1873 |
| Phase B | 1873–1897 |
| Phase A | 1897–1920 |
| Phase B | 1920–1945 |
| Phase A | 1945–1967 |
| Phase B | 1967–? |

One of the fundamental unresolved issues in the study of these waves is what, precisely, fluctuates. (The implications of this uncertainty are discussed in the next chapter.) There is agreement that in some general sense the level of economic activity or overall rate of economic growth varies in a regular pattern over time. But how that variation is measured has not been consistent. Researchers have tried to find some general index of the state of the economy. Early attempts to do so tended to focus on general price levels or the prices of particular commodities. More recently, those working in the Marxist tradition have focused on measures of the rate of profit. Wallerstein basically takes this latter position (Wallerstein, 1984a: 560–566).

What causes Kondratieffs? Wallerstein argues that they are an inherent and necessary part of the process of capitalist development. Periods of economic expansion and high profits inevitably set the stage for periods of economic stagnation and declining profits. There remains considerable uncertainty among world-system theorists about the exact mechanisms that cause economic fluctuations. Wallerstein has offered some tentative hypotheses (Wallerstein, 1984a: 560–566, 1984b: 62; Hopkins, Wallerstein et al., 1982a).

In his view, economic expansions are based on the creation of new economic activities and/or production techniques. Initially, the large, unfilled market for these new activities or techniques ensures high prices for them and profit opportunities for the firms engaged in producing them. For example, new technologies in steel production and steam engines set off a boom in railroad construction in the 1840s, 1850s, and 1860s.

The growth in the new sector then provides the economic stimulus for the rest of the economy, and phase A gets under way. In turn, high profits and increasing demand soon attract new firms to the market. But market demand cannot expand indefinitely because the existing distribution of income and wealth keeps the demand relatively fixed and existing sociopolitical arrangements keep that distribution relatively stable. Thus, as more firms enter the market, overproduction and oversupply occur. The resulting fierce competition among firms for a share of the market leads to declining prices and profits. With the new sector of the economy no longer providing economic stimulus, the economic stagnation of phase B sets in (Wallerstein, 1984a: 568, 1984b: 63). For example, the steel and rail boom of the nineteenth century ended after 1870 when English manufacturers exhausted the domestic market and faced growing competition for the world market from new producers, such as Germany and the United States (McMichael, 1985).

The conditions created by stagnation set the stage for a renewed economic upturn because stagnation creates pressures on core capitalists to find ways to intensify exploitation through broadening and deepening. One way this occurs is through accelerated "economic concentration." Mergers, acquisition, and the failure of smaller, weaker firms result in enterprises that are larger and command greater reserves of capital. In countries in which such reorganization is most successful, economic concentration also results in firms that have been restructured along more rational and efficient lines. For instance, during phase B in the late nineteenth century, large, centralized corporations (which had the appropriate organization, markets, and resources to implement mass production) successfully displaced smaller, family-owned enterprises in the United States (Bergesen, 1982).

During phase B core capitalists also have a greater incentive to maintain or improve profit margins by finding new sources of cheap raw materials and labor in the periphery. An accelerated rate of broadening results. For example, the late nineteenth century was a period of competition among the core powers for new colonies and investment rights in the periphery. The consequences were new sources of surplus with which to finance the next phase A.

Economic stagnation also intensifies class conflict. Workers and capitalists try to improve their economic position by increasing their share of national wealth. Initially, the greater political power of the capitalists may lead to increased economic inequality. In the longer term, however, political resolution of the conflict can only come when there is some redistribution of income toward workers and/or the middle classes (at least in the core). That resolution stimulates increased market demand (because workers have more income to spend), which can provide the basis for renewed economic expansion. (This redistributive process in the core helps to explain global polarization: Core workers end up better off, while broadening creates more semi-proletarians in the periphery.)

Finally, the search for new sources of profit during phase B puts a premium on economic innovation. That innovation can take several forms: improvements in productive efficiency through mechanization, changes in the organization of the labor process (for example, mass production), or the creation of new products or economic activities.

Out of this search, the set of innovations that will be the basis for the next phase A eventually emerges.

LOGISTICS

Kondratieff cycles may occur within the context of longer-term economic fluctuations called "logistics." Like Kondratieffs, logistics consist of a period of relative economic expansion (phase A) followed by a period of economic stagnation (phase B). Between phase A and phase B there may also be a significant transition period (phase T). Although Wallerstein is not completely certain, logistics *may* be identified by periods of generally rising (phase A) or falling (phase B) prices. The crucial goods whose prices fluctuated in response to logistics also *may* have varied historically. For example, in the preindustrial period (before 1800) the price of grain may have been most crucial. Afterward, industrial raw materials may have played the central role (Hopkins, Wallerstein et al., 1982a: 107–109).

Considerable uncertainty remains about the dating of logistics. Wallerstein feels relatively confident about the first logistic. Phase A began after 1450, ended in the early sixteenth century (the "long sixteenth century"), and was followed by the "crisis of the seventeenth century" (phase B), which persisted until the middle of the eighteenth century. After 1750, dating is less certain. Indeed, Wallerstein is willing to consider the possibility that logistics disappeared and only Kondratieffs continued. Nevertheless, he and his associates have proposed one simplified version of a dating scheme (Hopkins, Wallerstein et al., 1982a: 108):

| | |
|---|---|
| Phase A | 1750–1815 |
| Phase B | 1815–1897/1917(?) |
| Phase A | 1897/1917–1967(?)[1] |

What is the relationship between the timing of Kondratieffs and logistics? Because the dating of both kinds of cycles is uncertain, the answer is ambiguous. The timing of the sixteenth-century phase A does roughly correspond to a pair of Kondratieffs proposed by Hopkins and Wallerstein. They also find a rough correspondence between the seventeenth-century phase B and three pairs of Kondratieffs. After that the correspondence seems to disappear (Hopkins, Wallerstein et al., 1982a: 118). This is a somewhat "messy" result, which is why Hopkins and Wallerstein are willing to consider the possibility that logistics disappear after the eighteenth century (Hopkins, Wallerstein et al.,

1982a: 114). But Wallerstein has elsewhere continued to argue for logistics in the nineteenth and twentieth centuries (Wallerstein, 1984a).

In many ways Wallerstein and his associates see logistics as quite similar to Kondratieffs. Expansions come to an end when supply in crucial economic activities exceeds available demand. The following period of economic stagnation is characterized by the same processes of a Kondratieff phase B. In turn, these processes create the conditions necessary for a renewed phase A (Wallerstein, 1984a: 570).

Wallerstein does tentatively identify some differences between Kondratieffs and logistics. Logistics are "deeper" or more "fundamental" economic fluctuations. The first logistic ushered in the whole system of preindustrial, merchant capitalism in the sixteenth and seventeenth centuries. The second full logistic dovetailed with the initial appearance of industrialization. The current logistic appears to be associated with a set of basic changes in production technologies, products, and organizational arrangements that represents a new "stage" of industrial capitalism. In turn, each of these fundamental developments was associated with the creation of a new worldwide system of economic arrangements (such as trading patterns or international financial institutions) imposed by one great core power. Consequently, logistics are connected with another cycle: the cycle of "hegemonic ascent and decline" (Wallerstein, 1984a: 571).

## Cycles of Hegemony

At several points in the world-system's history, one core power achieved a position of economic and military superiority over the other core powers known as hegemony. Full hegemony exists when one state enjoys a major economic advantage over all other core states in the areas of production, commerce, and finance. Productive predominance means that the most technically advanced forms of production are disproportionately located in one core country, and thus the hegemonic country can export products at competitively advantageous prices to the world market. Commercial hegemony characterizes a situation in which one country carries on the largest volume of core international trade, and its transportation and trading companies provide the largest volume of services (for example, shipping, commercial insurance, and wholesaling). Financial hegemony exists when one core country is the largest source of capital for international investment and the largest provider of financial services such as banking. As a consequence, the financial industry of the hegemonic country dominates the provision of international credit, the setting of interest rates, and the setting of currency exchange rates, and the hegemonic state's currency is the

TABLE 5.1
Cycles of Hegemony

| Hegemonic Power | Dates | Part of Cycle |
|---|---|---|
| United Provinces | 1575–1590 | Ascending hegemony |
| of Holland | 1590–1620 | Hegemonic victory |
| | 1620–1650 | Hegemonic maturity |
| | 1650–1700 | Hegemonic decline |
| Great Britain | 1798–1815 | Ascending hegemony |
| | 1815–1850 | Hegemonic victory |
| | 1850–1873 | Hegemonic maturity |
| | 1873–1897 | Declining hegemony |
| United States | 1897–1913/1920 | Ascending hegemony |
| | 1913/1920–1945 | Hegemonic victory |
| | 1945–1967 | Hegemonic maturity |
| | 1967–? | Hegemonic decline |

*Source:* Hopkins, Wallerstein et al. (1982a: 118).

main medium of exchange employed in international trade and finance. Economic predominance enables the hegemonic state to maintain the largest "strategic" military forces (for example, naval forces or, currently, air forces) and thus, to intervene militarily all over the world more effectively than any other core state. But this military predominance has never been so great as to threaten the actual political independence of other core states (Hopkins, Wallerstein et al., 1982b: 62).

Periods of full hegemony have been both rare and fairly short in modern history. Wallerstein believes that there have been three such periods: (1) 1620–1650/1672 (United Provinces of Holland), (2) 1815–1850/1873 (Great Britain), and (3) 1945–1967 (United States) (Hopkins, Wallerstein et al., 1982b: 62).[2] Thus, world-system theory portrays the history of the modern era as a series of cycles of "ascending" and "declining" hegemony, with brief periods of full hegemony in each cycle. Wallerstein and his associates have suggested the cycles of hegemony summarized in Table 5.1. Each part of the cycle has distinct characteristics. "Ascending hegemony" is a period of conflict between rival core powers seeking hegemony. A previously hegemonic power is still a major core power, but it has lost its overwhelmingly predominant economic and military advantage. "Hegemonic victory" is the period in which one state emerges with a large productive and military advantage over the other states and bypasses the "old" hegemonic power in decline. "Hegemonic maturity" refers to the period in which "full hegemony" (productive, commercial, and financial) is enjoyed by one state. During "declining hegemony" the hegemonic power (while still the most militarily powerful state in the core) experiences a steady erosion of its economic and military position and faces increasing challenges to its power from other states. In the long periods outside these cycles (such as the eighteenth century), two or more powers are locked in a struggle for hegemony, but no one power is able to gain a clear advantage over the others (Hopkins, Wallerstein et al., 1982a: 116–117; Thompson, 1983a: 52–53).

What enables a core state to ascend to hegemony? Wallerstein and his associates provide an economic explanation that also takes into account the role of military power and state organization. Ascending powers have been those countries in a position to exploit new economic opportunities in the world-economy. A number of historically specific factors appear to have put the ascending country in this position: geographic location, available resources, an "appropriate" organizational structure in the economy, state policies actively supportive of the needs of the capitalist class, available sources of capital, the attitudes and values of the capitalist class, and so on. (The particular factors seem to have varied, and no exhaustive list is possible.) These advantages enabled the country to capitalize on new technologies and organizational forms at the beginning of a fundamental transformation of the world-economy (the beginning of a phase A or phase B logistic). Once the ascending country achieved an initial productive advantage, it was then in a position to achieve commercial advantage and, finally, financial advantage in the world-economy (Hopkins, Wallerstein et al., 1982b: 62–64; Bergesen, 1982; Tylecote, 1982; Chase-Dunn, 1978).

Productive advantage both reinforced and was itself enhanced by political and military factors in those states that rose to hegemony. Wallerstein argues that successful contenders for hegemony were characterized by "strong" states. Recall that state "strength" refers to a state's ability to effectively implement both internal and external policies in the face of opposition. This strength is not synonymous with arbitrary, centralized, "despotic" power. Indeed, the most effective contenders have *not* been states characterized by a high degree of political centralization, autocracy, or a powerful, autonomous bureaucracy. They were not militarized autocracies seeking power primarily through war. Rather, successful states have been dominated by groups favoring state policies that benefited those elements of the capitalist class representing the "new" productive activities. (Wallerstein quotes approvingly the description of the Dutch state as a "social dictatorship of the middle class" [Wallerstein, 1979b: 76].) In other words, the state and the capitalist class formed an alliance, and that occurred in states with some degree of "democratic" restraints on state power. Strong contenders for hegemony were those states with sufficient infrastructural power to assure stability and mobilize financial and military resources. They had political arrangements that generated mass support for the regime and the unified cooperation of the capitalist class (Rubinson, 1978; Wallerstein, 1979b, 1980: 113; Hopkins, Wallerstein et al., 1982a: 105; McMichael, 1985).[3]

Despite their economic and military strength, hegemonic powers maintain their positions only for a short period. Economic decline proceeds, according to Wallerstein, following the same order as ascent. First, the hegemonic power loses its advantage in productive efficiency. Then, it loses its commercial dominance in international trade. Finally, it loses its position as the center of world finance. With erosion of its economic position, it gradually loses its ability to support a superior military establishment (Wallerstein, 1982b: 62–64, 1983b).

Several reasons have been suggested for this apparently inevitable decline. Perhaps the most fundamental is that the hegemonic state is unable to maintain its near monopoly over the new economic activity that gave it a competitive advantage over its rivals in the core. Ultimately, other core states (or ascending semi-peripheral states) manage to emulate the productive techniques of the hegemonic power. For example, by the last third of the nineteenth century, Great Britain had lost its lead in steel, steam technology, and textiles and was faced with increasingly successful competition in those industries from Western European producers (especially Germany) and the United States (McMichael, 1985). Toward the end of the hegemonic cycle the economic balance shifts even further against the hegemonic power. One or more ascending states prove more successful in developing new economic activities. For example, by the beginning of the twentieth century, both Germany and the United States were poised to assume leadership in synthetic chemicals, electrical equipment, and automotive technology. Both countries' large industrial firms were also more appropriately organized than family-owned British firms to make the soon-to-come transition to large-scale, mass production (Wallerstein, 1982a; Mc-Michael, 1985; Bergesen, 1982).[4]

Loss of productive leadership has been only part of the story of hegemonic decline. Wallerstein and others have suggested additional factors as well. During the period of hegemonic maturity, firms in the leading country encounter little competition and consequently face few pressures to keep costs or prices down. Those firms tend to give into worker demands for rising wages, which ultimately contributes to the loss of competitive advantage in the world market. In addition, the costs of maintaining a large military establishment and/or supporting client states diverts economic resources, talented personnel, and technical expertise away from the productive sector of the economy. As the hegemonic power faces greater military challenges and becomes more overtly imperialistic, these burdens increase. Very importantly, as the relative military and economic power of the hegemonic country declines, it is less capable of acting to impose policies favoring its industries, commercial firms, and financial institutions on the rest of the core. Other core states gain in ability to protect their domestic industries, challenge existing commercial and financial arrangements, and seek special economic arrangements with areas of the periphery (Goldfrank, 1983; McMichael, 1985; Chase-Dunn, 1978; Hopkins, Wallerstein et al., 1982b: 62–64).

## Correlates of Hegemonic Cycles

World-system theorists regard hegemonic cycles as especially important because they appear to be associated with other important patterns of events. Analyses of these correlates of hegemonic cycles are among the most speculative aspects of world-system theory. They are also among its most provocative and potentially significant contributions.[5]

There is general agreement among world-system theorists that hegemonic cycles bear some relationship with economic cycles. As mentioned, Wallerstein argues that there is a rough correspondence between logistics and hegemonic cycles. Phase A of the sixteenth century was associated with the rise to "near" hegemony of the Spanish Hapsburg state. The end of that period also coincided with Spanish decline. Dutch hegemony was achieved and then lost during subsequent phase B stagnation. The rise of Great Britain corresponded to phase A of the nineteenth century, and its decline paralleled subsequent phase B. The hegemony of the United States corresponded to the twentieth-century phase A (Wallerstein, 1983b).

What accounts for this apparent connection with logistics? Note that it cannot be that phase A creates the conditions for hegemony. Dutch hegemony corresponded to a phase B. Rather, Wallerstein suggests that the phases of the logistics correspond to general changes in the basic economic problems and opportunities faced by core countries. Whether the period is one of general stagnation or expansion, some in the core deal with the economic circumstances better than others. "Winners" are those core countries that are able to achieve the greatest productive efficiency, regardless of how favorable or unfavorable the economic conditions at the time. Thus, Wallerstein describes Dutch success in these terms: "At the onset of the long economic downturn, the United Provinces [of Holland] was, among core powers, the most efficient agro-industrial producer by far. It was this productive efficiency which led

TABLE 5.2
The U.S. Hegemonic Cycle

| Kondratieff Phase | Time Period | Hegemonic Phase |
|---|---|---|
| A | 1897–1913/20 | Ascending hegemony |
| B | 1913/1920–1945 | Hegemonic victory |
| A | 1945–1967 | Hegemonic maturity |
| B | 1967–? | Hegemonic decline |

Source: Hopkins, Wallerstein et al. (1982a: 118).

to its commercial primacy, which in turn made possible its financial centrality" (1979b: 76).

The connection between cycles of hegemony and Kondratieff waves is presumably even closer. The period in which a hegemonic power begins to emerge (ascending hegemony) is one of Kondratieff upswing. The initial productive advantage of the emerging hegemonic power appears to be based on its lead in adopting new productive technology or techniques in phase A. The actual establishment of clear hegemony (hegemonic victory) occurs in the intensely competitive environment of the following phase B. After a "hegemonic war," the victorious hegemonic power then presides over a new phase A (hegemonic maturity). The hegemonic cycle draws to a close (hegemonic decline) in the midst of the following phase B (Hopkins, Wallerstein et al., 1982a: 112–120). Table 5.2 illustrates this pattern for the hegemonic cycle of the United States.

Other patterns are associated with this combined economic/hegemonic cycle. First, international economic relationships appear to alternate between periods of relative "openness" and periods of relative "restrictiveness." Open relationships exist when core states allow the free flow of goods and capital without such restrictions as tariffs, currency controls, import quotas, and the like. Restrictive relationships exist when such policies are imposed to protect each core country's markets from foreign competition. (Obviously, there are periods of transition from one mode to the other.) Open periods correspond to periods of hegemonic maturity; restrictiveness predominates the rest of the time (Hopkins, Wallerstein et al., 1982a; Chase-Dunn, 1978; McMichael, 1985).

Openness corresponds to hegemonic maturity because the leading power is in a position to use its military and economic capabilities to demand that other core states minimize their restrictive policies. The hegemonic power wants openness because it enjoys a competitive advantage in production, commerce, and finance. The more other countries' markets are open to its capitalists, the better off they are.

Openness provides them with export markets and investment opportunities and increases overall commercial activities. Foreign competition represents little threat to the hegemonic power's own domestic market. That hegemonic maturity corresponds to a period of expanding markets (phase A), when all core firms can enjoy economic expansion and high profits, makes the policy generally palatable to all core states.

Hegemonic decline and the accompanying phase B create pressures for increasing restrictiveness. All core capitalists face intense competition for markets and declining rates of profit. Core capitalists (and their workers) respond by putting pressure on their states to protect the domestic market and assist them in obtaining foreign markets. As the position of the hegemonic power deteriorates, it faces internal political pressure for protectionism, lacks the ability to stop such measures by its competitors, and is forced into defensive trade restrictions by the actions of other states. Thus, for example, the later part of the seventeenth century and most of eighteenth century (following Dutch decline) were characterized by a system of restrictive policies and cutthroat international economic competition known as mercantilism. That system gave way to a quite open one during British hegemony in the nineteenth century. A return to increasingly restrictive policies occurred after 1873, as British hegemony waned (Chase-Dunn, 1978).

Second, hegemonic cycles appear to be related to changing patterns in the relationships between the core and the periphery (Bergesen, 1980; Chase-Dunn, 1978). There seem to have been cycles in the degree to which core states have sought direct political control over areas in the periphery (either as formal colonies or as client states). During periods of direct control, core states create highly exclusive economic zones. Trade and investment in the peripheral area under control are limited to the "mother country," and capitalists from other core states are excluded. These periods of direct control alternate with those in which the periphery enjoys greater political autonomy from the core. The exploitative relationships with the core continue, but the relationship is one of multilateral investment and trade. Each area of the periphery maintains economic relationships with a number of core countries.

What accounts for this pattern? A hegemonic power benefits from access to the entire periphery and uses its power to break down economic barriers created by other core powers there. In a time of economic expansion (phase A of hegemonic maturity) the cost of direct control over part of the periphery is less attractive for all the core states, and there is less need for exclusive access to markets, sources of supply, and investment opportunities. Trade with dependent colonies becomes less important when intercore trade is expanding. Thus, for example, the British actively conspired to assist the independence movements in South America that destroyed the Spanish Empire there in the 1820s. The British thereby gained better access to South American markets and became a major investor in the region.

Declining hegemony creates conditions that favor the creation of exclusive, bilateral trading patterns between the core and the periphery. Economic stagnation puts a premium on carving out economic zones that provide protected markets, sources of supply, and investment opportunities. As we have seen, the search for profitable investment opportunities during a period of low profits leads to an attempt to increase exploitation in the periphery. That is accomplished by the incorporation of more of the global labor force into the world division of labor either by the addition of new geographic areas to the system or by the intensification of exploitation in existing peripheral areas. This process is facilitated by direct political control. Such control also provides a means of keeping competing capitalists from other core powers out of the controlled peripheral area. Because the declining hegemonic power loses its ability to impose a multilateral trading pattern, it joins other core powers in the search for exclusive economic zones. There have been two "waves" of these colonial expansions, whose "peaks" correspond to the end of Dutch hegemony after 1670 and British hegemony after 1873 (Chase-Dunn, 1978).

These cycles in core-periphery relationships are also apparently correlated with internal economic changes in the periphery. During periods of hegemony, economic expansion leads to a general increase in world trade, including core-periphery trade. Peripheral areas have open access to the core for markets, supplies of core-produced goods at competitive prices, and core capital. Hence, the export-oriented sectors of peripheral economies grow, and peripheral economies become more specialized in production for export. Export earnings make possible the purchase of more goods from the core; open trade exposes less efficient producers to core competition; traditional craft manufacturing declines; and the flow of core capital (to invest in the export sector) increases (Pamuk, 1982). For example, this appears to have been the pattern in the periphery during the period of U.S. hegemony in the 1950s and 1960s.

During times of hegemonic decline these trends are reversed. Exports to the core decline as part of the general reduction in world trade. The pressure to keep prices low in a stagnant market leads to increased exploitation (that is, reduced wages) in the export sector. The ability to pay off existing loans or incur new ones is reduced by the decline in export earnings. The supply of capital from the core dries up, and loan repayments lead to a flow of capital to the core. Lacking the ability to pay for imported goods, peripheral economies have to become more self-reliant and less specialized in export production. For example, despite rapid, export-oriented industrialization in the NICs, *overall* periphery-to-core exports were stagnant or declining in the 1980s. Similarly, a study of economic conditions in the Ottoman Empire during the period of British hegemonic decline reveals a clear pattern of decline in exports, core investments, and export specialization (Pamuk, 1982).

Hegemonic cycles may also correlate with the pattern of military conflict in the world-system (Thompson, 1983a). Escalating economic and military competition among rival core powers appears to precede hegemonic victory and culminates in a hegemonic or world war involving alliances of core powers. The result of this war is the final exhaustion of the old, declining hegemonic power, even though it may be part of the winning alliance. (Hegemonic wars may be quite lengthy and include periods of temporary peace. In the eighteenth century France and Great Britain fought a series of wars that was not finally resolved in Britain's favor until 1815.)

The new hegemonic power emerges with a clear economic and military advantage over the rest of the core.[6] This newly dominant power is able to impose a relative peace on the core states. The peace is always precarious, and numerous small wars and international crises continue, but these do not erupt into larger wars because the hegemonic power continually intervenes to maintain the international status quo. For example, Great Britain struggled to maintain the balance of power in Europe in the decades following 1815 and used its naval power to protect international trade and keep the periphery open to all core traders and investors.

Hegemonic decline ushers in another period of increasing tension and military competition. The core power's attempt to impose direct control over the periphery increases military tension and conflict there. Independent peripheral states may attempt to resist, and more importantly, the core states find themselves in competition for control over the periphery. International tension also results from the increasing competition for the (stagnant) world market, the rising tide of protectionism in the core, and the creation of exclusive zones in the periphery. Military buildups and the decline of the hegemonic power create an environment in which a military solution to conflicts among all states becomes both more possible and more likely. Minor wars between the states of the semi-periphery and periphery can no longer be prevented by the declining hegemonic power, which faces growing challenges from one or more "rising" core states. The core power struggles unsuccessfully to reimpose its will by military means (because the erosion of its economic position weakens its military capabilities), and as its decline continues, another hegemonic war looms on the horizon (Thompson, 1983a).

Finally, some world-system theorists also propose that one can find some correlates of the cycle of hegemony in domestic, social, cultural, and political developments within the core, semi-periphery, or periphery. (Kiser and Drass, 1987; Wuthow, 1980, 1983; Wallerstein, 1983b; Goldfrank, 1983; Weber, 1981). This area of world-system study is poorly explored, but a few hypotheses are worth brief mention here.

Various authors have proposed correlates of hegemonic maturity. Economic expansion and general rises in the standard of living should reduce class conflict and political tensions in the hegemonic society. Social reform should focus on gradual, evolutionary improvements of the status quo because the state can afford to be relatively nonrepressive and to support programs of social improvement. Prosperity, overwhelming military strength, and global economic dominance should provide broad domestic consensus for foreign policies that emphasize political and military interventionism and free trade. "Triumphalism"—the belief that the national culture is inherently superior and that the nation has a special, positive role to play in history—should predominate in national culture. Triumphalism's corollary—that one's culture and institutions should be adopted by other countries—also obtains. As Goldfrank (1983) points out, during their hegemonies, both Great Britain and the United States produced social theorists who proclaimed that their societies represented the height of human social and moral evolution: Herbert Spencer (Great Britain) and Talcott Parsons (United States).

Conversely, the expectation for periods of hegemonic decline would be that slow economic growth should lead to sociopolitical conflict over the relative share of national income enjoyed by the various classes and groups in society. At least initially, given the political power of the capitalist class, such a conflict should result in growing economic inequality. The resulting social tension and a lessened ability to afford the costs of social reform should lead to greater conservativism and repressiveness on the part of the state. The costs of interventionism abroad (for example, military expenditures) should also be a source of increasing political division, and political conflict should occur between those who continue to benefit from free trade and those who seek the security of economic protectionism. In place of triumphalism, growing doubts about the existing cultural and institutional arrangements of society should appear. These doubts might be expressed in a number of ways—for example, interest might grow in utopian ide-

TABLE 5.3
Examples of Ascent and Decline

| Periphery to Semi-Periphery | Semi-Periphery to Core | Core to Semi-Periphery |
|---|---|---|
| United States (1800–1860) | United States (1860–1900) | Spain (1620–1700) |
| Japan (1868–1900) | Japan (1945–1970) | Great Britain (1980–?) |
| Taiwan (1949–1980) | Germany (1870–1900) | |
| S. Korea (1953–1980) | | |

ologies and literature, and cults asserting utopian or "traditional" values might be on the rise.

## Ascent and Decline in the World-System

As we have seen in preceding chapters, countries have not always stayed in the same zones of the world-system. Some have ascended out of the periphery or semi-periphery to a higher status. A few core states have descended into the semi-periphery. (See Table 5.3.)

This recognition that ascent occurs, even from the periphery, is one of the major ways in which world-system theory differs from the dependency approach. Most of those employing that perspective do not expect countries in the periphery to overcome exploitation and dependent development within the existing system of political-economy imposed by the core.

At the same time, world-system theorists also reject the optimism of modernization theory. They do not think that the periphery and semi-periphery can follow the same path of development as the core by simply modernizing their economies with Western technology and increasing their participation in world trade. Rather, world-system theorists regard ascent as a fairly rare and difficult feat. Many countries try, but few can ever succeed; while some ascend, others decline. Consequently, membership in the core, semi-periphery, and periphery changes over time, but the basic division of the world-system into those three categories remains a stable feature of the system (Arrighi and Drangel, 1986).

Ascent and decline are the result of the normal functioning of the world-system. Because all states face an intensely competitive environment, each attempts to gain an economic and military advantage over the others. At any given time, each state has a stock of "resources" to employ in this competition, such as natural wealth, existing capital stocks, available infrastructure, geographic location, more or less "useful" cultural traditions, an existing industrial base, and military power. But the relative value of these resources changes, and states can pursue "bad" or "good" strategies (by luck or foresight) that damage or improve their opportunities in a rapidly changing environment. As a consequence, some states have access to the advantages that will improve their position in the world-system, whereas others confront the problems that will lead to decline (Friedman, 1982).

To some extent ascent or decline has been determined by factors specific to the countries involved. Nevertheless, some tentative generalizations have emerged from the study of these specific instances. So far, except in the case of hegemonic decline, most theorizing has focused on the process of ascent.

To ascend, states must somehow obtain more autonomy from the constraints of the world-economy than is normal. For example, they may need to establish tariffs to protect new industries from foreign competition. How and why ascending states have gained this freedom seems highly variable. For example, because of its desire to contain communism in Asia, the United States acted as a "sponsor" for both South Korea and Taiwanese industrialization. Both states were allowed to pursue highly independent economic policies, even at the expense of U.S. exports and investors (Crane, 1982). Japanese ascent in the nineteenth and early twentieth centuries was made possible in part by a strong state and military, which gave the Japanese a greater degree of autonomy in economic policy (Chirot, 1986: 124–126).

At the same time, the ascending country needs access to markets for its new core-like industries if those activities are to expand and replace the older, peripheral-like activities that perpetuate unequal exchange with the core. One possibility is the existence of a "domestic periphery." If domestic industry is protected from core competition, such an underdeveloped sector can provide the initial market for industrial production. For example, the United States enjoyed a massive, protected domestic market in the last half of the nineteenth century (Rubinson, 1978). After 1945 the United States, for geopolitical reasons, provided Japan, Taiwan, and South Korea with special access to its domestic market (Tylecote and Lonsdale-Brown, 1982; Crane, 1982). More generally, markets are more likely to be available during a time of expansion of the world-economy. For example, Rubinson (1978) argues that the ascent of the United States and Germany at the end of the nineteenth century was feasible because the geographic expansion of the world-system made a larger core possible.

At least in some cases, ascent also seems to rely on the availability of capital and technology transfers on unusually *favorable* terms. Germany and the United States relied heavily on the availability of British capital and technology during the nineteenth century (McMichael, 1985: 130–132). Industrialization of the NICs of Asia in the recent past was spurred on by readily available finance from and joint ventures with multinational firms. South Korea and Taiwan also enjoyed direct assistance from the United States (Chase-Dunn, 1984).

Although external conditions have to be favorable, internal developments and state policies are the keys to a state's ascendance. Successful ascendance has occurred in states dominated by coalitions of interests linked to domestic industry. (Previously dominant groups, such as large landowners, who profited from the export of agricultural commodities and the import of cheap goods from the core, lost control of state policy.) The ascending state is controlled by those who favor protection of domestic industries from the competition of (initially cheaper) core-produced goods. At the same time, agricultural policies assure low prices for and/or the heavy taxation of farmers, which provides cheap food for industrial workers and/or the funds for direct subsidies to industry.

Reliance on core capital, technology, and locally unavailable industrial equipment means some degree of dependence on and indebtedness to outsiders. But state regulation of core investment and imports limits borrowing and importation of productive technology to those levels necessary for industrialization. For instance, importation of luxury consumption goods is limited. At the same time, extreme forms of peripheral-style superexploitation (serfdom, slavery, tenant agriculture) are gradually phased out. For example, after 1945, Taiwan, South Korea, and Japan all went through agricultural land reforms whose eventual result was less overall economic inequality than in a typical peripheral country. This decline in inequality also reflects the growth of a wage-labor sector with sufficient income to begin providing a market for domestic industry. Nevertheless, wage levels are not allowed to rise fast enough to limit funds for investment or eliminate the cost advantage enjoyed by goods produced for export.

Finally, the relationship of the state to domestic capitalists is supportive, cooperative, but not subservient. Thus, in the three countries just mentioned, state subsidies for and cooperative planning with private corporations played a major role. On the other hand, policies often ran counter to the immediate interests of specific enterprises. For example, in the 1970s Taiwan stopped protecting certain industries that state authorities (and the World Bank) considered inefficient. In general, successful states do not control investment, prices, or the allocation of investment capital in detail. Rather, the state allows competitive market mechanisms to reward efficient producers and weed out inefficient ones. Only overall development is regulated by a general state strategy (Crane, 1982; Evans, 1985; Tylecote and Lonsdale-Brown,

1982; Chirot, 1986: 247–257; Wallerstein, 1979a: 76–83; McMichael, 1982).

## Application: Directions of Change in the Contemporary World-System

Perhaps the best way to understand and to appreciate the relevance of world-system theory is to apply what has just been discussed to the contemporary world situation. Where are we now in the unfolding trends and cycles of world-system history? What might we expect, based on past experience, to happen in the future? Wallerstein and his close associates provide one set of tentative answers to these questions.

### CURRENT CONDITIONS AND SHORT-TERM PROSPECTS

World-system theorists generally agree that the expansionary Kondratieff phase A that began in 1945 ended around 1970.[7] As we saw in Chapter 4, since that time the world has been in the period of relatively slow growth and economic instability that characterizes a Kondratieff phase B.

Economic trends and events typical of such a period accompanied these general economic conditions. Increasing production capacity in the core and the semi-periphery outran slowly growing demand in such basic industries as steel and autos. The result was intense international competition for markets. Economic concentration increased rapidly in the core through mergers and acquisitions. Core corporations sought to meet the increasing competition in part by demanding reduction in government social spending to reduce their tax burden and by reducing wage costs (through union busting, plant relocations, and so on). As one would expect at the beginning of phase B, economic inequality increased in the United States and the condition of the poor worsened. Two developments in the 1970s and 1980s could be considered evidence of the increased exploitation that can mark phase B: export-oriented industrialization using superexploited workers and the financial "bleeding" of the periphery through debt peonage.

Exactly when the current phase B will end is not certain; the potential remains for further economic crises. But if the pattern of Kondratieff waves runs true, the current phase B should be replaced by phase A some time in the 1990s. Accumulating technical advances in such areas as electronics, aerospace, or bioengineering might provide the basis for such an upswing.

If there is a Kondratieff upswing, the United States may not be its primary origin or beneficiary. Most world-system theorists agree that it has entered the period of hegemonic decline, whose first symptom has been evident for almost two decades. The United States has lost most of its competitive advantage over other countries of the core in industrial production, and that loss applies not only to the well-known examples of autos and steel but to most manufacturing activities, including most (nonmilitary) high-tech products. Following the sequence suggested by Wallerstein, commercial decline has been much less pronounced. Least affected, so far, has been financial activity; the United States is still the world's leading financial center (although it is worth noting that its international banks are no longer the largest, its currency has declined in value, and it has become the largest debtor nation in the world). Although militarily and politically it is still the leading core power, U.S. military and diplomatic freedom of action has begun to erode. Other core powers are less likely to automatically accede to its policy initiatives, peripheral countries have been more resistant to its demands, and it has been less successful in imposing peace on the periphery.

Walter Goldfrank (1983) suggests other symptoms of the U.S. hegemonic decline. He argues that its economic organization is no longer the most efficient or effective. Specifically, lack of coordination and planning on the part of business and government leaves the United States at a competitive disadvantage vis-à-vis countries that employ such methods to their fullest advantage. In addition, the increase in wage rates that the United States experienced during its period of hegemony puts it at a long-term competitive disadvantage.

Goldfrank also claims that the United States has chronically underinvested in education and research. It has been losing it technological leadership because it has diverted the resources needed for technological innovation into overinvestment in the military sector. Finally, he argues that the United States has failed to adapt to a world-economy in which most other core countries have in fact become increasingly protectionist in their trade policies. Like Britain before it, the United States has clung to the free-trade policies of the past; now such policies work primarily to the advantage of competitors seeking access to the huge U.S. market.

The expectation of most world-system theorists is that the decline of U.S. hegemony will continue. As a result, those trends and events associated with hegemonic decline are also expected: increasing protectionism in international trade, attempts to carve out economic and political spheres of influence in the periphery (but not actual colonies), and increasing military tension and conflict. At some future date another hegemonic war can be expected. Some world-system theorists see the Soviet Union as a classic "premature challenging state" (like Germany in the first half of this century) seeking hegemony through the "shortcut" of military strength and an authoritarian state. If so, the outcome of a hegemonic war (if it is not nuclear) or of an endless strategic arms race presumably would lead to the defeat of the Soviet Union at the cost of the economic and military exhaustion of the United States. Another "rising" power (Japan, Brazil, China?) would then be in a position to assume the hegemonic role (Bergesen, 1983b; Thompson, 1983a).

LONG-TERM PROSPECTS

Although a Kondratieff upswing may occur in the short term, Wallerstein believes that the world-system has entered into a period of fundamental crisis. He believes (although other world-system theorists are less sure) that this crisis will ultimately lead to the destruction of the existing world-system (Wallerstein, 1982a, 1984b).

As we have seen, the world-system has been able to overcome both short-term Kondratieff and long-term logistic phase Bs through the processes of broadening and deepening. Yet, Wallerstein points out, those processes have inherent limits. The geographical expansion of capitalism is now essentially complete. Deepening is still possible because large numbers of workers in the periphery have not been incorporated into the system as superexploited semi-proletarians. But as the percentage of all world workers in this category approaches 100 percent, there will be no "new" workers to incorporate into the world-system. At that point, two of the fundamental mechanisms for overcoming phase Bs will no longer be available.

Similarly, overcoming stagnation through an increase in effective demand has upper limits. The creation of an ever-larger strata of full proletarians and "middle-income" workers (mostly in the core) entails the redistribution of the available economic surplus from the capitalist class. Eventually, such a redistribution will reach the point at which the capitalist class will face a declining rate of profit.

Wallerstein also agrees with more conventional Marxist predictions of the demise of capitalism. Proletarianization of the labor force on a world scale, combined with world polarization of the income, has been creating an ever-larger class of extremely exploited workers. In this century this trend has already been the basis for the rise of anticapitalist and/or anticore revolutionary movements. Indeed, such movements (for example, the Communists in the Soviet Union) have yet to effectively challenge the survival of the world-system. To a large extent, they have been contained within particular countries, and over time they have been partially reincorporated into the world-system. Nevertheless, Wallerstein believes that these movements will continue to appear and will grow stronger. He expects them at some future date to be numerous enough and powerful enough to challenge a world-system weakened by its own inherent contradictions and limitations.

What will be the outcome of this crisis? Wallerstein is not sure. He hopes that a true, worldwide socialist system could replace capitalism: a socialist world government, production decisions based on social needs, social and economic equality, and full democratic control of all institutions. Other, less desireable (from Wallerstein's point of view) outcomes are just as possible. New forms of totalitarian domination might appear that would allow existing ruling elites to hold onto their power. Alternatively, the world might return to a situation in which the single world-system was replaced by a set of autonomous (culturally, economically, and politically distinct) "civilizations." Wallerstein sees evidence that any of these three outcomes could emerge from the final crisis. In any event, we can anticipate a long period of gradually intensifying instability and conflict.

## Summary and Conclusion

For world-system theorists the last five centuries have been characterized by a fairly orderly pattern of change contained within a single, overarching global system. The "orderliness" of those changes reflects the fact that they were the result of the relationships generated by a capitalist world-economy and interstate system. In the terminology of world-system theory, system dynamics are the result of the system structure that emerged during the sixteenth century.

Since that time, in terms of its fundamental defining characteristics, the world-system has stayed basically the same, but within that general structure, there have been a number of recurrent cycles of economic growth and stagnation, hegemony, colonialism, free or restrictive trade, war, and the like. Yet looked at from the point of long-term historical change, certain fundamental trends contained within the system promise to bring it to the point of crisis and collapse.

# Criticisms of the Theory

World-system theory has proven to be a highly controversial approach. No introduction to it would be complete without consideration of the critical responses it has evoked. This chapter will examine some of those criticisms. Besides summarizing them, the discussion will attempt to evaluate the issues raised and, where possible, examine proposals for reconciling the positions of the critics with those of world-system theorists. That discussion will provide much of the basis for the overall evaluation of the theory discussed in the next chapter.

The first part of this chapter will concern itself with criticisms made in regard to some of the specific claims about and interpretations of system structure and dynamics. The chapter will conclude with an examination of more general criticisms of the overall assumptions and intellectual strategies employed by world-system theorists.

## The Basis of the System: One Logic or Two?

We have seen that two of the defining characteristics of the world-system is that (1) it is capitalist and (2) it consists of an interstate system of competitive nation-states. A recurrent debate has been waged over the relative importance and degree of independence of these two features in shaping the nature of the world-system. On one side of the debate are those who appear to emphasize capitalist economic relations alone in explaining the system. On the other are those who criticize this approach as simplistic and argue for the independent causal role of "political" factors associated with the interstate system.

Wallerstein has been repeatedly criticized for overemphasizing economic relationships in explaining the underlying nature of the world-system. For example, Theda Skocpol (1977) argues that Wallerstein's definitions of the core and periphery imply that position in the world-system is determined solely by a society's level of technological development and world-market opportunities. These factors determine the society's position in the world division of labor and the method of labor control that it will employ. Skocpol also contends that Wallerstein sees a society's political and military position in the world-system as being determined solely by its relative position in the world-economy (1977: 1079–1080). William Thompson argues similarly that world-system theorists view the central relationship among parts of the system as that of the exploitation of the periphery by the core:

> The . . . core consists of those states in which agro-industrial production is the most efficient and where the complexity of economic activities and the level of capital accumulation is the greatest. As a consequence, the core receives the most favorable proportion of the system's economic surplus through its exploitation of the periphery, which, in turn is compelled to specialize in the supply of less well rewarded raw materials and labor (1983b: 12).

This system of exploitation is also the basic factor shaping economic, social, and political events in the periphery.

Other critics contend that world-system explanations of dynamics are also overly reliant on economic factors, especially those involving exchange relationships among countries (Zolberg, 1983; Ray, 1983). For example, we have seen that Wallerstein explains the causes of broadening almost entirely in economic terms. He has also been brought to task for his emphasis on economic factors in explanations of hegemonic cycles and wars. Recall that in Wallerstein's view, the struggle for hegemony has an essentially economic motivation, and the process of actually achieving hegemony depends upon obtaining economic predominance in production, commercial relations, and international finance.

What do these critics of Wallerstein propose as an alternative approach? Most argue that a more adequate analytical strategy would consider the independent role of those political factors that shape relationships among states in the world-system (for example, Modeski, 1978; Skocpol, 1977, 1985; Zolberg, 1983). A typical statement of this view is that of Aristide Zolberg:

> Contrary to Wallerstein's theoretical intention . . . the "basic linkage between parts of the system" was at no time merely economic. From the

very beginning, another identifiable structure is interacting with the structural linkage he shows us—a structure he does not or will not see. . . . The structural linkage I have in mind encompasses a set of politico-strategic actors (1983: 258).

In this view, the relationship among states in the world-system is not merely one of a struggle for economic advantage. War is not simply part of that economic struggle. Instead, the search for military security and territorial expansion represents an independent explanation for relationships in the world-system. For example, Charles Tilly provides this account of the emergence of European nation-states:

The people who controlled European states and states in the making warred in order to check or overcome their competitors and thus enjoy the advantages of power within a secure or expanding territory. To make more effective war, they attempted to locate more capital. In the short run, they might acquire that capital by conquest, by selling off their assets, or by coercing or dispossessing accumulators of capital. In the long run, the quest inevitably involved establishing regular access to capitalists who could supply and arrange credit and in imposing one form of regular taxation or another on the people and activities within the sphere of their control (1985: 172).

The most fully elaborated approach that emphasizes the independent role of geopolitical factors in the struggle for hegemony is the "long cycle of world leadership" perspective advanced by George Modelski and others. They argue that cycles of hegemony are primarily explainable by the functioning of the interstate system itself, although there may be a temporal relationship between those cycles and Kondratieff waves (Thompson, 1983a; Modelski, 1978, 1981, 1983, 1987; Kumon, 1987). (See the next chapter for more discussion of this theory.)

Wallerstein dismisses these criticisms as mere "semantic juggling" (1983a: 307). He maintains that the division between political and economic analysis simply has no place in world-system theory. The world-economy and the interstate system are interrelated aspects of a single, unitary system. Neither can be considered more important than the other nor the sole cause of the other. Rather, both must be considered together in analyzing the system.

Chase-Dunn (1981) elaborates this basic position. He argues that capitalism and the interstate system are interdependent and reinforcing features of the world-system. Each depends on the other for its continued existence. The operation of the interstate system, argues Chase-Dunn, means that any one state cannot control the investment activities of all capitalists. If one state were to regulate private business activity in a way that reduced the ability of its national capitalist class to accumulate surplus, it would only hurt itself. In response, investment would flow out of that country to others with less restrictive policies and more profit opportunities. Even preventing the flight of domestic capital would not work. Entrepreneurs in the country that was regulating investment activity would be at a competitive disadvantage in the world market. Their competitors in other countries would take advantage of the investment opportunities in the more favorable locations. The result would be relative economic decline for the country that was regulating its capitalists. Thus, one of the defining features of capitalism—relative freedom to invest for maximum private profit—is protected and maintained by the existence of the interstate system.

At the same time, says Chase-Dunn, continuation of the interstate system depends on the existence of a capitalist world-economy. As we have seen, competition among the capitalists of different countries results in some countries being more successful than others. But the winning nations of one period do not remain so in subsequent periods. The previous winners lose out to competitors in other countries. Thus, no one country has been able to amass sufficient resources to impose its military control over all the others. Rather, the system of competitive capitalism has prevented the creation of a single world-empire controlled by one state.

EVALUATION. This attempt to argue that there is no problem with the overemphasis on economic factors in world-system theory has not convinced the critics. Overall, the consensus of opinion remains that Wallerstein does primarily rely on economic factors to account for world-system structure and dynamics. Such an approach, most agree, provides an incomplete explanation of the system.

The resolution of the problem would seem to lie in a more systematic incorporation of political and geopolitical factors in the analysis of the dynamics of the world-system. Peter Evans, Dietrich Rueschemeyer, and Evelyne Huber Stevens suggest the direction such a strategy would take in examining the relationship between states and the world-economy (also see Evans, Rueschemeyer, and Skocpol, 1985): "[There is a] . . . tension inherent in the world-system in which the logic of state action cannot be subsumed by the analysis of capital accumulation, but in which the global logic of capitalist markets continually makes and breaks geopolitical strategies" (1985: 12).

James Ray also suggests a way to resolve the question of the relative role of political and economic factors. He argues that the theoretical emphasis either on economic or political factors is probably premature. We are not yet in a position to make general statements about the relationship between and the relative importance of the two explanatory factors. It would be better to accept the possibility of a reciprocal relationship between them as a *general* principle. Scholars should then attempt to specify the nature of that relationship in particular time periods:

> While one obvious path to the resolution of this type of controversy points in the direction of reciprocal or dialectical relationships, what is needed now is a synthesis of traditional scholarship concerning the global political system and Wallerstein's analysis of the world-system which will specify on which occasions and under which circumstances economic or political processes are more fundamental. . . . It is probably true that the operations of the global political system and the modern world [economic] system are at times relatively independent, but there is little doubt that more often the relationship between the two is crucial (1983: 30).

## The Nature of the State

A fundamental assertion of world-system theorists is that the state operates to assist the capitalist class in capital accumulation: "States are organizations . . . which are utilized by the classes that control them to expropriate shares of the world surplus product" (Chase-Dunn, 1980: 506). World-system theorists adopted this essentially Marxist view of the state just as Marxist theorists themselves became involved in a new debate about the nature of the capitalist state. At least initially, this debate was between those who took an "instrumental" view of the state and those who took a "structural" one.

In the instrumental view capitalists more or less directly control state policy by their direct influence over government officials ("state managers"). They do so by such means as participating in the selection of state managers (for example, through campaign contributions), corrupting or coopting state managers, and serving in government themselves. Thus, the state is the passive agent or instrument of the capitalist class. Most U.S. Marxists adopted an essentially instrumental view of the state prior to the 1970s (Marger, 1987: 42–43; Carnoy, 1984: 211–213).

In the 1970s the instrumental view came under increasing attack by both Marxists and non-Marxists. In part, that criticism rested on evidence that there were many instances in which state policy appeared to run counter to the immediate wishes of elements of the capitalist class. Instrumental theory was also criticized for assuming that the capitalist class functioned as a fully self-aware, rational, and unified group that actively conspired with state managers to shape state policies in their immediate, short-term interests. Critics argued that the evidence in-dicated that the capitalist class was not nearly so well organized, unified, or rational in its political behavior (Marger, 1987: 42–43; Carnoy, 1984: 208–218).

To correct these apparent deficiencies in instrumental theory, U.S. Marxists, following the lead of a number of European theorists, devised a structural theory of the state. Structuralists argue that it is not necessary for the capitalist class to have direct control over the behavior of state managers. Instead, these theorists look for constraints (structural features) built into the capitalist system of political-economy that require state managers to act in the long-term interests of the capitalist class (by preserving the capitalist system itself). The key feature for most of these theorists is that the state is dependent on continued investment by the capitalist class. This investment generates the economic growth that provides revenues for the state and creates mass support for the political system. State leaders consequently cannot act in ways that would consistently discourage capitalist investment because this would undermine both the financial basis of and mass support for the state. In fact, leaders need to encourage and assist investment activities (Carnoy, 1984: 218–245; Marger, 1987: 42–43; Szymanski, 1978).

At the same time, argue structural theorists, the state is not merely the passive agent of the capitalist class. For the survival of the state and the capitalist system as a whole, the state must be "relatively autonomous" from the capitalist class. Relative autonomy allows state managers to pursue policies necessary to maintain the legitimacy of both the state and the capitalist system. Such actions often involve policies that at least appear to favor the masses at the expense of elements of the capitalist class, who therefore may actually oppose those policies. For example, all core states have allowed the formation of labor unions and have established extensive systems of social welfare. In addition, state managers must also have some freedom to protect the long-term power of the state in competition with other states, which is also in the long-term interest of the capitalist class but may require that the state take actions that hurt specific capitalists in the short term. For example, heavy taxation may be necessary to maintain military strength.

Many structural theorists also maintain that there are good reasons to think that state managers are motivated to maintain their own autonomy, to increase their own power by increasing state power. In democratic systems, they are also concerned with maintaining mass popularity, not just pleasing the capitalist class (Marger, 1987: 42–43; Carnoy, 1984: 218–245; Szymanski, 1978).

These competing views of the state are reflected in the evolution of world-system theorizing about it. Early criticisms of Wallerstein's first book on world-system theory (1974a) included the charge that he took an overly instrumental view of the state. For example, Block (1978) interprets Wallerstein's analysis of state strategies in the international arena as one in which such strategies are the result of a conscious general decision of the capitalist class. In a similar vein, Skocpol contends that Wallerstein reduces the system of domination between the core and the periphery to the "vulgar expression of market-class interests . . . [in which] . . . we are forced to assume that these [capitalist] classes always get what they want, reshaping institutions and their relations to producing classes to suit their current world market opportunities" (1977: 1080).

World-system theorists generally respond to these charges by denying that they are "vulgar instrumentalists" but are, in fact, positing an essentially structural view of the state (Chase-Dunn, 1980: 506). This view acknowledges the factors employed by other structural theorists in explaining the behavior of the state. World-system theorists also put special emphasis on two particular constraints on the nature of state actions: (1) the world division of labor and each state's position in it and (2) the system of interstate political-military competition (Chase-Dunn, 1980: 506). Both constraints lead the state to act in ways generally favorable to the interests of the capitalist class without necessarily doing the bidding of individual capitalists. For example, given the international competition for markets, acting contrary to the interests of the capitalist class (for example, by imposing expensive regulations) will only give the capitalists of another country a competitive advantage that will weaken the nation's economic position in the world-economy. Because the struggle for power in the international arena requires economic resources, state managers are motivated to protect and encourage their national capitalist class to maximize growth of the national economy (Chase-Dunn, 1980: 507; Block, 1978).

This essentially neo-Marxist position does not represent the only possible version of theorizing about the state in the world-system. Evans, Rueschemeyer, and Stephens (1985) argue for a view of the state that includes even more emphasis on state autonomy than is typical of neo-Marxist formulations. In this view, the interstate system and the imperatives of capital accumulation represent real, independent constraints on state behavior. At the same time, these factors by themselves are not adequate to explain the origins of state policies. State managers act creatively and autonomously in pursuit of their own goals. In doing so, their behavior is not only constrained by the world-system but is also a factor in shaping and changing it. This position closely approximates that of the neo-Weberian theorists discussed in the next chapter and represents an attempt to reassert the independent role of the state in shaping events that goes substantially beyond that of Marxian formulations.

EVALUATION. World-system theorists have followed the lead of other neo-Marxist theorists in moving toward some version of a structural view of the state. Nevertheless, major differences among various theorists remain in regard to the relative importance attached to the independence of state managers in relation to the constraints imposed by the world-system and the capitalist class. In turn, this uncertainty reflects growing dissatisfaction with Marxist-inspired theories of the state. The direction of theoretical movement seems to be toward an even greater emphasis on the independent role of the state. As such, it represents another aspect of the concern to avoid interpretations that are economically based (that is, class based in the case of theories of the state) and that consider the independent role of political factors. As the previous section indicated, it is not clear that world-system theory, as it is currently formulated, has yet adequately accommodated this theoretical movement.

## Peripheral Societies: Dependency or Mode of Production?

As we have seen, world-system analysis basically accounts for conditions in the periphery in terms of its position in the world division of labor and explains the poverty of the periphery by its continued exploitation and unbalanced development. Peripheral class systems, systems of labor control, forms of government, and other social arrangements are likewise an outgrowth of the nature of the periphery's position in the world-system. This position is a relatively straightforward extension of and elaboration on the position taken by dependency theorists.

In approaching the conditions in the periphery in this way, world-system theorists have provoked sharp criticism from more "traditional" Marxist scholars. The resulting debate between world-system theorists and these Marxist scholars has forced world-system theorists to move toward at least a partial modification of their dependency-theory-derived view. The heart of these Marxist criticisms can be summarized in terms of three basic flaws Marxists find in the dependency approach.

First, more traditional Marxist theorists claim that the dependency approach incorrectly attributes conditions in the periphery almost exclusively to factors or forces external to those societies, especially to the actions of core capitalists and core states in their attempts to exploit it. Such an approach, according to this view, entirely ignores the role of internal factors, particularly indigenous classes, in shaping and maintaining conditions in peripheral societies. Instead, dependency theorists portray indigenous groups as the passive victims, pawns, or agents of core capitalists and states (Ahmad, 1983: 40).

Second, according to these critics, world-system theory focuses solely on the periphery's unfavorable exchange relationship with the core to account for its problems. This emphasis on processes of economic "circulation" (exchange or trade relationships) is inconsistent with traditional Marxist theorizing, which focuses on capitalism primarily as an exploitative mode of production. What defines the system is the appropriation of surplus value from workers engaged in labor for the capitalist owners of the means of production. The sphere of productive relationships, not exchange relationships, is the proper focus of the analysis of capitalist exploitation. Hence, one must look at peripheral production relationships and the class relations created by them (C. Johnson, 1983; Brenner, 1977).

Third, these Marxist critics argue that to describe peripheral economies as a special form of capitalism is wrong. The label "capitalism" should be restricted to those economies whose relations of production conform to the criteria suggested originally by Marx. Namely, workers must be "free" (uncoerced) and solely supported by wage labor. Because so much of the labor in the periphery has been, and is, coerced and is not supported solely by wage labor, the periphery does not have a capitalist mode of production. Therefore, dependency theorists are guilty of confusing export and trade of commodities for cash (again, "circulation") with real capitalism based on the exploitation of "true" proletarians (free wage laborers) (D. Johnson, 1983).

If conditions in the periphery are not the result of a system of "dependent capitalism," what is their cause? These Marxists (who are known as "mode-of-production" theorists) essentially answer with what they believe is a logical extension of classical Marxian theory: that more than one mode of production can be identified in peripheral societies. Specifically, they argue that peripheral societies are a combination of capitalist and specific varieties of precapitalist, feudal modes of production. The feudal modes especially characterize rural areas and are the result of the failure of these countries to replace their historical modes of production. The aspects of their economies that display a capitalist mode of production represent the gradual introduction of capitalism to these societies in the last century or so. Eventually, it will become dominant, but that will take time. Meanwhile, the continuation of the feudal modes has contributed to slow economic growth. The dominant classes connected with those modes (such as large landowners) have resisted the introduction of capitalism. The simultaneous existence of different modes of production in one society is also the source of numerous social and cultural inconsistencies, which have given rise to recurrent political and social conflict (Chinchilla, 1983). John Taylor summarizes the situation:

> As a result of being determined . . . by a [combination] . . . of modes of production, the Third World social formation is characterized by a whole series of *dislocations* between various levels of the social formation. As opposed to the previous period of determinancy . . . by a particular non-capitalist mode, in which the different levels were *adapted one to another,* the latter are now dislocated with respect to each other and with respect to the existing economic structure itself. Imperialist penetration intervenes . . . to ensure the increasing dominance of the capitalist mode of production, and to create that restricted and uneven form of economic development (1979: 163).

Bill Warren (1980), the most extreme exponent of mode-of-production analysis, even argues that the spread of capitalism to the periphery has been a force for "progressive" change. In Warren's view, imperialism and colonialism were good things for the periphery because they introduced the more advanced mode of production of capitalism. He maintains that capitalism brings technological advance, which makes possible industrialization, urbanization, democratization, and the general social transformation of peripheral societies. These societies are thus better off materially and socially than they would have been if they had retained their feudal modes of production.

Critics of mode-of-production analysis, in and out of world-system theory, are quick to respond. They reaffirm their argument that the periphery is now organized along capitalist lines but concede that much of the rural sector of these societies contains surviving elements of precapitalist economic relationships. These critics admit that most of the labor force does not survive exclusively through free wage labor. Nevertheless, even the most traditional aspects of these societies have been modified to meet the needs of a capitalist world-economy (D. Johnson, 1983; Petras, 1984d: 25). Critics also reject the requirement that an economy be based on the exploitation of free wage labor to be considered capitalist:

> If there is any single overriding feature of the capitalist mode of production . . . it is the appropriation of value wherever and however it is produced for accumulation. If wealth is accessible, it is plundered and used to facilitate capitalist development (D. Johnson, 1983: 237).

Marx was historically wrong: capital accumulation, reproduction, and expansion occurred under a variety of experiences, which included slavery, peonage, forced labor, etc. Indeed, these social forms were more common and contributed a very great proportion of the surplus to the initial and even advanced stages of accumulation (Petras, 1984d: 25–26).

Critics of mode-of-production analysis also contend that to characterize all the relations of production in the periphery according to Marx's original scheme of "Asiatic" or "feudal" modes of production is an oversimplification. Such a crude classification scheme does real violence to the complex reality of peripheral societies' economic organization: slavery, peonage, serfdom, small-farm commercial production, and so on.

Finally, almost all these observers of the periphery vehemently reject Warren's positive characterization of the penetration of capitalism into the periphery. Such a characterization ignores both the long history and the contemporary reality of harsh exploitation, oppression, and poverty in the periphery and grossly exaggerates the extent of real economic progress there (Ahmad, 1983).

EVALUATION. The debate between defenders of the dependency approach and their mode-of-production critics has often been shrill and bitter. The debate about what capitalism "really" is cannot be resolved in a way that will satisfy either side, but at least some in both theoretical camps have attempted to modify their views to accommodate criticisms coming from their opponents. For example, Dale Johnson (1983), while basically identifying with the dependency approach, advances a way to reconcile the two approaches. Following Petras (1981), he suggests that a reciprocal relationship exists between the mode of production present in a society and the economic forces of the world-system. Johnson labels as "general determinants" of the internal structure of peripheral societies the pressures originating out of the operation of the world-economy. "Proximate determinants," on the other hand, are those class relationships created by a particular mode of production. Johnson argues that a complete analysis of the conditions in a peripheral society requires explanations that incorporate both the general and proximate determinants. He further argues that the relationship between the two sets of determining factors is "asymmetrical" and "dialectical":

The external/internal nexus is unraveled if it is viewed as a dialectic of asymmetrical processes. The structuring impulses are international in scope, but the actual outcomes are the result of localized conditions and struggles. The method is historical-structural, involving analysis of political economy and class relations under conditions of dependency, where dependency itself is a class relationship among parties of unequal power. . . . Thus, while territorial class struggles are the proximate causes of events, the forces forming classes and providing a context for their clashes are international in scope (1983: 242, 244).

Consequently, world-system theory can accommodate what is probably a valid criticism. Its theorists do need to pay more attention to peripheral class relationships and other internal factors that account for conditions there. They could do so without surrendering the basic claims of the theory that the operation of the world-system creates the general conditions under which internal structures emerge.

## The Nature of Unequal Exchange

As we have seen, world-system theorists' whole explanation of change in the modern era rests on the claim that the core has extensively exploited the periphery. Emmanuel's theory of unequal exchange is usually cited as the explanation for how this exploitation occurs. Most world-system theorists are content to stop there, and the focus of most world-system interpretations has been on the specific forms of trading and financial relationships that supposedly have assured the continuation of unequal exchange (Bernstein, 1982: 235). This complacency is more than a little curious given that the theory of unequal exchange is the source of considerable controversy among both Marxian theorists and their critics.

The existence of systematic peripheral exploitation has always been hotly disputed by "classical" economists who argue that under conditions of unrestricted free trade, both trading partners end up better off than if they had not traded. Consequently, there is nothing inherently exploitative about trade between the core and the periphery. This view, known as the theory of comparative advantage, remains the dominant view among U.S. economists and such international financial agencies as the World Bank. The debate between these advocates of world free trade and various Marxist scholars on the validity of comparative advantage has been lengthy and complex.[1] Suffice it to say that neither side has succeeded in convincing the other.

Other non-Marxist scholars also reject on empirical grounds claims that the trading relationship between the core and periphery is exploitative. In fact, they argue that there is evidence the periphery is better off because of its economic ties with the core than it would have been had those ties not existed (Chirot and Hall, 1982).[2] For example, some economic historians question whether the process of incorporation into the periphery through colonization in the nineteenth century invariably retarded economic development in those areas. Typical of this line of argument is the work of Morris Morris et al. (1969); they argue that the industrialization of India was not delayed by British colonial rule. (Recall also that even a Marxist theorist such as Warren [1980] claims that incorporation into the world-economy has resulted in economic progress for the periphery.)

The discussion of unequal exchange among Marxist theorists has also been contentious.[3] Most of the debate has not been about whether some of the surplus produced in the periphery ends up in the core. Rather, the debate has centered on the proper application of Marx's theory of value to international exchange to explain *how* the transfer of surplus happens.

Recall that Emmanuel's explanation is based on different wage rates in the core and the periphery. That claim and a number of assumptions that underlie his argument are strongly criticized by other Marxist scholars. Proceeding from different initial assumptions, Ernest Mandel (1975) provides a counterexplanation: that the different level of productivity of core and peripheral workers account for unequal exchange. Peripheral workers labor in activities that employ less capital (making them less productive). Peripheral goods consequently require more labor to produce that core goods do. The result is the exchange of peripheral commodities produced with a lot of labor for those of the core involving much less. Mandel attempts to demonstrate that transfer of surplus to the core is the result. Thus, in his view, low wages are not the cause of unequal exchange but the result of labor-intensive production in the periphery, when the goods so produced are exchanged for capital-intensive core goods.

The details of this debate between Emmanuel and Mandel need not concern us here. The important thing to note is that their ultimate explanations of unequal exchange rest on completely different explanatory factors (in addition to very different initial assumptions). The resulting controversy has never been settled.


EVALUATION. The debate about the existence or nature of unequal exchange cannot be resolved here. The important thing for our purposes is that it continues. Consequently, at the very least, we must recognize that one of the most fundamental claims of world-system theory remains to be demonstrated. Failure to explicitly address the issues raised by the debate has to be considered a serious shortcoming of the theory.

## The Significance of Peripheral Exploitation for the Core

What about the consequences of unequal exchange? As we have seen, world-system theory argues that the exploitation of the periphery has been beneficial and necessary for the core in a number of ways. A number of Marxist and non-Marxist critics challenge that claim, whether or not they accept the notion of unequal exchange.

Robert Brenner (1977) is one of the most scathing Marxist critics of Wallerstein. Brenner argues that even though unequal exchange may occur, it cannot be used as the primary explanation for the successful development of capitalism in the core. He contends that core economic expansion was the result of the inherent dynamics of a capitalist mode of production. Capitalism created conditions that required and made possible the endless accumulation of capital for the purpose of raising labor productivity (through investment in increasingly technologically sophisticated production equipment). This accumulation process was internal to the core countries and derived from the core's particular relations of production (exploitation of wage labor by private owners of the means of production). Brenner argues that by focusing on peripheral exploitation, Wallerstein simply ignores the central process that accounts for the origins of capitalist development.

A large number of critics, both Marxist and non-Marxist, also challenge the importance of peripheral exploitation for the core on essentially empirical grounds. They say that the magnitude of the surplus extracted from the periphery was not large enough to have the far-reaching consequences that world-system theorists claim it had. Therefore, other factors must account for the economic development of the core. For example, one of Wallerstein's better known non-Marxist critics, Chirot, takes this view. In his early work (1977), Chirot was more closely aligned with the world-system view, but recently (1986; Chirot and Hall, 1982) he has explicitly rejected most of world-system theory in general and has been particularly critical of the notion that peripheral exploitation is necessary for the success of the core.

One of Chirot's criticisms focuses on the world-system view of the rise of capitalism in Europe. As we have seen, Wallerstein regards the exploitation of South America and Eastern Europe in the sixteenth century as having been crucial to the resolution of the crisis of feudalism and the rapid transformation of the core in Western Europe thereafter. Chirot argues that in fact the development of the core after 1500 can be explained primarily by various internal factors: geography, political organization, and cultural values (1986: 11–28). Chirot agrees strongly with those (such as Weber) who argue that the diffusion of a "rational" orientation in Western culture was central to the process of change in the core. (Indeed, Wallerstein's failure to focus on this internal cultural change is one of Chirot's central complaints about the world-system account of the modern era [Chirot and Hall, 1982].)

Chirot does acknowledge that contact with the new periphery did play some minor role in European development. That role was not, he argues, primarily one of providing increases in core wealth. Instead, the effects were more subtle and not directly economic. First, the opportunities to acquire wealth rapidly through overseas trade and/or conquest helped create a new class of innovative entrepreneurs and venture capitalists. Second, overseas expansion did bring considerable wealth to particular core states, such as Spain, which set off a wave of colonization and exploration efforts by other core states seeking to copy Spanish success. In the process, an intensely competitive environment was created that encouraged both economic competition and state building in the core (Chirot, 1986: 34).

Chirot also challenges the contention that the imperialist expansion of the late nineteenth century was based on actual economic necessity for the core. Core political leaders may have sincerely believed that economic success depended on the acquisition of colonies; they certainly acted on that belief in the rush for colonies at the end of the nineteenth century. But, Chirot believes that they were wrong. Core investment in peripheral areas was a very small percentage of the total of all core investments, and overall the new colonies never provided markets or investment opportunities of sufficient size or profitability to justify the cost of acquiring and administering them (1986: 83). What finally rescued the core from the economic slump of the late nineteenth century, he argues, was the creation of new industries based on new technologies (1986: 84–92).

When he turns to current world economic system, Chirot does acknowledge that trade with the periphery is important to the core. Almost one-third of core imports and exports are with the periphery, and a major loss of that trade would cripple core economies. But, he maintains, the core does not need to engage in direct political, military, or economic imperialism to maintain that trading relationship. Peripheral countries need to trade with the core as much as the core needs to trade with the periphery. They need core capital and technology for their economies. Attempts to develop without trade to the core (as in China under Mao) have been failures. Even revolutionary, socialist regimes have come to recognize that fact. In turn, the only way a country can participate in core-peripheral trade is to accept the rules of the highly competitive system of international trade, which means that peripheral countries must export what the core needs at prices constrained by international market conditions (1986: 209–223). Indeed,

Chirot argues that the decline of colonialism in this century and the concurrent continued prosperity of the core demonstrate that the core does not need imperialism to succeed (1986: 213–214). (A more detailed version of this argument can be found in Feinberg [1983].)

EVALUATION. How telling are these criticisms against world-system theory? A careful reading of the work of world-system theorists suggests they have anticipated and/or attempted to accommodate most of them. World-system theory does argue that peripheral exploitation by core capitalists was an integral part of the success of core capitalism (Hopkins, Wallerstein et al., 1982b: 49–50). At the same time, some world-system theorists make clear that they consider the *quantitative* amount of wealth removed from the periphery an unresolved empirical issue that is not central to their argument about the periphery's role in core development. For instance, Terence Hopkins calls the extent of peripheral exploitation a "theoretically open matter" (1982a: 17) and is willing to concede that peripheral exploitation "may have played . . . a *quantitatively* subordinate role in accumulation, however qualitatively important its directional role in [core] development may have been" (1982a: 17). Similarly, Chase-Dunn acknowledges that the central accumulation process in the core has been internal (1983: 75). Hopkins and Wallerstein also concede that the precise nature of the effect of peripheral exploitation on the core is an unresolved issue in world-system theory (Hopkins, Wallerstein et al., 1982b: 50).

Chirot's discussion of the role of new technologies and industries in rescuing the core from stagnation in the late nineteenth century is also not fundamentally incompatible with world-system theory. As we saw in the previous chapter, a major element of the world-system explanation of economic cycles is the notion that introduction of new productive techniques and products acts as a stimulus to capitalist expansion.

World-system theorists also do not see direct imperialism and colonialism as constant and necessary features of the world-system. In their view, these are simply two modes of core exploitation of the periphery that have appeared (and disappeared) at different times in history. In fact, the decline of direct rule in the periphery is the normal consequence of periods of hegemony. The end of direct rule and participation in a relatively open world market does not end the economic exploitation of the periphery.

Finally, world-system theorists need not prove that the core as a whole benefited from peripheral exploitation. (Chirot's argument is essentially that imperialism is not in the general interests of the core.) Recall that the capitalist class is politically dominant in the core and is in a position to strongly influence the nature of state policy toward the periphery. Consequently, theorists need only demonstrate that peripheral exploitation benefits important elements within that class.

Thus, this line of criticism is not by itself grounds for immediate rejection of world-system theory. On the other hand, it does raise a valid question. World-system theory has not actually demonstrated that peripheral exploitation is of central importance to the success of the core or even its capitalist class. Unless and until more systematic evidence is assembled to prove that claim, it will remain one of the central unproved assertions of the theory, about which critics can appropriately raise questions.

## Emiseration of the Periphery?

The other issue in regard to peripheral exploitation is its effects on the periphery. Hopkins and Wallerstein maintain that as part of the general trend toward polarization in the world-economy, "the long-term level of well-being of the world-system's and the globe's work forces has been declining" (Hopkins, Wallerstein et al., 1982b: 70). By so asserting, these theorists are explicitly incorporating the basic claim of classical Marxist theory that capitalist exploitation leads to the progressive "emiseration" of the working class (which is caused primarily by superexploitation of peripheral workers). Hopkins and Wallerstein differ from the classical Marxist view in applying emiseration to a global scale rather than to individual core societies.

The claim of absolute declines in well-being for most of the world's population is a controversial one. Most conventional measures of economic conditions indicate a slow but real increase in per capita income in all but a handful of extremely poor countries (World Bank, 1987). Admittedly, as we have seen, in many countries a great and even growing inequality in the distribution of income means that much of the increase in national income has actually gone to the rich and/ or a small urban middle class. It is also true that inflation and/or economic austerity measures have led to a drop in "real" (inflation-adjusted) wages in a number of countries during the 1980s (for example, Brazil and Mexico). Yet, even if one takes into account such things, the weight of the available evidence is still on the side of those who claim a real trend toward greater material well-being in the world during this century (for example, Morris, 1979).

Wallerstein and his associates simply dismiss this evidence as flawed and inadequate. They contend that more careful measurement would validate the emiseration hypothesis. Thus, when speaking of India, Wallerstein asserts that "a *careful* [emphasis added] study would show that in the year 1900, direct producers received significantly less for comparable types of work than they did in 1600" (Wallerstein, 1982b: 99).

EVALUATION. There is no way to resolve this debate between incomplete data on the one side and nonexistent, hypothetical data on the other. One simply should be aware that the emiseration hypothesis is one aspect of the general polarization hypothesis that is highly controversial and not generally supported by the limited available data.

## Global Polarization?

The issue of absolute emiseration is an analytically separate issue from that of global economic polarization. All that is required for global polarization to occur is that incomes in the periphery grow more slowly than in the core. If that occurs, the gap between the average income in the core and the periphery will continue to increase.

As we discussed in Chapter 4, measured in terms of per capita GNP, economic growth of the core has been faster than that of the periphery for the last four decades. When examined during the course of the modern era, the increasing average income of the core relative to the periphery is even more striking.

On the face of it, these findings would suggest that global economic polarization is, in fact, a fundamental trend in the world-system. Despite this evidence, a number of critics of world-system theory (and dependency theory, which also makes this claim) raise the issue of whether such polarization is an *inherent* and *necessary* aspect of world capitalism. In other words, they reject the reasons given by world-system theorists for global income trends. They further reject the notion that these trends must necessarily continue in the future. These criticisms have taken several forms.

The most important of these has already been addressed. Those who reject the existence of unequal exchange deny the inevitability of global polarization. As we have seen, part of their argument against unequal exchange is that there is evidence that incorporation was not always detrimental to the periphery.

Another criticism revolves around the issue of population growth. Daniel Chirot and Thomas Hall (Chirot and Hall, 1982: 101; Chirot, 1986: 256–261) argue that at least for a large portion of the periphery, much of the slow increase in per capita GNP can be explained simply by the fact that populations have been growing so rapidly that most of the increased economic output has been diverted to support increased population sizes. Indeed, absolute rates of peripheral economic growth (the annual percentage growth in total GNP) have been higher than those that have historically prevailed in the core (Chirot, 1986: 248).

In addition, both Chirot and others point to the success of the NICs (such as Taiwan and South Korea), which have enjoyed per capita GNP increases much in excess of those of the core for the last two decades. If polarization is inherent in the capitalist world-system, these theorists ask, why have these semi-peripheral countries been growing rapidly and closing the economic gap between themselves and the core? For these observers, the success of the NICs indicates that proper development strategies make possible rapid industrialization *and* full integration into the world-system (Chirot, 1986: 247–255).

EVALUATION. How damaging are these criticisms of the global polarization thesis in world-system theory? Note, first, that the basic empirical trend is not being challenged. How to interpret that trend is the issue. Second, these alternatives to the world-system interpretation are either themselves not above challenge or are not necessarily incompatible with the world-system perspective.

The role of population growth in retarding economic development in the periphery is itself a source of major theoretical and empirical debate. One simply cannot take the position that it is a well documented and generally accepted conclusion that population growth has been a major cause of the economic difficulties of the periphery. (See National Research Council, Working Group on Population and Economic Development [1986]; Kelley et al. [1986]; Salvatore [1988]; and World Bank [1984] for examples of differing views on this issue.) To casually dismiss world-system theory because it is obvious that the "real" problem of the periphery is overpopulation and rapid population growth is to substitute one debatable claim for another.

That a small number of NICs appear to have achieved impressive growth rates does not by itself run counter to the expectations of world-system theory. Recall that one aspect of world-system dynamics is the occurrence of some ascent and descent. Only if one has evidence that the success of the NICs indicates that the periphery is in the process of disappearing is the notion of polarization effectively refuted. So far, world-system theorists and others have raised considerable doubts about how fundamental a change the success of a few NICs represents. Therefore, the claim that the world-system of capitalism leads inevitably to global economic polarization remains a plausible, but controversial, position.

**Crisis of Capitalism?**

As we have seen, world-system theory predicts that the capitalist world-system will ultimately experience a crisis so severe that it will not survive (this is consistent with the theory's Marxist ancestry). That crisis is inherent in the evolution of the world-system. Supposedly, it has begun to appear in this century and will become severe in the next.

Unfortunately, the grounds on which this claim is based are perhaps among the most ephemeral and speculative of the whole theoretical edifice. Most often cited as evidence of the growing crisis is the emergence of anticore, anticapitalist revolutionary movements and regimes in this century.

Chirot (1986) explicitly challenges this view of recent history and its implications for the future. He maintains that existing Leninist regimes offer no fundamental threat to world capitalism. The Soviet Union is technologically and economically backward, and its state apparatus is repressive. Peripheral countries in which Leninist regimes have come to power have not been notably successful. Leninist regimes consequently no longer provide attractive "role models" for peripheral societies trying to modernize rapidly. A few, but not many, more countries may experience Leninist revolutions; those that do will be small, weak countries that offer no real threat to the core. Consequently, barring nuclear war, the core is no longer threatened by the rapid spread of Leninist regimes or by the economic or military power of those that already exist (Chirot, 1986: 286–287).

Moreover, Chirot does not consider present economic or geopolitical trends as indications that the world-system is experiencing any fundamental crisis. Rather, he regards the present period as one in which the world-system is making a transition from one industrial technology to another. The process will be disruptive and cause difficulties for particular industries and/or countries, but it will result in yet another "industrial cycle" of rising production and improving material conditions. Governments in the periphery, whatever their political ideology, will discover that economic development is only possible if they trade, borrow capital, and import technology from the core. Therefore, the core will be in no danger of losing the periphery as a market and source of raw materials and agricultural commodities (1986: 222–230).

Even world-system theorists debate the nature, timing, and outcome of the supposed crisis. Some emphasize the economic basis of the crisis; others focus on the role of antisystemic forces in the periphery. Some see the crisis evolving rapidly; others are unsure that capitalism is in any immediate crisis. Some feel reasonably confident that the crisis will end with the creation of a world socialist system; others are less confident (Amin et al., 1982). This singular lack of agreement reflects the ambiguity of the evidence used to interpret the crisis.

EVALUATION. Overall, this whole debate about the "crisis of capitalism" is almost entirely speculative in nature. One cannot determine whether Wallerstein or Chirot is correct based on the evidence either one marshalls. Yet again, one has to conclude that world-system theory has raised an interesting question and proposed an interesting hypothesis. It remains to be seen if that hypothesis is supported by the available evidence.

## Socialist States: In or Out of the System?

The issue of the revolutionary potential of antisystemic movements brings us to the role of existing socialist states. As we saw in Chapter 4, most world-system theorists generally regard such states as an integral part of the world-system. Indeed, they consider the Soviet Union and its European satellites as essentially capitalist in their internal systems of political-economy and as increasingly incorporated into the world division of labor. The basic role of the Soviet Union in the world-system is that of a "rising" semi-peripheral state on the verge of attaining core status.

This view of the Soviet system as being a form of "state capitalism" has elicted a strong response from those more traditional Marxists who feel that the Soviet Union is basically a socialist society. A particularly forceful rebuttal is advanced by Albert Szymanski (1979, 1982), who argues that the economic relationship between the Soviet Union (and its Eastern European allies) and the core is not evidence of integration with the capitalist world-economy. The total volume of trade is quite small, and the Soviet economy still remains virtually self-contained. Trade is carefully limited and controlled by state import-export organizations whose goals are to obtain specific goods needed by the economy. At the same time, the state explicitly avoids permanent dependence on core sources of supply, insulates the economy from direct contact with capitalist competition, and limits Western investment to specific needed facilities. All joint ventures are Soviet owned. In short, trade with the core is neither very large nor crucial to the Soviet economy. The economic relationship between the core and the Soviet Union is that of limited, nonvital trade between two fundamentally different economic systems. The trade that does occur is similar to the trade between the European core and the agrarian empires of Asia prior to their incorporation into the world-system.

In Szymanski's view, the political relationship of the Soviet Union with the core is not that of a rising semi-peripheral state *within* the system. Instead, he argues, it is one of hostility between two fundamentally different world-systems. This hostility is in part the consequence of the core's repeated attempts to destroy the Soviet Union in the first decades of its existence. As a result, it has had to match core military power as a defensive measure. The USSR's relationship with the periphery is essentially one of supporting anticapitalist movements and progressive regimes resisting core exploitation. This bears no resemblance to the traditional core-periphery relationship of oppression and exploitation. Similarly, the Soviet relationship with Eastern Europe, rather than one of exploitation, is one of assistance.

Szymanski argues that internally the Soviet Union is qualitatively different from a capitalist society. Despite many flaws and problems, it has a socialist mode of production geared toward long-term societal needs. Centralized planning and state ownership of the means of production assure this socialist form of economic decisionmaking. The immense investment of economic resources in education and social services and the very low level of economic inequality are evidence of this commitment to socialism. Although repression does occur, the actual level of repression is much less than is usually claimed by Western observers, and the state enjoys genuine mass support.

Criticism of the world-system position is not limited to orthodox Marxists. Chirot's (1986) critical revision of world-system theory also includes a much different interpretation of the nature of the Soviet Union. For Chirot, the Soviet Union is neither capitalist nor socialist. Rather, it is a historical "throwback" quite similar to the ancient agrarian empires. Like all such empires, the purpose of the state is to protect and expand its control over subject peoples. To that end, the central activities of the state are the mobilization of military resources and the maintenance of internal security. The costs of maintaining this empire are high. Military expenditures drain the economy, and the price of subsidies to client states in the empire is burdensome. Heavy investment in militarily important industry results in low levels of production for domestic consumption. Military mobilization and frustration of the population's material desires require elaborate controls over behavior and an extensive system of state repression. Military expenditures and domestic repression contribute, in turn, to scientific and technological stagnation, which renders problematic the USSR's transition to a high-technology economy (Chirot, 1986: 270–275, 279–287).

EVALUATION. Recent changes in the Soviet Union can be used to support the positions of world-system theorists, Szymanski, or Chirot. Internal economic reforms (emphasis on enterprise profitability, productivity incentives, and small-scale private enterprise; less emphasis on collective agriculture; encouragement of direct core investment; and growing trade with the West) can be viewed as evidence of "creeping capitalism" and growing integration into the world-economy. Less repression and more political responsiveness can be interpreted as evidence of movement toward democratic socialism (in support of Szymanski's view). The whole reform effort can be evaluated as evidence of an attempt to deal with the dilemmas Chirot points out. The direction of change in the Soviet Union is still ambiguous enough to provide ample opportunities for different interpretations.

Perhaps the closest thing to a resolution of this debate are those interpretations of the Soviet experience that reject neat categorizations of the Soviet Union as essentially one kind of social system or another. These interpretations emphasize the unique historical circumstances of Soviet development and their contradictory results. Among those sympathetic to the world-system perspective, Goldfrank (1982) perhaps comes closest to this view.

Goldfrank agrees that the Soviet Union does function in the world much like an upwardly mobile, semi-peripheral state that has actually achieved core status militarily. In that sense, he accepts the standard world-system view. But he argues that Soviet development contains historically unique peculiarities. Some aspects of the Soviet system are genuinely socialist: a centrally planned economy, greater economic equality, and the contribution to revolutionary movements in the periphery. Yet, the Soviet Union clearly cannot be considered a "true" socialist system because of such aspects as the absence of democratic worker political control, extreme cultural repression, failure and exploitation in the agricultural system, the emergence of a bureaucratic political elite, and the failure to support revolutionary movements when it does not serve the immediate interests of the Soviet state.

Goldfrank sees this particular mix of results as a reflection of the circumstances and historical legacy facing the revolutionary Soviet regime when it came to power: a tradition of overcentralized, bureaucratic government; long, vulnerable borders to defend against hostile states; the population and resources that made self-sufficient industrialization possible; and a population consisting of diverse ethnic minorities. Given these circumstances, the Soviet state had two strategic priorities: to build a strong, stable central state and to protect itself from foreign intervention. These policies required rapid, heavy industrialization, collectivization of agriculture, and a strong repressive apparatus. In turn, they precluded and were in conflict with the achievement of many of the goals of socialism, especially democratic control. In short, the Soviet Union made some steps toward socialism but did not achieve it.

## Historical Accuracy

The world-system theory is an attempt to create a comprehensive account of the history of the world-system during the last five centuries. Such an account necessarily depends upon interpretations of the original scholarship of scores of historians. So far, most of the historical interpretation in world-system theory has relied on the work of Wallerstein and his close associates.

A number of reviewers of the first two volumes of Wallerstein's history of the world-system (1974a, 1980) raise objections to his handling of historical issues. For example, in the first volume (1974a) he argues that the second serfdom of Eastern Europe in the sixteenth century arose as a response to the incorporation of that region into the world-system as a peripheral producer of agricultural commodities. In fact, the historical record is not clear about the exact timing, nature, or causes of this new system of serfdom (Skocpol, 1977). Chirot and Hall (1982) also criticize Wallerstein for greatly oversimplifying historical changes prior to 1500. Other critics point to other additional lapses in Wallerstein's historical interpretations (Ray, 1983: 16).

EVALUATION, There is no way to resolve these debates about historical interpretations here. Readers of world-system analysis must understand that the historical interpretations on which world-system theory is based are selective in their use of the available historical evidence and are often highly controversial.

## Operationalizing Cycles

It is clear that capitalist economies fluctuate between periods of growth and periods of stagnation or decline and that there have been periods when one core state has been substantially more influential militarily and economically than other core states. Unfortunately, such general observations are not sufficiently precise to sustain a systematic theory of economic or geopolitical cycles. Such a theory would require specification of what is fluctuating, how one measures it, and the method of determining its timing. In other words, to use sociological jargon, one must be able to provide a clear "operational" definition of cycles that defines them in terms of the way in which they are measured.

World-system theorists are still not in a position to offer such clear definitions. Considerable inconsistency in conceptualization and measurement continues to plague the discussion of cycles. Wallerstein himself admits to these problems in his discussion of economic cycles. Indeed, the actual existence of medium and long-term economic cycles is one of considerable debate among economists. The majority of U.S. economists currently question their existence, considering them empirically and theoretically implausible (Wallerstein, 1984a).

Underlying this debate is the fact that the attempt to identify and study economic cycles has run into a number of empirical problems, as Wallerstein himself freely admits. First, there is no agreement on what is fluctuating. Most early work on economic cycles employed commodity price fluctuations (grain, gold). More recently, Wallerstein (1984a) has suggested profit rates. Second, most evidence used to establish the existence of cycles has been limited to one or to a few countries, and the data are not of very high quality. Obtaining reliable global information for five centuries seems an almost impossible task.

Third, when indicators have been proposed (which would presumably measure some sort of general economic conditions), they have not always correlated very well with other indicators of economic conditions. Those that have been proposed do not always fluctuate together at the same times in different countries. Wallerstein implicitly acknowledges this problem when he admits that the meaning of phase A and phase B may not be clear because such phases may be economically "good" for some countries or social strata but "bad" for others (1984a: 572). The tendency in much of the world-system literature is to use the common-sense notion of phase A as a period of prosperity and phase B as a period of general stagnation. Yet, that usage may not capture what is actually meant by the concepts.

Fourth, a major unresolved issue is whether Kondratieffs happened prior to the Industrial Revolution. Wallerstein appears to think that they did. Others argue that preindustrial cycles were of a fundamentally different sort (Wallerstein, 1984a: 566–567). Finally, all these problems of definition and measurement have led to inconsistency in attempts to date economic cycles, which has led to wide variations in the starting and ending points specified by the various theorists. In turn, that problem has made it difficult to be sure how the Kondratieffs relate to the logistics over time and has created considerable difficulty in trying to specify what other social, economic, or political events should be expected to correlate with phase B or phase A of either Kondratieffs or logistics.[4]

The attempt to define and measure hegemonic cycles has encountered similar difficulties. Albert Bergesen summarizes the situation:

> There are unresolved disagreements over the exact number of these hegemony/competition cycles the world-system has passed through. Hopkins and Wallerstein . . . and Modelski . . . suggest four, Chase-Dunn . . . three, and Bergesen . . . only two. There is agreement on the hegemonic powers of the nineteenth and twentieth centuries—Britain and the United States—but disagreement on the importance of the Dutch during the seventeenth century, and Spain versus Portugal during the sixteenth century (1983a: 79).

In part, these disagreements appear to stem from whether the primary measurement of hegemony is based on economic criteria or political/ military criteria. Even those who agree on accenting the economic dimension cannot agree on what constitutes clear hegemony. To add to the confusion, there are further serious disagreements on when to date hegemonic periods (Thompson, 1983a).

These problems of operationalizing economic and hegemonic cycles are part of a larger problem in the study of cycles. Not only are the cycles themselves ambiguously operationalized; the various social, political, and economic correlates of these cycles have yet to be defined in a way that would allow measurement and dating. (See McGowan [1985], Bergesen [1985], and Chase-Dunn [1985].)

EVALUATION. The existence of cycles is at the heart of the world-system approach to the study of change on a global scale. That definition and measurement of so fundamental a theoretical construct as cycles are at such a tentative stage is a good indicator of the preliminary nature of the study of system dynamics. That "something" out there in the world-system does seem to fluctuate in a way that *resembles* regular cycles appears to be a plausible hypothesis. If it is a correct one, it would have to be considered one of the major contributions of world-system theory to the study of social change. At this point, however, it still an interesting, but unconfirmed, hypothesis.

## Comparability of Cycles

A related, but separate, issue is whether economic and hegemonic cycles are "comparable" over time. If cycles are comparable, one can identify characteristics and patterns of relationships between events that occur again and again. For instance, world-system theorists assert that what is happening now to the United States during its period of hegemonic decline is basically similar in its nature and causes to what happened to Great Britain in the nineteenth century and to Holland in the eighteenth century.

Yet, even world-system theorists recognize that the degree of similarity may be open to dispute. A number of different observers of the modern era raise doubts about the degree of comparability of cycles. For instance, both Samir Amin (1982) and Giovanni Arrighi (1982) argue that each cycle of hegemony has unique properties and causes, particularly in the case of the United States. Supposedly, during this period of decline, the whole world capitalist system is facing an unresolvable, final crisis that will end in its destruction. Consequently, Amin and Arrighi conclude that a general theory of hegemonic cycles is much too general and abstract to explain what is and will be happening in the late twentieth century.

Phillip McMichael (1985) has a less apocalyptic view of the current world situation, but he does argue that British hegemony in the nineteenth century was quite different from U.S. hegemony in the twentieth. He maintains that British hegemony created a system based on free trade, whereas U.S. hegemony was based less on free trade and more on a system of open international investment. Thompson also questions the similarity of U.S. hegemony to previous hegemonies:

It appears that military superiority preceded economic superiority in the Dutch and British eras of leadership. Contrarily, economic superiority preceded military predominance in the American era. Alternatively, the decay of Dutch and British military superiority appears to have been more rapid than that of their relative economic positions. While the American case is awkward because its leadership history is still in progress, it appears that the relative American economic position peaked in the early 1950's and has continued to decline since that time. This relative economic decline either precedes the decline of relative American military power or roughly parallels the decay in military position (1983a: 57).

Finally, Michel Morineau (1984) raises fundamental questions about the whole attempt to talk about economic cycles. He has concerns about the regularity of economic fluctuations in terms of their duration. Rather than cycles of roughly equal duration, he argues for much more irregular fluctuations. Moreover, his research suggests that instead of a single, unified pattern of economic fluctuations, there are, in fact, dissimilar patterns of fluctuation for different parts of the economy. Even more fatal to the notion of comparable economic cycles, argues Morineau, are the causes of economic fluctuations, which have been fundamentally different over time because of the vast changes in technology, among other factors.

EVALUATION. Where do all these doubts about the real similarity of cycles leave the attempt of world-system theorists to create a theory of economic and hegemonic cycles? At the very least, these doubts raise the question of whether such a general theory is possible. If cycles are really quite different in terms of their basic features and causes, no theory can be postulated. Rather, each cycle would have to be regarded as a relatively unique pattern of events only roughly analogous to a previous period of time. One could compare the two periods for similarities and differences that might shed light on what happened and why. On the other hand, one could not expect that events would merely repeat themselves in some predictable way.

Whether cycles are comparable or merely interesting historical analogies is an open question. The existence of a real cyclical pattern in modern world history cannot be assumed but must be proven. To date, world-system theory has not marshalled the evidence for that proof. We must conclude that the notion of cycles remains another interesting, but unproven, hypothesis.

## Teleological Arguments

World-system theory, because of its concern with history, is an exercise in post hoc (after the fact) theorizing. That, by itself, is not necessarily a problem. But there is some question as to whether world-system theorists (especially Wallerstein) approach historical theorizing in an appropriate manner. Specifically, some critics charge that Wallerstein's accounts of the development of the world-system are teleological. In Skocpol's view, "Repeatedly he [Wallerstein] argues that things at a certain time and place had to be a certain way in order to bring about later states or developments that accord (or seem to accord) with what his system model of the world capitalist economy requires or predicts" (1977: 1088).

In other words, according to Skocpol, Wallerstein believes that one can identify the "purpose" that an event or trend serves for the evolution of the world-system as a whole. Because the system "required" or "needed" that trend or event in order to develop, that event or trend "had" to occur the way it did. The system "required" certain developments for it to become what it has become. Such theorizing, because it explains events by identifying their purpose for some larger entity or end-state, is teleological reasoning. For example, Wallerstein argues that semi-peripheral states appeared in the world-system because the world-system needed such states in order to operate smoothly (1979a: 21). Or recall a previous example. Eastern Europe had to create a "new serfdom" because to prosper, the core needed peripheral regions to exploit (Wallerstein, 1974a).

This reasoning provokes two kinds of criticism. On the one hand, scholars who interpret the historical record differently challenge Wallerstein's teleological explanations of specific historical events. (We have already discussed this kind of criticism in regard to serfdom in Eastern Europe.) On the other hand, other scholars criticize the telelogical approach to theorizing in general. These critics regard such reasoning as unscientific because it is inherently "circular" and therefore not subject to disproof by contrary evidence. This is one of Skocpol's (1977) major methodological criticisms of Wallerstein's first volume of world-system history (1974a).

EVALUATION. This critique of teleological theorizing raises serious questions about the whole attempt to formulate a theory. The world-system approach assumes that one can identify inherent tendencies in the system (system "requirements"), which then unfold as specific historical trends and cycles. If, in fact, this line of reasoning is flawed by teleological historical interpretations, then the whole approach may be flawed. Wallerstein is aware of this criticism but dismisses it by arguing that he is creating a new approach to social science theorizing that is scientifically valid and has an analog in other sciences (1983a: 307).

## The Holistic Assumption

The tendency toward teleological arguments is related to a fundamental assumption of world-system theory that has also drawn sharp criticism. That assumption has been variously labeled "globalism" (Petras and Brill, 1986), "systems theory" (Aronowitz, 1981), and "holism" (Hall, 1984). Holism is the assumption that the characteristics of societal subsystems (such as social classes and state structures) can best be explained by the imperatives of the all-encompassing world-system (Hall, 1984: 44; Petras and Brill, 1986: 4; Aronowitz, 1981: 505).

Critics argue that this assumption leads to a general kind of analytical error in world-system theory—namely, it exaggerates the degree to which events and characteristics within societies can be explained by the characteristics and tendencies of the world-system as a whole. For example, Hall's (1984) examination of the nature of Brazilian colonial agriculture reveals that it could only be partially accounted for by Brazil's position in the world division of labor. This agricultural system had its roots in a form of "patrimonial" capitalism that existed in empires predating the appearance of global capitalism. Stanley Aronowitz (1981) and Petras and Brill (1986) argue in a similar vein that the holistic assumption leads to a static, overdeterministic view of the possibilities of change. Significant social movement in societies is possible only if factors essentially external to the world-system change so that the system itself changes. Aronowitz contends that this leads Wallerstein to devise an ad hoc interpretation of the rise of capitalism in Western Europe that ignores the internal contradictions of the feudal mode of production. Petras and Brill claim that world-system theorists cannot account for recent changes in the periphery and must dismiss them because the concept of the world-system cannot accommodate such changes.

EVALUATION. It is difficult to ignore this criticism because it is closely related to the issue of world-system theory neglect of the independent causal importance of such factors as internal class relationships. Yet, as Hall points out, one can accept this criticism and still believe that global, systemic factors are among the major causal variables that account for events in societies. He suggests that

> the reconstruction of the world-system perspective substitutes a differentially connected set of spheres, both within and beyond a capitalist domain, as constituting the world social formation. Such a reconstruction does not assume any single and universal time; it acknowledges instead multiple streams of history in relatively autonomous spheres that occasionally puncture, interpenetrate, or come into conjuncture with one another (1984: 61).

## Is a Theory Possible?

The world-system approach is essentially an attempt to create a theory of history. It is a more limited effort than many others because the theory is meant "only" to apply to those parts of the world within the capitalist world-economy and "only" during the period following 1500. Despite its more limited scope, the theory is still an ambitious attempt to encompass a long and complex historical period, and, as such, is subject to the general criticism of all attempts at historical theorizing and to specific criticisms made of its version of historical analysis. Many sociologists are simply unsure that theories of history are appropriate in sociology.

For example, C. Wright Mills, who strongly favored the incorporation of historical materials and concerns in sociology, was equally dubious of the effort to construct general theories of history. He characterized previous theories of history as "transhistorical straitjackets into which the materials of human history are forced and out of which issue prophetic views (usually gloomy ones) of the future" (1961: 22–23). Mills argued that there can be no general theory of history because each social structure displays its own unique mechanisms of change. Given that a wide variety of social structures have existed throughout history, there have been a variety of principles by which historical change has occurred (1961: 150).

Arthur Stinchcombe, another sociologist much concerned with the study of historical change, is convinced that the attempt to create general theories of history is an invalid intellectual strategy. For Stinchcombe, such "epochal" theories of whole historical eras are too abstract and general. They are unable to account for the actual events in an era in a way that is historically accurate: "Epochal theories have a merely literary function. They are produced for the . . . [purpose] . . . of giving a specious sense that we understand the nature of society . . . by providing a myth about how it came about" (1978: 10). Instead of general historical theorizing, argues Stinchcombe, sociologists should concentrate on interpretations of specific major historical developments that have transformed the organization of societies at different points in time. Any more general historical theorizing should await the accumulation of these specific studies.

The political scientist Zolberg (1983) agrees with world-system theorists that historical processes should be studied on a global scale. At the same time, he rejects the notion that there is such an entity as the "world-system" about which one can formulate general laws of change, and he considers it unrealistic to attempt devising a meaningful, historically well-grounded theory that covers events spanning five centuries of world history. Like Stinchcombe, Zolberg argues that the result of such historical theorizing is a set of explanatory propositions that is too general and too abstract to account for specific historical events accurately:

> Such a very large slice of time encompasses an overly broad range of variation among the factors, conditions and outcomes that must be taken into account for the purposes of macroanalytic theory. . . . Theoretical efforts lead inexorably toward formalism, the statement of propositions concerning extremely abstract properties such as "rhythms" and "cycles" (1983: 275).

Zolberg also argues that the world-system approach is inherently unscientific. Science, he asserts, proceeds by examining multiple cases to find recurrent events that are the result of essentially the same cause. Such an approach is not possible in world-system analysis because there is only one "case" to examine, the world-system of the present era (1983: 287).

Wallerstein is aware of these criticisms and dismisses them. He denies that he is creating the theory of history criticized by Mills and Stinchcombe because world-system theory confines itself to a consideration of one era in history with the same global social structure (1983a: 300). Wallerstein also reaffirms his belief that scientific generalizations about a single world-system can be tested. In his view, the social sciences are based on an outmoded conception of science derived from classical (Newtonian) physics. In this outmoded approach one examines the phenomena in the observable world and seeks to find valid generalizations that apply to a large number of observations. Wallerstein suggests another approach:

> We presently start from complex empirical description and try to reduce it to simple general statements. Instead we ought to start with simple general statements, cross-cut such statements with ever more specifications, until we arrive at utilizable concrete complex descriptions of historical structures. The test of the utility of our heuristic theorizing would lie in our consequent ability to explain and manipulate a complex reality (1983a: 307).

EVALUATION. The debate about the appropriateness of and/or the proper approach to historical theorizing has been a recurrent one in the social sciences. To a large extent it revolves around what constitutes an adequate explanation of historical phenomena. On one side of the debate are those who favor a high degree of specificity in the explanation of historical events. On the other are those who believe it is possible to identify very general historical regularities. The debate is not likely to be resolved in favor of either side any time soon. But significant numbers of sociologists will continue to be predisposed to dismiss world-system theory as an attempt to do something that should not be done because it cannot be done.

## Summary and Conclusion

The issues that have been examined here far from exhaust the controversy in regard to world-system theory. They do, however, illustrate fairly well the nature of the debate about it. Much of the criticism of the theory originates from two general sources: Marxist theorists and neo-Weberian theorists. World-system theory represents a major revision of some core elements in Marxian theory. Those who seek to remain within the main tradition of Marxian analysis are not likely to be comfortable with world-system theory. The theory also remains sufficiently close to the Marxian tradition to make non-Marxian scholars equally uncomfortable, especially those scholars who look at large-scale change from a neo-Weberian perspective. As we have seen, these scholars are concerned with what they regard as the inadequate attention world-system theory gives to the independent role of political factors within and between societies. The next chapter will examine some of the alternative formulations those with this orientation have proposed.

The study of the world-system is essentially at the stage of speculation and hypothesis formulation. Issues of definition and measurement are unresolved. Serious debates about the historical record rage. Vagueness and uncertainty pervade attempts to specify the relationship between various events. The explanations that have been advanced have been subjected to strong criticism for theoretical omissions and misinterpretations of the historical record. As a consequence, any generalizations that have emerged so far need to be treated with caution and approached with a healthy degree of skepticism.

# An Assessment of World-System Theory

**A**s we saw in Chapter 1, world-system theory is part of a larger theoretical movement that emerged in U.S. sociology in the 1970s. It represented part of an attempt to replace the then-dominant structural-functionalist theory with models derived from the Marxist theoretical tradition. At the same time, world-system theory grew out of a general feeling that the previous efforts of Marxist scholars also were, by themselves, not satisfactory. A new approach was needed. For a rapidly growing number of sociologists that new approach was world-system theory. At least among the generation of sociologists who entered the profession after the 1960s, world-system theory can be considered the "new orthodoxy" in the study of social change. Overall, how should that new orthodoxy be evaluated?

First, world-system theory is a response to the real inadequacies of previous models of social change. For all its manifest problems, world-system theory represents an important attempt to correct a number of serious shortcomings in those models. In evaluating world-system theory, therefore, one should not forget what theoretical approaches it replaced. That modernization theory was hopelessly inadequate to account for conditions in the periphery seems fairly well accepted by all but a small minority of sociologists. (Nevertheless, the theory is alive and well in the rhetoric of most core leaders, and as an ideology it continues to be useful.) Within the context of contemporary sociology, despite the fact that there are some adherents of previous models, relatively few sociologists would argue that we need to go back to the early theoretical efforts. They are just too badly flawed and have been too convincingly criticized.

Instead, a more fruitful strategy might be to identify the strengths and the weaknesses of world-system theory. Such an assessment would then provide the basis either for its modification or for the development of an alternative theory. By addressing many of the criticisms of world-system theory, the previous chapter laid the groundwork for such a strategy. All that remains to do is to pull those threads together into an overview and assessment, which is the task of this chapter.

## Strengths

Most theorizing in U.S. sociology about large-scale, long-term social change prior to world-system theory was virtually ahistorical. Despite some notable individual practitioners, "historical sociology" was only a minor subtopic in U.S. sociology. As we saw in Chapter 1, modernization theory was only weakly grounded in what was a superficial view of the historical experience of Western Europe in the nineteenth century. One of the key contributions of world-system theory has been to affirm the necessity of relatively detailed historical analysis as a central part of the study of social change. In doing so, world-system theory has become part of a more general revival of historical analysis in U.S. sociology. Even among those who question the specific historical interpretations of world-system theorists, there now seems to be a more general recognition that sociology must "bring history back in" if it is ever to formulate adequate theories about change in large-scale social structures.

World-system theory has also altered the general way in which sociologists think about the process of large-scale change. Previous general models of social change (including both classical Marxism and modernization theory) conceptualized it primarily at the societal level. The focus was on factors internal to a society that account for social change. In contrast, world-system theory has forced sociologists to consider the role of the relationships between societies in generating change within them. Thus, for example, world-system theory has insisted on viewing the rise of capitalism in the core within the context of core penetration and exploitation of the periphery. One need not accept the detailed claims of world-system theory or neglect the independent causal role of internal factors to acknowledge that at least a consideration of external factors belongs in the study of societal change.

In addition, the basic idea that there is something called a world-system, with its own general characteristics and dynamics, seems to be an enduring contribution of world-system theory. It is a logical extension of the general sociological insight that social relationships of all sorts display recurrent patterns and general tendencies toward change. Whether that world-system is as the current theory characterizes it is a separate issue. Further theorizing will have to include a consideration of the possibility that there are relatively enduring global structures and dynamic processes that help shape events at the societal level.

World-system theory also overcomes dependency theory's flawed conclusion that continued integration into the world-economy assures that a peripheral society will always remain a "dependent" peripheral society; "development" is always "dependent development." This view implicitly suggests that successful industrialization can be achieved only by withdrawing from the world-system. Unfortunately (for dependency theory), this view does violence to the historical record. As we have seen, not all societies in the periphery have stayed in the periphery. Moreover, it is not clear that withdrawal from the world-system is necessarily the route to successful modernization (as the uneven success of some socialist states seems to attest). World-system theory avoids this theoretical pitfall by postulating the process of ascent (and decline) as part of the basic dynamics of the world-system. Ascent is not something accidental or unexpected but something that results from the basic functioning of the world-system (albeit, rarely).

Another central focus of world-system theory has been on the process of peripheral exploitation. One may legitimately argue about the nature, causes, extent, and importance to the core (and periphery) of that exploitation. In fact, it (and the accompanying coercion) may have varied in fundamental ways during the last five centuries; there may be no single, general process of unequal exchange. Diffusion of core technology and scientific knowledge may have had many long-term positive benefits for the periphery. Nevertheless, it is hard to read the historical record and not be struck by the extent to which core behavior toward the periphery has been motivated by the desire to exploit it and has been characterized by brutality and coercion. Whatever the shortcomings of their interpretation, world-system theorists have been right to make peripheral exploitation a central issue.

The world-system view that the periphery has been incorporated into a capitalist world-system and that peripheral societies are thus "essentially capitalist" is a controversial one among mainstream Marxist scholars. As we have seen, it requires that one broaden the definition of capitalism beyond circumstances in which free wage labor prevails. But the world-system approach (if it does not lead to a neglect of internal factors) represents a theoretical improvement over previous Marxist theorizing about the periphery. The world-system view is more consistent with the evidence concerning the extent to which traditional economic and social structures were transformed during the colonial period. (This view also avoids the pitfall of modernization theory, which sees the problems of the periphery primarily in terms of its degree of traditionalism or historical backwardness.) The world-system notion of different forms of capitalist labor control in the periphery allows for a more precise, parsimonious description of different economic systems in the periphery and thereby avoids awkward, imprecise, and complex efforts to define seemingly endless modes of production simultaneously operating in a single system of political-economy.

Despite its overemphasis on economic explanations, world-system theory does argue for a necessary (and reciprocal) relationship between capitalism and the interstate system. Although the theory's account of this relationship may not be adequate, the concurrent emergence of both systems strongly suggests that such a connection does exist. To their credit, world-system theorists address the issue. Most conventional theorists of international relations may consider specific sources of international tension generated by economic competition, but they have curiously ignored the general connection between capitalism and the interstate system.

Finally, and perhaps most importantly in the long run, world-system theory is valuable because it identifies and addresses a set of issues that are essential to an understanding of the modern era. In the process, the theory has helped to refocus the sociological study of large-scale social change. Even a partial list of these issues conveys the scope and importance of the world-system theory as an intellectual enterprise:

1. What accounts for the dynamism and instability of the societies of the modern era?
2. What explains the rise and decline of great powers?
3. Why is capitalism so unstable and subject to recurrent crises?
4. Why have most countries in the periphery failed to achieve widespread, sustained economic development?
5. What are the underlying trends and forces that have shaped the modern era?
6. What accounts for the rise of capitalism and the success of the core?

The appeal of world-system theory in part rests on its identification of these very basic (and immensely complex) issues as the proper concern of sociological theorizing about the nature of modern social change.

## Weaknesses

As we have seen, world-system theory has evoked a fair amount of criticism, much of it well founded. A number of the issues raised in the previous chapter simply cannot be dismissed. Even the most basic concepts of the theory are imprecisely defined and very difficult to operationalize. Criteria for determining the status of states in the system, the nature of economic and political cycles, the dating of cycles, and so forth are all in need of major clarification and specification. The theory's failure to systematically address the issue of the nature and causes of unequal exchange is especially troubling. The current formulation in world-system theory is both empirically and theoretically questionable, and the continued attempt to divide the world more or less neatly into core, semi-periphery, and periphery may do violence to the current diversity among contemporary states. Particularly troublesome is the attempt to categorize the Soviet Union as a rising semi-peripheral state that is basically capitalist. The complex reality of the Soviet state and society would seem better captured by acknowledging it as a relatively unique social formation.

Moreover, despite the attempts to achieve better theoretical balance that were discussed in the previous chapter, the charge that world-system theory overemphasizes economic explanations still seems applicable. In particular, the role of various political and geopolitical factors in shaping events and trends in the world-system remains insufficiently explored. In the recent past scholars outside world-system theory have provided convincing evidence of the importance of the independent causal role of political factors. World-system theory seems in need of much more significant modification than most of its adherents have yet been willing to make.

So far at least, the basic issue raised by mode-of-production theorists has also not been sufficiently addressed by most world-system theorists. Not enough attention has been given to various internal factors, particularly internal class relationships and political structures, in accounting for either the problems of peripheral societies or change in core societies. Moreover, very limited attention has been given the role of culture in shaping developments in particular societies. For example, might it be relevant to include a systematic consideration of cultural factors in the analysis of why some peripheral societies have "ascended" and others have not? Overall, world-system theory suffers from a tendency to overemphasize core actions and interests in accounting for the conditions in the periphery. This "Eurocentric bias" (which world-system theory shares with Lenin's theory of imperialism) also seems to account for the limited discussion of interperipheral relationships.

The previous chapter identified a number of basic claims of world-system theory that are empirically shaky and/or controversial. The evidence for absolute emiseration in the periphery, the actual existence of global Kondratieff waves, the extent of wealth extraction from the periphery, the nature and sequencing of hegemonic cycles, and the nature and timing of the "second serfdom" in Eastern Europe are all examples of the empirically questionable nature of world-system theory.

We have also discussed the fact that the whole analytical strategy of world-system theory is subject to challenge. The problems of teleological arguments and historical overgeneralization are very real concerns. For a significant number of scholars, the entire intellectual approach of world-system theory is questionable.

Reflection on the previous chapters also cannot fail but to convince one of the extremely preliminary and tentative nature of world-system theory. Even some of the most basic issues remain unresolved. A reading of the world-system literature reveals major inconsistencies among various theorists and, not infrequently, inconsistencies among different claims of the same theorist.

Overall, the numerous criticisms of world-system theory seem to point to one general conclusion: As it stands, world-system theory does not constitute a generally satisfactory account of modern social change. At the very least, it would require major modifications to overcome its current shortcomings. In the interim, readers of world-system theory need to approach it cautiously and with a full awareness that it is neither a finished nor an accepted theory. Rather, it is an interesting, very preliminary interpretation whose most basic claims remain unproven and/or the subject of major debates among scholars.

## Other Directions in the Study of Global Change

World-system theory is part of a general revival of concern about the nature of global historical change. Some theorists propose approaches explicitly intended as alternatives to world-system theory and designed to correct many of its shortcomings. Others are less explicitly concerned with correcting world-system theory, and their work represents an independent attempt to deal with some of the same issues considered in world-system analysis. These efforts merit brief mention here because they suggest that whatever the specific merits of world-system theory, the issues it considers are regarded as important by a wide range of scholars. In a few cases, these approaches also point to other directions the study of the modern era might take and may even suggest useful additions to or modifications of world-system theory.

Despite the almost universal distrust of generalizations and theories among most historians, the study of the "rise and fall" of great powers has recently been reinvigorated by Paul Kennedy (1987). While denying he has any general theory of the process and acknowledging the historical uniqueness of the experience of every great power, he comes to some tentative conclusions that are somewhat similar to those of world-system theory. Namely, he argues that the long-term power potential of a nation-state ultimately rests on the economic resources it can command for warmaking. The states that enjoyed a period of geopolitical predominance were those that first achieved economic superiority relative to their rivals. Likewise, their decline was associated with the loss of this advantage and their refusal to admit it by continuing to overextend themselves militarily relative to their real economic resources.

A few economic historians also show a renewed interest in economic cycles. Walter Rostow (1978) argues that Kondratieff waves are a useful way to summarize the pattern of change in modern economies. But his dating, measurement, and explanation of Kondratieffs differ significantly from those proposed by Wallerstein and his associates. Political scientist Joshua Goldstein (1983, 1984, 1987) takes the analysis of Kondratieffs even further by examining the link between them and cycles of war. He also examines the available evidence on the measurement and dating of Kondratieffs.

Theories of hegemony and cycles of global war have also become a subfield, primarily in political science. Modelski's theory of "long cycles of world leadership," which was mentioned in the last chapter, differs fundamentally from world-system theory (Modelski, 1987; Kumon, 1987). He is willing to concede that the cycle of Kondratieff waves and cycles of leadership may have a temporal relationship to one another. (When issues of world leadership come to the fore, economic resources are absorbed in interstate conflict and are not available to invest in economic activity. Such a period is associated with a Kondratieff phase B.) He also acknowledges that world leadership is associated with a state's economic importance. Nevertheless, he contends that the interstate system and the world-economy each operate autonomously. His focus is on the demand of the interstate system for order as a "public good" and the ability of a particular power to provide it. According to this view, state policy agendas are shaped primarily by a combination of concerns about international order, national security, territorial rights, and trade stability. A state's ability to effectively pursue its geopolitical goals depends not only on economic strength but on the ability to employ it to maximize "global reach." Historically, such an ability has been based on seapower, rather than on continental land armies. Consequently, Modelski argues, the dynamics of cycles of leadership are independently determined and are not reflections of economic cycles (Modelski, 1978, 1981, 1983, 1987; Kumon, 1987; Thompson, 1983a).

An approach somewhat closer to world-system theory, "hegemonic stability" theory, is associated with the work of Charles Kindleberger (1975, 1977, 1981), Stephen Krasner (1976, 1978, 1985), and Robert Gilpin (1981). In this view, hegemony derives from a preponderance of material resources. Periods of hegemony create international political and economic institutions, relative peace, and free trade.

During the last decade a growing number of sociologists, known as neo-Weberians, have attempted to provide an alternative to neo-Marxism in general and world-system theory in particular. They are highly critical of models that overemphasize economic and class-based factors and thus generate much of the non-Marxist criticism of world-system theory (the last chapter addressed some of those criticisms). At the same time, they seek to examine some of the same issues of historical analysis.

Their theoretical starting point is the work of the great classical sociological theorist Max Weber.[1] From him they derive a concern for charting the rise of modern societies, an interest in comparative history, a concept of the state as an autonomous structure (rather than an adjunct of class relations), and a belief in the independent importance of cultural factors in accounting for historical change. Like him, they do not deny the importance of economic factors (such as capitalism) or class relations or the usefulness of much of the Marxian theoretical tradition. Rather, they view the Marxist perspective as unbalanced and incomplete.

Neo-Weberians offer an alternative view of the emergence of capitalism and the nation-state in the core that addresses the cultural component in these developments. They argue that Weber's notion of "rationality" as an increasingly pervasive element in Western culture is central to understanding the process by which capitalism and the nation-state developed (Chirot, 1986; Collins, 1980). In regard to the rise of the nation-state, they argue for an examination of such factors as the emergence of bureaucratic organization, the constraints imposed and opportunities created by the interstate system (especially the demands imposed to improve warmaking capability), and the goals of ruling elites (Chirot, 1986; Tilly, 1975, 1985).[2]

Other neo-Weberians seek to make the modern state the focus of their theorizing. These sociologists argue that the state must be viewed as an autonomous actor whose functioning is an important independent factor in accounting for historical change and variations in the social structures of different societies. The state's characteristics cannot be reduced to or solely explained by the nature of the mode of production or of class relations (Skocpol, 1977; Evans, Rueschemeyer, and Skocpol, 1985). Rather than theorizing about the nature of the capitalist state, in general, "scholars from various disciplines must use the findings of wide-ranging comparative studies to improve conceptualizations and generate new hypotheses about the structures and activities of states (plural) in various social structural and transnational settings" (Evans, Rueschemeyer, and Skocpol, 1985: 363).

Most recently, Mann (1986a) has proposed an approach to interpreting historical change that attempts to transcend both the neo-Marxian and neo-Weberian perspectives. His position is that both oversimplify the nature of society and the explanation of social structure and why it changes. Mann begins with a redefinition of society. He argues that societies are not well-bounded systems composed of subsystems, dimensions, and levels. Therefore, the distinction between social change within societies and between societies is not useful. On the other hand, he explicitly rejects the notion that there is (as world-system theorists argue) some form of global social structure because its various elements (states, culture, economies) almost never coincide. (For example, some states exclusively rule a single cultural group, others rule multiple cultural groups, and still others share the rule of a single cultural group with other states.) Rather, he regards societies as made up of "multiple overlapping and intersecting socio-spatial networks of power" (1986a: 1).

What then explains the nature of a particular society? Mann asserts that the networks that make up a society are based on four kinds of power: economic, political, military, and ideological. Such networks are systems of interaction and institutionalized organizations. They represent attempts to organize and control behavior. The central problems they therefore face are those of creating organization, control, and logistics (obtaining resources) and establishing communication networks (1986a: 2–3).

Mann argues that contrary to the neo-Weberian and the neo-Marxian positions, one cannot generalize as to which of these sources of power are "primary" in determining the nature of all societies and in shaping the direction of social change. Rather, different kinds of power have had greater importance than others at various times in history. Moreover, concrete organizations, while primarily oriented toward the power that gives them a specific organizational form, often combine two or more forms of power; they are "promiscuous" in their use of power. For instance, what the "state" is or does depends on the historical circumstances. Hence, at best, one can determine that at particular times in history particular forms of power and types of organizations have had a preponderant role in shaping the general direction of historical change (1986a: 2–28).

Mann consequently sees the process of long-term historical change as relatively, but not completely, indeterminate. His theoretical model only claims to identify certain sources of power and kinds of organizations that have at different times played the largest role in shaping events. But he does tentatively suggest some general trends and patterns. For example, he argues that there has been a long-term tendency for organizations to increase their power capacities. He also identifies a possible alteration in history between two general kinds of power configurations and speculates about the process that accounts for that alteration. But he acknowledges that these only very roughly correspond to the historical record. Thus, Mann does not believe that it is possible to put together a model of social change that specifies in detail the basic processes (and their causes) that shape events throughout long periods of times. But he believes it is possible to develop specific explanations of historical change within the framework of his more general model that can satisfactorily account for events (1986a: 518–541).

## Summary and Conclusion

World-system theory is part of a more general attempt to overcome the shortcomings of previous sociological theorizing about modern social change. The theory has much to recommend it. Certainly it raises the right issues and points out the kind of theoretical effort that will be needed. It provides a coherent (if incomplete) account of important aspects of the events in the modern era. It is probably the most fully elaborated effort in sociology so far to grapple with the issues of truly large-scale, long-term social change.

Yet, it is also clearly a flawed and controversial theory. Scholars working in the world-system theoretical framework have an immense unfinished agenda. Much correction and modification seem to be in order. Even correcting and modifying the theory may not be enough. Ultimately, a new theoretical formulation (such as Mann's) may be required. If a new theory can be developed that builds on the very real strengths of world-system theory, then world-system theory will have contributed to the overall enterprise of historical sociology.

# Notes

## Notes to Chapter 1

1. Marx's precise view of the nature of the periphery is a matter of heated debate among Marxist scholars. His scattered statements during several decades were contradictory and incomplete, which led to a number of different conclusions about his position. For examples of the nature of the current debate see Gellnor (1986) and C. Johnson (1983). As we will see in Chapter 6, world-system theory is part of this debate.

2. The following discussion is based primarily on Lenin (1939), Addo (1984), Chirot (1977: 48–51), and Meldolesi (1984).

3. The following discussion of this work is based primarily on Makkai (1983) and Meldolesi (1984).

## Notes to Chapter 3

1. The following discussion is based on Wolf (1982: 24–72) and Lenski and Lenski (1978: 188–220).

2. The following discussion is based on Wallerstein (1974a), Wolf (1982), Frank (1978a, 1984), Knapton (1958), Bendix (1978), Kennedy (1987), and Sanderson (1988).

3. The following discussion is based on Wallerstein (1980, 1988), Frank (1978a, 1984), Wolf (1982), Kennedy (1987), and Knapton (1958).

4. Unless otherwise indicated, the factual basis of the discussion of the world-system is based on Chirot (1977, 1986) and Kennedy (1987). The interpretations of those facts are my own.

## Notes to Chapter 4

1. This section is based on a selective reading and interpretation of Chirot (1977, 1986), Chase-Dunn (1984), Frank (1980), Petras (1984c), Amin et al. (1982), and Wallerstein (1979a).

2. This section is based on a selective reading and interpretation of Chase-Dunn (1984), Chirot (1977, 1986), Frank (1981), Amin et al. (1982), Feinberg (1983), and Wallerstein (1979a).

3. The possibility of alignment with the Soviet bloc is an available alternative to continued dependence on the core, but it has not proven to be an attractive one. Trade with and aid from the Soviet Union offer few advantages: Soviet technology and equipment are often inferior, aid is often contingent on accepting large numbers of Soviet advisers (who have often not been effective and frequently have attempted to dictate policy and/or subvert the regime), and Soviet resources are limited. Alignment with the Soviets also leads to core sanctions. In fact, many former Soviet allies in the periphery have elected to sever ties and improve relations with the core. Only a few avowedly Communist regimes in the periphery have maintained long-term alignment with the Soviet Union (Feinberg, 1983: 130–176; Chirot, 1977: 230–231).

4. There are only limited discussions of semi-peripheral class systems in the world-system literature. The present discussion relies heavily on Wallerstein's general discussion (1979a: 102–105) and is also based on the author's interpretation of the situation in major semi-peripheral countries. See Frank (1981), Chirot (1986), Evans (1979), D. Johnson (1985), and Thomas (1984) for a description of the class systems in some of these countries.

5. Further discussion of these issues from different Marxist perspectives can be found in Szymanski (1979) and Sweezy (1980).

6. Brevity requires that I omit discussion of Yugoslavia here. Suffice it to say that Yugoslavia is a member of the semi-periphery with a system of political-economy that is a mixture of market mechanisms and relatively decentralized socialist arrangements. It is fairly well integrated into the world-economy. The Yugoslavs were initially relatively successful at avoiding the effects of peripheralization and other problems of countries in the semi-periphery. Until the 1980s the country managed a rapid rate of economic growth, but this was followed by growing economic difficulties (such as external debt problems) and political conflict. Yugoslavia has avoided political alignment with either the Soviet Union or the core.

## Notes to Chapter 5

1. As we will see in the next chapter, dating of cycles is one of the unresolved issues of world-system theory. Wallerstein and others have not yet committed themselves to a firm dating scheme. The scheme presented here is one of several suggested in the world-system literature. Even more uncertain is the dating of phase Ts; discussion of these phases has been omitted here.

2. Spain under the Hapsburgs in the sixteenth century enjoyed a period of military ascendancy, and the state enjoyed immense wealth (because of American gold and silver), but it did not achieve the sort of overall economic predominance necessary to achieve full hegemony.

3. Many critics of Wallerstein (for example, Chirot [1986] and Skocpol [1977]) argue that he views state strength in terms of how much centralized power

is in the hands of state leadership. Hence, one would expect that absolutist France—not relatively decentralized Great Britain—should have been the most successful capitalist state in the eighteenth century. In fact, as we saw in Chapters 2 and 3, this is not what Wallerstein means, and he explicitly argues that Great Britain was the stronger of the two states.

4. The reasons for this failure to innovate and adapt to changing conditions on the part of the hegemonic power are poorly understood and subject to lengthy debate. See Tylecote (1982), Chirot (1986), Rubinson (1978), and Bergesen (1982).

5. What follows is a highly selective interpretation of a complex and contradictory literature. Major summaries of these issues can be found in Chase-Dunn (1978), McMichael (1985), Wallerstein (1979b, 1983b), Bergesen (1982), Bosquet (1980), and Thompson (1983a).

6. One view is that the hegemonic war is the result of particular kind of power challenging the old hegemonic state. The "challenging state" is trying to take a shortcut to world power by mobilizing its national resources through a highly centralized state apparatus and by emphasizing military power (rather than economic competitiveness). But this state makes the mistake of mounting the challenge prematurely—before it has sufficient economic and military resources to win. Hence, it loses, and the state that emerges as the new hegemonic power is part of the alliance that defeats it. For example, in the first half of the twentieth century Germany was the challenging power to British hegemony. It lost and the United States (with greater economic resources) emerged as the new hegemonic power after World War II. See Thompson (1983a).

7. The following is loosely based on Amin et al. (1982), Sylvan et al. (1983), Frank (1980), Boswell and Bergesen (1987), and the materials discussed in Chapter 4.

## Notes to Chapter 6

1. The debate is further complicated by those who accept the general claims of the theory of comparative advantage but point to ways in which the core can, in fact, take advantage of the periphery, even when the preconditions of the theory are met. For example, Kindleberger (1975, 1977, 1981) accepts "mainstream" economic interpretations of international trade but also points out that national power can be used to obtain a favorable trading position. Gilpin (1981) addresses the "distortions" created in core-periphery economic relations by multinational corporations.

2. They also have been especially critical of the notion of some dependency theorists that the periphery has consistently suffered from unfavorable "terms of trade" (the prices it receives for its goods relative to what it pays the core) (Chirot and Hall, 1982: 93; C. Smith, 1987: 607; Meier, 1976; Bairoch, 1977). But the concept of unequal exchange proposed by Emmanuel is not based on statements about the terms of trade, and consequently these criticisms are not directly relevant to world-system theory.

3. For an introduction to the issues in this complicated and technical debate, see Mandel (1975), Brewer (1980), Pilling (1973), and Kay (1975).

4. For a recent attempt to address some of these issues, see Goldstein (1983, 1987).

## Notes to Chapter 7

1. As we have seen, world-system theorists also borrow from Weber, particularly his concept of "status group." Their concern with exchange relationships in capitalism has Weberian overtones. As we saw in Chapter 1, the overall intellectual agenda of world-system theory also owes much to all "classical" theorists who attempted to make sense of the modern era.

2. Tilly would probably dislike being labeled a neo-Weberian (or anything else). Nevertheless, he is cited frequently and with approval by those who do call themselves neo-Weberians.

# Bibliography

Abraham, M. Francis. 1980. *Perspectives on Modernization: Toward a General Theory of Third World Development.* Washington, DC: University Press of America.

Addo, Herb. 1984. "On the Crisis in the Marxist Theory of Imperialism." *Contemporary Marxism* 9: 123–147.

Ahmad, Aijaz. 1983. "Imperialism and Progress." Pp. 33–74 in *Theories of Development,* edited by R. Chilcote and D. Johnson. Beverly Hills, CA: Sage.

Amin, Samir. 1984. "Income Distribution in the Capitalist System." *Review* 8: 3–28.

_____ . 1982. "Crisis, Nationalism, and Socialism." Pp. 167–232 in *Dynamics of Global Crisis,* by S. Amin, G. Arrighi, A. G. Frank, and I. Wallerstein. New York: Monthly Review Press.

_____ . 1980. "Class Structure of the Contemporary Imperialist System." *Monthly Review* 31(8): 9–26.

_____ . 1976. *Unequal Development.* New York: Monthly Review Press.

Amin, Samir, Giovanni Arrighi, Andre Gunder Frank, and Immanuel Wallerstein. 1982. *Dynamics of Global Crisis.* New York: Monthly Review Press.

Applebaum, Richard. 1970. *Theories of Social Change.* Chicago, IL: Markham.

Aronowitz, Stanley. 1981. "A Metatheoretical Critique of Immanuel Wallerstein's *The Modern World-System.*" *Theory and Society* 10: 503–520.

Arrighi, Giovanni. 1982. "A Crisis of Hegemony." Pp. 55–108 in *Dynamics of Global Crisis,* by S. Amin, G. Arrighi, A. G. Frank, and I. Wallerstein. New York: Monthly Review Press.

Arrighi, Giovanni, and Jessica Drangel. 1986. "The Stratification of the World-Economy: An Exploration of the Semi-Peripheral Zone." *Review* 10: 9–74.

Bairoch, Paul. 1977. *The Economic Development of the Third World Since 1900.* Berkeley: University of California Press.

Bendix, Reinhard. 1978. *Kings or People: Power and the Mandate to Rule.* Berkeley: University of California Press.

_____ . 1956. *Work and Authority in Industry.* New York: Harper & Row.

Bergesen, Albert. 1985. "How to Model Cyclical Dynamics of the World-System: A Reply to McGowan." *Review* 7: 501–513.

———— . 1983a. "Modeling Long Waves of Crisis in the World-System." Pp. 73–92 in *Crises in the World-System,* edited by A. Bergesen. Beverly Hills, CA: Sage.

———— . 1983b. "1914 Again? Another Cycle of Interstate Competition and War." Pp. 255–276 in *Foreign Policy in the Modern World-System,* edited by P. McGowan and C. Kegley. Beverly Hills, CA: Sage.

———— . 1982. "Economic Crisis and Merger Movements: 1880's Britain and 1980's United States." Pp. 27–40 in *Ascent and Decline in the World-System,* edited by E. Friedman. Beverly Hills, CA: Sage.

———— . 1980. "Cycles of Formal Colonial Rule." Pp. 119–126 in *Processes of the World-System,* edited by T. Hopkins and I. Wallerstein. Beverly Hills, CA: Sage.

Bernstein, Henry. 1982. "Industrialization, Development, and Dependence." Pp. 218–235 in *Introduction to the Sociology of "Developing" Societies,* edited by H. Alavi and T. Shanin. New York: Monthly Review Press.

Block, Fred. 1978. "Marxist Theories of the State in World-System Analysis." Pp. 27–38 in *Social Change in the Capitalist World-Economy,* edited by B. Hockey Kaplan. Beverly Hills, CA: Sage.

Bloom, David, and Richard Freeman. 1986. "The Effects of Rapid Population Growth on Labor Supply and Employment in Developing Countries." *Population and Development Review* 12: 381–414.

Bollen, Kenneth. 1983. "World System Position, Dependency, and Democracy: The Cross-National Evidence." *American Sociological Review* 48: 468–479.

Bosquet, Nicole. 1980. "From Hegemony to Competition: Cycles of the Core?" Pp. 46–83 in *Processes of the World-System,* edited by T. Hopkins and I. Wallerstein. Beverly Hills, CA: Sage.

Boswell, Terry, and Albert Bergesen (eds.). 1987. *America's Changing Role in the World-System.* New York: Praeger.

Braudel, Fernand. 1981, 1982, 1984. *Civilization and Capitalism: 15th–18th Century,* vols. 1–3. New York: Harper & Row.

Brenner, Robert. 1977. "The Origins of Capitalist Development: A Critique of Neo-Smithian Marxism." *New Left Review* 104: 25–92.

Brewer, Albert. 1980. *Marxist Theories of Imperialism: A Critical Survey.* London: Routledge & Kegan Paul.

Bromley, Robert. 1978. "Introduction—The Urban Informal Sector: Why It Is Worth Discussing." *World Development* 6: 1033–1039.

Brown, Lester. 1987. *State of the World.* New York: Norton.

Buckley, Walter. 1967. *Sociology and Modern Systems Theory.* Englewood Cliffs, NJ: Prentice-Hall.

Burns, E. Bradford. 1980. *The Poverty of Progress: Latin America in the Nineteenth Century.* Berkeley: University of California Press.

Caporaso, James. 1981. "Industrialization in the Periphery: The Evolving Global Division of Labor." Pp. 140–171 in *World-System Structure: Continuity and Change,* edited by W. L. Hollist and J. Rosenau. Beverly Hills, CA: Sage.

Carnoy, Martin. 1984. *The State and Political Theory.* Princeton, NJ: Princeton University Press.

Chase-Dunn, Christopher, 1985. "Introduction." *Review* 7: 445–450.

———. 1984. "The World-System Since 1950: What Has Really Changed?" Pp. 75–106 in *Labor in the Capitalist World-Economy,* edited by C. Berguist. Beverly Hills, CA: Sage.

———. 1983. "The Kernel of the Capitalist World-Economy: Three Approaches." Pp. 35–78 in *Contending Approaches in World-System Analysis,* edited by W. Thompson. Beverly Hills, CA: Sage.

———. 1982a. "Introduction." Pp. 9–20 in *Socialist States in the World-System,* edited by C. Chase-Dunn. Beverly Hills, CA: Sage.

———. 1982b. "Socialist States in the Capitalist World Economy." Pp. 21–57 in *Socialist States in the World-System,* edited by C. Chase-Dunn. Beverly Hills, CA: Sage.

———. 1982c. "The Transition to World Socialism." Pp. 271–296 in *Socialist States in the World-System,* edited by C. Chase-Dunn. Beverly Hills, CA: Sage.

———. 1981. "Interstate System and Capitalist World-Economy: One Logic or Two?" Pp. 30–53 in *World-System Structure: Continuity and Change,* edited by W. Hollist and J. Rosenau. Beverly Hills, CA: Sage.

———. 1980. "Socialist States in the Capitalist World-Economy." *Social Problems* 27: 505–525.

———. 1978. "Core-Periphery Relations: The Effects of Core Competition." Pp. 159–177 in *Social Change in the Capitalist World-Economy,* edited by B. Hockey Kaplan. Beverly Hills, CA: Sage.

Chinchilla, Norma. 1983. "Interpreting Social Change in Guatemala: Modernization, Dependency, and Articulation of Modes of Production." Pp. 139–180 in *Theories of Development,* edited by R. Chilcote and D. Johnson. Beverly Hills, CA: Sage.

Chirot, Daniel. 1986. *Social Change in the Modern Era.* New York: Harcourt Brace Jovanovich.

———. 1985. "The Rise of the West." *American Sociological Review* 50: 181–195.

———. 1977. *Social Change in the Twentieth Century.* New York: Harcourt Brace Jovanovich.

Chirot, Daniel, and Thomas Hall. 1982. "World-System Theory." *Annual Review of Sociology* 8: 81–106.

Collins, Randall. 1980. "Weber's Last Theory of Capitalism: A Systematization." *American Sociological Review* 45: 925–942.

Coser, Lewis. 1956. *The Functions of Social Conflict.* Glencoe, IL: Free Press.

Crane, George. 1982. "The Taiwanese Ascent: System, State, and Movement in the World-Economy." Pp. 93–114 in *Ascent and Decline in the World-System,* edited by E. Friedman. Beverly Hills, CA: Sage.

Dahrendorf, Ralf. 1959. *Class and Class Conflict in Industrial Society.* Stanford, CA: Stanford University Press.

Deutch, Karl. 1966. *Nationalism and Social Communication.* Cambridge, MA: MIT Press.

Duvall, Raymond, and John Freeman. 1981. "The State and Dependent Capitalism." Pp. 223–242 in *World-System Structure: Continuity and Change,* edited by W. Hollist and J. Rosenau. Beverly Hills, CA: Sage.

Eitzen, D. Stanley. 1988. *In Conflict and Order: Understanding Society.* Boston: Allyn and Bacon.

Emmanuel, Arrighi. 1972. *Unequal Exchange.* New York: Monthly Review Press.

Evans, Peter. 1985. "Transnational Linkages and the Economic Role of the State: An Analysis of Developing and Industrialized Nations in the Post–World War II Period. Pp. 192–226 in *Bringing the State Back In,* edited by P. Evans, D. Rueschemeyer, and T. Skocpol. Cambridge: Cambridge University Press.

————. 1979. *Dependent Development: The Alliance of Multinational, State, and Local Capital in Brazil.* Princeton, NJ: Princeton University Press.

Evans, Peter, Dietrich Rueschemeyer, and Evelyne Huber Stephens. 1985. "Introduction." Pp. 11–30 in *States Versus Markets in the World-System,* edited by P. Evans, D. Rueschemeyer, and E. Huber Stephens. Beverly Hills, CA: Sage.

Evans, Peter, Dietrich Rueschemeyer, and Theda Skocpol. 1985. "On the Road to a More Adequate Understanding of the State." Pp. 347–366 in *Bringing the State Back In,* edited by P. Evans, D. Rueschemeyer, and T. Skocpol. Cambridge: Cambridge University Press.

Feinberg, Richard. 1983. *The Intemperate Zone: The Third World Challenge to U.S. Foreign Policy.* New York: Norton.

Fischer, Claude. 1984. *The Urban Experience,* 2nd ed. New York: Harcourt Brace Jovanovich.

Frank, Andre Gunder. 1984. "The Unequal and Uneven Historical Development of the World Economy." *Contemporary Marxism* 9: 71–98.

————. 1981. *Crisis: In the Third World.* New York: Holmes and Meier.

————. 1980. *Crisis: In the World Economy.* New York: Holmes and Meier.

————. 1978a. *World Accumulation, 1492–1789.* New York: Monthly Review Press.

————. 1978b. *World Accumulation and Underdevelopment.* New York: Monthly Review Press.

————. 1967. *Capitalism and Underdevelopment in Latin America.* New York: Monthly Review Press.

————. 1966. "The Development of Underdevelopment." *Monthly Review* 18(7): 17–31.

Freedman, Robert (ed.). 1961. *Marx on Economics.* New York: Harcourt Brace.

Friedman, Edward. 1982. "Introduction." Pp. 9–26 in *Ascent and Decline in the World-System,* edited by E. Friedman. Beverly Hills, CA: Sage.

Gellnor, Ernest. 1986. "Soviets Against Wittfogel: On the Anthropological Preconditions of Mature Marxism." Pp. 78–108 in *States in History,* edited by J. Hall. New York: Basil Blackwell.

Giddens, Anthony. 1971. *Capitalism and Modern Social Theory.* New York: Cambridge University Press.

Gilpin, Robert. 1981. *War and Change in World Politics.* New York: Cambridge University Press.

_____ . 1975. *U.S. Power and the Multinational Corporation.* New York: McGraw-Hill.

Goldfrank, Walter. 1983. "The Limits of Analogy: Hegemonic Decline in Great Britain and the United States." Pp. 143–155 in *Crises in the World-System,* edited by A. Bergesen. Beverly Hills, CA: Sage.

_____ . 1982. "The Soviet Trajectory." Pp. 147–156 in *Socialist States in the World-System,* edited by C. Chase-Dunn. Beverly Hills, CA: Sage.

Goldstein, Joshua. 1987. *Long Cycles.* New Haven, CT: Yale University Press.

_____ . 1984. "Long Cycles of Economic Growth and War." Paper presented at the annual meeting of the American Political Science Association, Washington, D.C.

_____ . 1983. "Long Waves and War Cycles." M.S. thesis, MIT.

Hall, John. 1984. "World-System Holism and Colonial Brazilian Agriculture: A Critical Case Analysis." *Latin American Research Review* 19: 43–65.

Harrison, David. 1988. *The Sociology of Modernization and Development.* London: Unwin Hyman.

Hopkins, Terence. 1982a. "The Study of the Capitalist World-Economy: Some Introductory Considerations." Pp. 9–38 in *World-System Analysis: Theory and Methodology,* by T. Hopkins, I. Wallerstein, R. Bach, C. Chase-Dunn, and R. Mukherjee. Beverly Hills, CA: Sage.

_____ . 1982b. "Notes on Class Analysis and the World-System." Pp. 83–90 in *World-System Analysis: Theory and Methodology,* by T. Hopkins, I. Wallerstein, R. Bach, C. Chase-Dunn, and R. Mukherjee. Beverly Hills, CA: Sage.

Hopkins, Terence, and Immanuel Wallerstein. 1987. "Capitalism and the Incorporation of New Zones into the World-Economy." *Review* 10: 763–780.

Hopkins, Terence, Immanuel Wallerstein, and Associates. 1982a. "Cyclical Rhythms and Secular Trends of the Capitalist World-Economy: Some Premises, Hypotheses, and Questions." Pp. 104–120 in *World-System Analysis: Theory and Methodology,* by T. Hopkins, I. Wallerstein, R. Bach, C. Chase-Dunn, and R. Mukherjee. Beverly Hills, CA: Sage.

_____ . 1982b. "Patterns of Development of the Modern World-System." Pp. 41–82 in *World-System Analysis: Theory and Methodology,* by T. Hopkins, I. Wallerstein, R. Bach, C. Chase-Dunn, and R. Mukherjee. Beverly Hills, CA: Sage.

_____ . 1982c. "Structural Transformations of the World-Economy." Pp. 121–141 in *World-System Analysis: Theory and Methodology,* by T. Hopkins, I. Wallerstein, R. Bach, C. Chase-Dunn, and R. Mukherjee. Beverly Hills, CA: Sage.

Johnson, Carlos. 1983. "Ideologies in Theories of Imperialism and Dependency." Pp. 75–106 in *Theories of Development,* edited by R. Chilcote and D. Johnson. Beverly Hills, CA: Sage.

Johnson, Dale. 1985. *Middle Classes in Dependent Countries.* Beverly Hills, CA: Sage.

_____ . 1983. "Class Analysis and Dependency." Pp. 231–255 in *Theories of Development,* edited by R. Chilcote and D. Johnson. Beverly Hills, CA: Sage.

Kay, Geoffrey. 1975. *Development and Underdevelopment.* London: Macmillan.

Kelley, Allen, Julian Simon, Joseph Potter, and Herman Daly. 1986. "Review Symposium: Population Growth and Economic Development." *Population and Development Review* 12: 563–586.

Kennedy, Paul. 1987. *The Rise and Fall of the Great Powers.* New York: Random House.

Kindleberger, Charles. 1981. "Dominance and Leadership in the International Economy." *International Studies Quarterly* 25: 242–254.

———. 1977. *America in the World-Economy.* Foreign Policy Association Headline Series 237. Ephrata, PA: Science Press.

———. 1975. "The Rise of Free Trade in Western Europe, 1820–1875." *Journal of Economic History* 35: 20–55.

Kiser, Edgar, and Kriss Drass. 1987. "Changes in the Core of the World-System and the Production of Utopian Literature in Great Britain and the United States, 1883–1975." *American Sociological Review* 52: 286–293.

Knapton, Ernest. 1958. *Europe: 1450–1815.* New York: Charles Scribner's Sons.

Krasner, Stephen. 1985. *Structural Conflict: The Third World Against Global Liberalism.* Berkeley: University of California Press.

———. 1978. *Defending the National Interest.* Princeton, NJ: Princeton University Press.

———. 1976. "State Power and the Structure of International Trade." *World Politics* 28: 317–348.

Kumon, Shumpei. 1987. "The Theory of Long Cycles." Pp. 56–84 in *Exploring Long Cycles,* edited by G. Modelski. Boulder, CO: Lynne Rienner.

Laumann, Edward. 1966. *Prestige and Association in an Urban Community.* Indianapolis, IN: Bobbs-Merrill.

Lenin, Vladimir I. 1939. *Imperialism, the Highest Stage of Capitalism.* New York: International Publishers.

Lenski, Gerhard, and Jean Lenski. 1978, 1987. *Human Societies: An Introduction to Macrosociology.* New York: McGraw-Hill.

Levy, Marion. 1966. *Modernization and the Structure of Societies.* Princeton, NJ: Princeton University Press.

Magdoff, Harry. 1986. "Third World Debt." *Monthly Review* 37(9): 1–10.

———. 1969. *The Age of Imperialism: The Economics of U.S. Foreign Policy.* New York: Monthly Review Press.

Magdoff, Harry, and Paul Sweezy. 1984. "The Two Faces of Third World Debt." *Monthly Review* 36(8): 1–10.

Makkai, Laszlo. 1983. "Ars Historica: On Braudel." *Review* 6: 435–454.

Mandel, Edward. 1981. "Laws of Motion of the Soviet Economy." *Review of Radical Political Economics* 13: 35–39.

Mandel, Ernest. 1975. *Late Capitalism.* London: New Left Books.

Mann, Michael. 1986a. *The Sources of Social Power,* vol. I: *A History of Power from the Beginning to A.D. 1760.* New York: Cambridge University Press.

———. 1986b. "The Autonomous Power of the State: Its Origins, Mechanisms and Results." Pp. 109–136 in *States in History,* edited by J. Hall. New York: Basil Blackwell.

Marger, Martin. 1987. *Elites and Masses: An Introduction to Political Sociology.* Belmont, CA: Wadsworth.

Marshall, T. H. 1950. *Citizenship and Social Class.* Cambridge: Cambridge University Press.

McGowan, Pat. 1985. "Pitfalls and Promise in the Quantitative Study of the World-System: A Reanalysis of Bergesen and Schoenberg's 'Long Waves' of Colonialism." *Review* 8: 477–500.

McMichael, Phillip. 1985. "Britain's Hegemony in the Nineteenth Century World Economy." Pp. 117–150 in *States Versus Markets in the World-System,* edited by P. Evans, D. Rueschemeyer, and E. Huber Stephens. Beverly Hills, CA: Sage.

_____. 1982. "Social Structure of the New International Division of Labor." Pp. 115–146 in *Ascent and Decline in the World-System,* edited by E. Friedman. Beverly Hills, CA: Sage.

Meier, George. 1976. *Leading Issues in Economic Development.* New York: Oxford University Press.

Meldolesi, Luca. 1984. "Braudel and Lenin: Capitalism Is a 'Superlative.'" *Contemporary Marxism* 9: 99–122.

Mills, C. Wright. 1961. *The Sociological Imagination.* New York: Grove.

Mintz, Beth, and Michael Schwartz. 1981a. "The Structure of Intercorporate Unity in American Business." *Social Problems* 29: 87–103.

_____. 1981b. "Interlocking Directorates and Interest Group Formation." *American Sociological Review* 46: 851–859.

Modelski, George. 1987. "The Study of Long Cycles." Pp. 1–15 in *Exploring Long Cycles,* edited by G. Modelski. Boulder, CO: Lynne Rienner.

_____. 1983. "Long Cycles of World Leadership." Pp. 115–140 in *Contending Approaches to World-System Analysis,* edited by W. Thompson. Beverly Hills, CA: Sage.

_____. 1981. "Long Cycles, Kondratieffs, Alternating Innovations and Their Implications for U.S. Foreign Policy." Pp. 117–148 in *The Political Economy of Foreign Policy Behavior,* edited by C. Kegley, Jr. and P. McGowan. Beverly Hills, CA: Sage.

_____. 1978. "The Long Cycle of Politics and the Nation-State." *Comparative Studies in Society and History* 20: 14–35.

Moore, Wilbert. 1974. *Social Change,* 2nd ed. Englewood Cliffs, NJ: Prentice-Hall.

Morineau, Michel. 1984. "Juglar, Kitchin, Kondratieff, et Compagnie." *Review* 8: 577–598.

Morris, Morris D. 1979. *Measuring the Condition of the World's Poor: The Physical Quality of Life Index.* New York: Pergamon.

Morris, Morris D., Toro Matsui, Bipan Chandra, and Tapan Raychaudhuri. 1969. *The Indian Economy in the Nineteenth Century.* Delhi, India: Economics, Sociology, and History Association.

Mugubane, Bernard. 1985. "The Evolution of Class Structure in Africa." Pp. 198–227 in *Political-Economy of Contemporary Africa,* 2nd ed., edited by C. W. Gutkind and I. Wallerstein. Beverly Hills, CA: Sage.

National Research Council, Working Group on Population and Economic Development. 1986. *Population Growth and Economic Development: Policy Questions.* Washington, DC: National Academy of Sciences.

Pamuk, Sevket. 1982. "World Economic Crises and the Periphery: The Case of Turkey." Pp. 147–164 in *Ascent and Decline in the World-System,* edited by E. Friedman. Beverly Hills, CA: Sage.

Parsons, Talcott. 1966. *Societies: Evolutionary and Comparative Perspectives.* Englewood Cliffs, NJ: Prentice-Hall.

———. 1951. *The Social System.* Glencoe, IL: Free Press.

Petersen, William. 1975. *Population,* 3rd ed. New York: Macmillan.

Petras, James. 1984a. "Toward a Theory of Industrial Development in the Third World." Pp. 71–94 in *Capitalist and Socialist Crises in the Late Twentieth Century,* by J. Petras, with R. Carroll-Seguin, M. Correa, S. Gundle, R. Korzeniewicz, M. Morley, and M. Seldon. Totowa, NJ: Rowman and Allanheld.

———. 1984b. "The New Cold War: Reagan's Policy Toward Europe and the Third World." Pp. 7–43 in *Capitalist and Socialist Crises in the Late Twentieth Century,* by J. Petras, with R. Carroll-Seguin, M. Correa, S. Gundle, R. Korzeniewicz, M. Morley, and M. Seldon. Totowa, NJ: Rowman and Allanheld.

———. 1984c. "The 'Peripheral State': Continuity and Change in the International Division of Labor." Pp. 117–138 in *Capitalist and Socialist Crises in the Late Twentieth Century,* by J. Petras, with R. Carroll-Seguin, M. Correa, S. Gundle, R. Korzeniewicz, M. Morley, and M. Seldon. Totowa, NJ: Rowman and Allanheld.

———. 1984d. "Marxism and World-Historical Transformations." *Contemporary Marxism* 9: 18–34.

Petras, James, and Howard Brill. 1986. "The Tyranny of Globalism." Pp. 3–20 in *Latin America: Bankers, Generals and the Struggle for Social Justice,* by J. Petras, H. Brill, D. Engbarth, E. Herman, and M. Morley. Totowa, NJ: Rowman and Littlefield.

Pilling, Geoffrey. 1973. "Imperialism, Trade, and Unequal Exchange: The World of Arghiri Emmanuel." *Economy and Society* 2: 164–185.

Portes, Alejandro. 1983. "The Urban Informal Sector: Definition, Controversy, and Relation to Development." *Review* 7: 151–174.

Portes, Alejandro, and John Walton. 1981. *Labor, Class, and International System.* Orlando, FL: Academic Press.

Ray, James. 1983. "The 'World System' and the Global Political System: A Crucial Relationship?" Pp. 13–34 in *Foreign Policy in the Modern World-System,* edited by P. McGowan and C. Kegley. Beverly Hills, CA: Sage.

Ritzer, George. 1983. *Sociological Theory.* New York: Knopf.

Rostow, Walter. 1978. *The World-Economy: History and Prospect.* Austin: University of Texas Press.

Rubinson, Richard. 1978. "Political Transformation in Germany and the United States." Pp. 29–74 in *Social Change in the Capitalist World-Economy,* edited by B. Hockey Kaplan. Beverly Hills, CA: Sage.

Salvatore, Dominick. 1988. *World Population Trends and Their Impact on Economic Development.* Westport, CT: Greenwood.

Sameter, Ibrahim. 1984. "From Growth to Basic Needs." *Monthly Review* 36(5): 5–13.

Sanderson, Stephen. 1988. *Macrosociology: An Introduction to Human Societies.* New York: Harper & Row.

Selden, Mark. 1985. "State, Market, and Sectoral Inequality in Contemporary China." Pp. 275–291 in *States Versus Markets in the World-System,* edited by P. Evans, D. Rueschemeyer, and E. Huber Stephens. Beverly Hills, CA: Sage.

Shannon, Thomas. 1983. *Urban Problems in Sociological Perspective.* New York: Random House.

Skocpol, Theda. 1985. "Bringing the State Back In: Strategies of Analysis in Current Research." Pp. 3–42 in *Bringing the State Back In,* edited by P. Evans, D. Rueschemeyer, and T. Skocpol. Cambridge: Cambridge University Press.

_____ . 1977. "Wallerstein's World Capitalist System: A Theoretical and Historical Critique." *American Journal of Sociology* 82: 1075–1090.

Smelser, Neil. 1973. "Toward a General Theory of Modernization." Pp. 268–284 in *Social Change,* edited by A. Etzioni. New York: Basic Books.

Smith, Carol. 1987. "Regional Analysis in World-System Perspective: A Critique of Three Structural Theories of Uneven Development." *Review* 10: 597–648.

Smith, David. 1987. "Overurbanization Reconceptualized: A Political Economy of the World-System Approach." *Urban Affairs Quarterly* 23: 270–294.

Smith, Joan, Jane Collins, Terence Hopkins, and Akbar Muhammed. 1988. *Racism, Sexism and the World-System.* Westport, CT: Greenwood.

Stinchcombe, Arthur. 1982. "The Growth of the World System." *American Journal of Sociology* 87: 1389–1395.

_____ . 1978. *Theoretical Methods in Social History.* New York: Academic Press.

Sweezy, Paul. 1980. *Post-Revolutionary Society.* New York: Monthly Review Press.

Sylvan, David, Duncan Snidal, Bruce Russett, Steven Jackson, and Raymond Duvall. 1983. "The Peripheral Economies: Penetration and Distortion, 1970–1975." Pp. 79–114 in *Contending Approaches to World-System Analysis,* edited by W. Thompson. Beverly Hills, CA: Sage.

Szymanski, Albert. 1983. *Class Structure: A Critical Perspective.* New York: Praeger.

_____ . 1982. "The Socialist World-System." Pp. 57–74 in *Socialist States in the World-System,* edited by C. Chase-Dunn. Beverly Hills, CA: Sage.

_____ . 1981. *The Logic of Imperialism.* New York: Praeger.

_____ . 1979. *Is the Red Flag Flying? The Political Economy of the Soviet Union.* London: Zed.

_____ . 1978. *The Capitalist State and the Politics of Class.* Cambridge, MA: Winthrop.

Taylor, John. 1979. *From Modernization to Modes of Production.* Atlantic Highlands, NJ: Humanities Press.

Thomas, Clive. 1984. *The Rise of the Authoritarian State in Peripheral Societies.* New York: Monthly Review Press.

Thompson, William. 1983a. "The World-Economy, Long Cycles, and the Question of World-System Time." Pp. 35–62 in *Foreign Policy and the Modern World-System,* edited by P. McGowan and C. Kegley. Beverly Hills, CA: Sage.

———. 1983b. "Introduction: World System With and Without the Hyphen." Pp. 7–26 in *Contending Approaches to World-System Analysis,* edited by W. Thompson. Beverly Hills, CA: Sage.

Tilly, Charles. 1985. "War Making and State Making as Organized Crime." Pp. 169–191 in *Bringing the State Back In,* edited by P. Evans, D. Rueschemeyer, and T. Skocpol. Cambridge: Cambridge University Press.

———. 1975. "Conclusion." Pp. 456–481 in *The Formation of National States in Western Europe,* edited by C. Tilly. Princeton, NJ: Princeton University Press.

Timberlake, Michael, and Kirk Williams. 1984. "Dependence, Political Exclusion, and Government Repression: Some Cross-National Evidence." *American Sociological Review* 49: 141–147.

Tivey, Leonard. 1981. "Introduction." Pp. 1–13 in *The Nation-State,* edited by L. Tivey. New York: St. Martin's Press.

Tylecote, Andrew. 1982. "German Ascent and British Decline, 1970–1980: The Role of Upper Class Structure and Values." Pp. 41–68 in *Ascent and Decline in the World-System,* edited by E. Friedman. Beverly Hills, CA: Sage.

Tylecote, Andrew, and Marian Lonsdale-Brown. 1982. "State Socialism and Development: Why Russian and Chinese Ascent Halted." Pp. 255–288 in *Ascent and Decline in the World-System,* edited by E. Friedman. Beverly Hills, CA: Sage.

Wallerstein, Immanuel. 1988. *The Modern World-System III: The Second Era of Great Expansion of the Capitalist World-Economy, 1730–1840.* San Diego, CA: Academic Press.

———. 1984a. "Long Waves as Capitalist Process." *Review* 4: 559–576.

———. 1984b. "Patterns and Prospectives of the Capitalist World-Economy." *Contemporary Marxism* 9: 59–70.

———. 1984c. "The States in the Institutional Vortex of the Capitalist World-Economy." Pp. 27–46 in *The Politics of the World-Economy,* by I. Wallerstein. Cambridge: Cambridge University Press.

———. 1983a. "An Agenda for World-Systems Analysis." Pp. 299–308 in *Contending Approaches to World-System Analysis,* edited by W. Thompson. Beverly Hills, CA: Sage.

———. 1983b. "Crises: The World-Economy, the Movements, and the Ideologies." Pp. 21–36 in *Crises in the World-System,* edited by A. Bergesen. Beverly Hills, CA: Sage.

———. 1982a. "Crisis as Transition." Pp. 11–54 in *Dynamics of Global Crisis,* by S. Amin, G. Arrighi, A. G. Frank, and I. Wallerstein. New York: Monthly Review Press.

———. 1982b. "World-System Analysis: Theoretical and Interpretative Issues." Pp. 91–103 in *World-System Analysis: Theory and Methodology,* by T. Hopkins, I Wallerstein, R. Bach, C. Chase-Dunn, and R. Mukherjee. Beverly Hills, CA: Sage.

_____. 1980. *The Modern World-System II: Mercantilism and the Consolidation of the European World-Economy.* New York: Academic Press.

_____. 1979a. *The Capitalist World-Economy.* Cambridge: Cambridge University Press.

_____. 1979b. "Underdevelopment and Phase B: The Effect of Seventeenth Century Stagnation on the Core and Periphery of the European World-Economy." Pp. 73–83 in *The World-System of Capitalism,* edited by W. Goldfrank. Beverly Hills, CA: Sage.

_____. 1974a. *The Modern World-System: Capitalist Agriculture and the Origins of the European World-Economy in the Sixteenth Century.* New York: Academic Press.

_____. 1974b. "The Rise and Future Demise of the World Capitalist System: Concepts for Comparative Analysis." *Comparative Studies in History and Society* 16: 387–415.

Waltz, K. 1979. *Theory of International Politics.* Reading, MA: Addison-Wesley.

Ward, Kathryn. 1985. "The Social Consequences of the World Economic System: The Economic Status of Women and Fertility." *Review* 8: 561–593.

_____. 1984. *Women in the World-System: Its Impact on Status and Fertility.* New York: Praeger.

Warren, Bill. 1980. *Imperialism: Pioneer of Capitalism.* London: New Left Books.

Weber, Robert. 1981. "Society and Economy in the Western World-System." *Social Forces* 59: 1130–1147.

Weeks, John. 1986. *Population,* 3rd ed. Belmont, CA: Wadsworth.

White, Lynn. 1962. *Medieval Technology and Social Change.* Oxford: Clarendon.

Williams, Robin. 1970. *American Society: A Sociological Interpretation,* 3rd ed. New York: Knopf.

Wolf, Eric. 1982. *Europe and the People Without History.* Berkeley: University of California Press.

World Bank. 1987. *World Development Report 1987.* New York: Oxford University Press.

_____. 1984. *World Development Report 1984.* New York: Oxford University Press.

_____. 1981. *World Development Report 1981.* New York: Oxford University Press.

Wuthow, Robert. 1983. "Cultural Crises." Pp. 57–72 in *Crises in the World-System,* edited by A. Bergesen. Beverly Hills, CA: Sage.

_____. 1980. "World Order and Religious Movements." Pp. 57–76 in *Studies in the Modern World-System,* edited by A. Bergesen. New York: Academic Press.

Zolberg, Aristide. 1983. "'World' and 'System': A Misalliance." Pp. 269–290 in *Contending Approaches to World-System Analysis,* edited by W. Thompson. Beverly Hills, CA: Sage.

_____. 1980. "Origins of the Modern World System: A Missing Link." *World Politics* 33: 253–281.

# Index